The Drea

Dedication

I dedicate this book to Alison Shaughnessy.

I must not forget the others who have suffered, nor those to whom I owe apologies or thanks:

Alison's parents, Bobby and Breda Blackmore, and their children Susan, Richard and Robert, whose loss and pain I cannot comprehend.

Debra and our children, who endured years of misery caused by my wilful blindness in helping to free the Taylor sisters.

My solicitor Caroline Kean, formerly of Olswang, now of Wiggin and Company, who believed in me, understood my need to fight this fight and saw ways forward when others had given up hope.

Former Detective Superintendent Chris Burke and the other members of the murder squad (especially Gerry Gallagher, Angela Thomas Coren Smith, Trevor Heard, Sean Gleeson and Adrian Summers) whose integrity I helped publicly and falsely to cast doubt upon.

Mick McGovern, who endured my rantings, dodged flying objects, drowned my sorrows and celebrated each and every victory with me.

Thanks, too to the journalists who didn't believe the Taylors' lies: Gary Jones, Jo-Ann Goodwin, Peter Rose, Mike Sullivan, Marcus Powell and Claire Powell.

Thanks to Emma, Ian Mill QC, Gavin Millar QC, Michael Burton QC, Tom Beeton, and my publisher Bill Campbell, who all helped, advised or inspired me at various stages of the long struggle to tell this story.

Last, and certainly least, I'd like to give a special word of thanks to the Taylors' many friends in the media, especially Nick Davies of *The Guardian*, whose efforts to discredit me did so much to strengthen my resolve to continue. Without you, the truth might never have been told.

www.bernardomahoney.com

the DREAM SOLUTION

THE MURDER OF ALISON SHAUGHNESSY –
AND THE FIGHT TO NAME HER KILLER

BERNARD O'MAHONEY
WITH MICK McGOVERN

MAINSTREAM
PUBLISHING

EDINBURGH AND LONDON

First published in Great Britain in 2001 by
MAINSTREAM PUBLISHING COMPANY (EDINBURGH) LTD
7 Albany Street
Edinburgh EH1 3UG

ISBN 1 84018 467 1

A catalogue record for this book is available
from the British Library

Typeset in Garamond
Printed and bound in Great Britain by
Mackays of Chatham

Contents

ONE

Freedom

I parked my stolen vehicle in an underground car park before heading off on foot towards the Royal Courts of Justice. I'd bought the red Ford Sierra from a fellow doorman at the Essex nightclub where I was head of security. For a sum smaller than the list price, I now possessed – if not quite owned – an almost-new car. I could only hope its false number plates would withstand the scrutiny of PC Plod. I'd been working the night before until the early hours, but I'd still managed to get into central London and park the car by 8.30 a.m. I had more than an hour before I met up with the family of the two young sisters who were about to find out whether the Court of Appeal would quash their convictions for murder.

It was Friday, 11 June 1993. I walked into a newsagent's. The shopkeeper greeted me warmly as I brought to the till seven or eight newspapers – all the tabloids plus a few broadsheets. I felt sure they'd all contain reports from the first day of the appeal hearing. I found a café in Shaftesbury Avenue, about ten minutes' walk from the court complex. I ordered a mug of tea and a couple of slices of toast, then sat down at one of the few tables not occupied by a man in a suit. I flicked expectantly through the pile of newspapers in front of me. I made sure at a glance that each carried a story about the extraordinary revelations of the day before, then I settled down to read each article in full. Perhaps because of my besuited company, I chose to start with *The Independent*. The headline shouted: POLICE 'HID FACTS' FROM SISTERS' MURDER TRIAL.

Police officers concealed evidence that could have pointed to the innocence of two sisters serving life sentences for the murder of Alison Shaughnessy, the Court of Appeal was told yesterday.

An acquittal appeared one step nearer for the sisters, Michelle and Lisa Taylor – who have spent nearly two years in jail.

I was pleased the writer agreed with my own optimistic view of the appeal's likely outcome. The sisters' parents had been a little gloomy when we'd said goodbye the day before. Although I'd confidently predicted their girls would soon be home, they weren't convinced. I read on with satisfaction. The article described how a witness whose evidence 'went to the core' of the convictions had changed his story. He had also sought a reward offered by the murdered woman's employers. Yet, as the article said, the police had not disclosed these facts to the defence at the time of the trial.

Mrs Shaughnessy, 21, died from 54 stab wounds after being attacked at her home in Vardens Road, Battersea, south London, in June 1991.

The prosecution alleged Michelle, who had once had an affair with Mrs Shaughnessy's husband, John, was motivated by jealousy and that her sister, Lisa, 19, had helped her.

Even now, almost a year after I'd first become familiar with the case, the words '54 stab wounds' still unnerved me. I knew what being stabbed felt like: in the past I'd had a knife rip into my own flesh. But I was a doorman, used to violence. For me, being attacked was an occupational hazard. I lived in a different world from that of the victim, who by all accounts had been a sweet and gentle bank clerk, recently married, struck down in the quiet of her own flat. I knew Michelle and Lisa couldn't have murdered her. The sisters I had grown to know and like over the last 11 months didn't seem capable of the freakish violence to which Alison had been subjected. I felt certain the killer was a man – only a man could have done something like that. It was true, of course, that Michelle had been having an affair with Alison's husband, John, with whom she worked, but that affair, as Michelle had often told me, had dwindled to nothing by the time of the murder. Unfortunately for her though, seven months before the murder she'd written something in her diary which the prosecution used against her to devastating effect: 'I hate Alison, the unwashed bitch. My dream solution would be for Alison to disappear as if she never existed and then maybe I could give everything I want to the man I love.' The prosecution said this diary entry proved Michelle's mad obsession with the man who'd supposedly taken her virginity. In Michelle's twisted mind, it was alleged, Alison had been the interloper in Michelle's relationship with John. And, wanting to possess John for herself, she'd murdered Alison in a jealous rage. To me, that story was nothing but fevered nonsense concocted by the police.

> The sisters were convicted in July last year, after the jury heard Dr Michael Unsworth-White's evidence that he saw two white girls – one of them with a blonde pony-tail – running from the murder house, carrying a laundry bag at around the time of the fatal attack.

What the jury hadn't been told was that almost a year earlier Dr Unsworth-White told the police that one of the girls 'may have been black'. But at the trial the doctor – a clean-cut, middle-class professional with no link to either party – had appeared very credible.

> The court was told his account was crucial because it fitted what was otherwise a flimsy prosecution case. 'It is impossible to over-emphasise the evidence of this witness and the impact it would have on the jury.' Yet the defence was denied a chance to challenge the credibility of his evidence, nor to ask him about seeking a reward.

Although I'd led the campaign to free the sisters, I'd had nothing to do with the discovery of the crucial document that had exposed the police's shortcomings. I'd spent my time trying to discredit other witnesses and produce new evidence about the supposed identity of the real murderer. I'd come up with strands of new evidence which the defence had thought useful. However, I didn't tell the legal team that, despite the apparent plausibility of my new evidence, it consisted largely of fabrications I knew would collapse under serious prodding. Also, the methods I'd used to gather my material might well have landed me in prison if the police had discovered what I'd been up to. Still, I was pleased to read the article's last paragraph which referred to the fruits of my labour: 'They were told other grounds of appeal include fresh evidence "to suggest the murderer was someone other than the appellants".'

As I chewed my toast I couldn't help smiling. I read through the other newspapers' stories. They all said much the same. Certain sentences brought me back to the events of the day before. The oak-panelled court had been much smaller than I'd imagined it would be. I remembered how we, the sisters' supporters, had crammed ourselves onto the wooden benches. The parents had sat behind me with their eldest son. I had let their youngest daughter, 14-year-old Tracey, sit on my knee. We'd all sat silently in an air of tense expectancy. Suddenly the silence had been broken by noises from below: the jangling of keys, the slamming of a steel door, then footsteps on a wooden staircase. Michelle had entered the dock first, closely followed by Lisa. They looked startled to see so many people staring at them. I'd been pleased they'd followed my instructions about what to wear – smart but casual. There had been many discussions about the correct attire. At the time of their original trial Lisa's exercising of her right to remain silent had led to her being compared to a hard-faced IRA terrorist, while Michelle had been portrayed as a sex-crazed mistress capable of frenzied murder. I'd suggested that for the appeal they needed to look like normal, girl-next-door types. We agreed they had to avoid wearing anything that might make them look hard (baggy street jeans and loud jewellery) or tarty (mini-skirts and low-cut tops). Moreover, the wrong sort of clothes might make them appear somehow disrespectful of the court. Everything had to be just so. As soon as they'd sat down I'd watched their eyes flashing around the court in search of familiar faces. Tracey had bounced on my knee as she'd waved frantically to catch their attention. They'd seen her and smiled. Michelle had caught my eyes and nudged Lisa, but before we could properly acknowledge one another the usher rose to his feet, tugged at his gown and announced solemnly: 'The court shall rise.'

Everyone stood as the three judges entered the room and took their places on the bench.

I may have had little respect for the justice system, but I'd certainly warmed to the appeals system. I knew from my own experience that it had little to do with justice and much to do with technicalities. To my cynical eye it seemed the system had been designed for the benefit of intelligent criminals and their wily lawyers. I'd told the Taylors from my very first dealings with them that in order to win an appeal they only had to remove one important brick from the wall of evidence to bring the whole construction crashing down. I'd said that, for example, if ten people testified to having witnessed a brutal murder, yet it was later discovered that one of them had lied, then theoretically the whole of the rest of the evidence, however otherwise indisputable, might be disregarded – and the convicted murderer might walk free. Obviously, I'd said, in their case they were innocent. But the principle was the same. I'd worked to find that brick, but with the discovery of the undisclosed police document the Taylors' legal team had pulled out their own brick – and now the wall was about to collapse. When the prosecution barrister had conceded that the police's failure to disclose that document at the original trial had been a 'material irregularity' I had looked excitedly at Michelle and Lisa, but their faces hadn't seemed to register the significance of his words.

For the next hour I sat in the café reading the newspapers. Then at about 9.40 a.m. I packed them into a plastic carrier bag and set off on the short walk to the court. As I walked down The Strand I could see that a small crowd had already formed outside the Royal Courts of Justice. As I got nearer I saw several television crews and newspaper photographers – far more than the day before. Another good omen, I thought. I recognised a few faces in the gathering crowd. I didn't want to bump into any media people who might know something about my criminal background, so I wasn't pleased to see one particular photographer. Until then, I hadn't realised he had anything to do with the media: I'd known him as a tipper-truck driver. He saw me and said hello. He told me he was now taking photographs for one of the sisters' local papers. He asked me what I was doing there. I said I was just a friend of the family. I moved away from him and said hello to a few campaign supporters. I asked where the parents were. Someone said: 'Here they are now.' A mini-bus pulled up near us. The doors opened and members of the Taylor family started getting out. Their arrival provoked a frantic burst of activity from the waiting newspeople, who rushed to the assembling group. I started moving away, because I didn't want to be filmed with them, but the sisters' father, Derek, saw me. He waved me over. I embraced him and his wife, Ann. They looked nervous, but I felt their nervousness had more to do with the developing media scrum than any doubts about the appeal's outcome. In case I was wrong I said: 'Don't worry. They're going to walk.' I'd grown close to Ann and Derek over the previous 11 months while I'd sought out new evidence that might help free their girls. I'd been honest with them about my criminal background. They'd treated it as unimportant. It had been agreed that my own experiences on the wrong side of the law would give me an edge in challenging the police's case against their daughters.

We didn't stand for long on the pavement. A group of about 12 of us moved as one towards the entrance. Reporters threw questions at the parents, but they said nothing. Within seconds we'd passed under the grey stone arch into the lobby. To get to our court we had to pass through an airport-style security barrier of metal detectors supplemented by hand-searches of bag and body. Once through, we swept down the length of the majestic great hall, passing black-gowned and bewigged barristers, their cargo-bearing clerks scurrying in their wake. We negotiated our way through the maze of corridors and stairs until we found our court. There seemed twice as many people as the day before trying to get in. Supporters of the Taylors had arrived early to try to save seats for family and friends. I filed in next to Ann Taylor as the public benches filled up. A whisper started going around that the family of the murdered woman had arrived to witness the judgment that would certainly be delivered that day. Ann turned to me and said angrily: 'What do they want? They've got no bloody business here.' I thought her comments were unnecessary, but I could understand her anger. The victim's family had always made plain they regarded the sisters as murderers. In our eyes this belief put them on the side of the police – the enemy who had conspired to lock up two innocent girls. We sat down and, as other people from our side joined us, we all spread out deliberately to give the usher the impression there was no more room. Outside, looking through a glass pane in the door, was Alison's mother. She was waiting for the usher to find her a seat, but we'd ensured she wouldn't get one. The door to the court was closed, leaving Alison's mother and family outside as the proceedings got underway once again.

Over the next few hours a fog of legal jargon filled the air and clouded understanding. Ann kept asking me to translate what was being said. I was often unsure myself, but one thing I could tell for sure was that the prosecution barrister, John Nutting, had about him an air of defeat. He seemed to be putting up little resistance to the defence's case. On the other side, Michelle's barrister, Richard Ferguson QC, seemed to be enjoying himself. An enjoyable moment for me came when a police officer connected with the investigation had to stand up and apologise for the document that hadn't been disclosed to the defence. I felt this was tantamout to the police acknowledging in public that they'd conceal evidence to obtain a conviction. I thought of the times when I had told magistrates and jurors the truth about how the police really went about their business – and had received in return only blank looks of disbelief. The officer who'd led the investigation, Detective Superintendent Chris Burke, was also in court. Ann had pointed him out to me the day before. Until then he'd only been a name that all the Taylors spat out with disgust. I could tell by his face that he was finding the proceedings difficult and painful. I loved every minute of them.

Soon after the detective sat down the senior judge, Lord Justice McCowan, began reading the bench's judgment. He started by saying that on 24 July 1992 at the Central Criminal Court before Mr Justice Blofeld a jury had unanimously convicted the sisters of murder: 'The appellant Michelle Ann Taylor was sentenced to life imprisonment and the appellant Lisa Jane Taylor was ordered to be detained at Her Majesty's pleasure.' With a clear and measured delivery he outlined briefly the essence of the prosecution's case against the sisters. Then he seemed to spend a huge portion of time going through the tortuous ins and outs of the evidence given by the now-discredited witness. An air of barely stifled boredom filled the court. It only dissipated when the judge moved to the second major ground for appeal – the media's coverage of the original trial. He said:

> In giving leave to appeal, the single judge described that coverage as 'unremitting, extensive, sensational, inaccurate and misleading'. Having had the opportunity of reading a substantial selection of the newspaper reports in question, we see no reason to dissent from the view. Indeed, Mr Nutting has not sought to persuade us otherwise.
>
> One notable characteristic is this. A video had been made of Mr Shaughnessy's wedding to the deceased. It had no relevance to the trial and was not played at it. Somehow or other a copy fell into the hands of the media, and we are told that it was shown on television. Among other things it showed Michelle coming along the receiving line and kissing first the bride, and then the bridegroom. Her kiss of the latter was described to us as a 'peck on the cheek', such as any friend might give in those circumstances. What certain elements in the press did, however, was to show in their newspapers stills taken from the video, but in addition they froze a frame so that the peck on the cheek was made to appear a mouth-to-mouth kiss. This was accompanied in one newspaper by the headline, CHEATS KISS, and another by the headline, JUDAS KISS, and in another by the headline, TENDER EMBRACE – THE LOVERS SHARE A KISS JUST A FEW FEET FROM ALISON.
>
> Nothing like any of that, of course, had been said in court. Indeed,

the newspapers concerned did not limit themselves in any way to reporting what had been said in court. These are some of the headlines we have seen: TILL DEATH US DO PART, BUTCHERED BRIDE, and LOVE CRAZY MISTRESS BUTCHERED RIVAL WIFE, COURT TOLD. The court had been told no such thing.

All of this was being published as the trial proceeded. As Mr Ferguson put it – with considerable restraint – they do not appear to have appreciated that the issue at the trial was whether the appellants had killed the deceased.

What, in fact, they did was not reporting at all; it was comment, and comment which assumed guilt on the part of the girls in the dock. But the press is no more entitled to assume guilt in what it writes during the course of a trial, than a police officer is entitled to convince himself that a defendant is guilty and suppress evidence, the emergence of which he fears might lead to the defendant's acquittal.

During the trial, defence counsel complained to the judge about the press coverage, although they were not, they tell us, aware of the extent of it. During the trial the judge gave several warnings to the jury to decide the case on the evidence alone, and he gave a further appropriate warning to them in the summing-up.

Mr Nutting points out that the jury did not deal with the case in a cavalier fashion. On the contrary, they took five hours to consider their verdicts. He points also to the fact that the jury at one stage returned to ask a question related to the possibility that the killer might have been an intruder who had broken into the flat. He points this out, as showing that the jury had not approached the matter with closed minds.

But we find it quite impossible to say that the jury were not influenced in their decision by what they read in the press.

The principle is that, if the media coverage at trial has created a real risk of prejudice against the defendants, the convictions should be regarded as unsafe and unsatisfactory.

The court was filled with the silence of intense concentration. Everyone could tell the conclusion to which the judge's words were heading. He continued:

We were troubled, at one stage, by the fact that defence counsel did not, at trial, ask the judge to discharge the jury because of the press coverage. Mr Nutting has, however, with typical fairness, provided the answer. This is what he said: 'Asking for a retrial puts defence counsel in a hopeless situation, where young girls had spent considerable time in custody, and where to dispel the publicity, it would be necessary to postpone the trial for a further long period.'

We accept that. We are satisfied that the press coverage of this trial did create a real risk of prejudice against the defendants, and, for this second reason, as well as the first, the convictions are unsafe and unsatisfactory and must be quashed.

The word 'quashed' was the cue for an eruption of emotion. Everyone on the public benches began to cheer and clap; some stamped their feet. Lord Justice McCowan looked up sternly and called for order. He said he would clear the court if there were any further disruptions. Michelle straightened her back and stared straight ahead. She showed no emotion. Lisa's face, however, was full of excitement. She smiled broadly at the public gallery. Our only fear now was that the judge would order a retrial. I knew there was evidence against the sisters which was difficult to counter. Some of that evidence – which the appeal judges had seemed to glide over – had caused me at times to have doubts about the sisters' innocence, but I just couldn't believe they were capable of murder. In my mind I saw only the cynicism of police desperate to get a result in a high-profile case. That focus had distorted my approach to the case: I'd become so determined to prove the sisters' innocence and the police's guilt that I'd stifled any niggling doubts. Behind me I could hear one of the sisters' friends whispering a prayer repeatedly: 'Please God, let them come home. Please God, let them come home.' Everyone settled down again and silence returned. Lord Justice McCowan continued: 'Moreover, by reason of the view we take of the way in which this case was reported, we do not think that a fair trial could now take place. Hence we do not order a retrial.'

The public benches erupted once again. This time we all stamped our feet on the wooden floors and clapped and cheered wildly, ignoring all calls for order. Michelle looked at Lisa, but neither of them showed any emotion. After what seemed like five minutes of uproar the court became silent once again to listen to the judge's final words: 'In allowing the appeal, we further order that the papers in the case be sent to the Attorney-General, for him to consider whether he thinks it appropriate to take any action in respect of the newspapers concerned.'

We all stood up and walked out of the court into the great hall. An official led us into an annexe. He pointed to a studded wooden door from which, he said, Lisa and Michelle would emerge. A peculiar-looking little man called Dick was sweating with excitement. He was flailing his arms around and loudly denouncing the police and press to anyone who would listen. Dick had not known the sisters before their trial, but had contacted the family and offered to assist them in getting people to sign petitions. At first, the Taylors had regarded him as a harmless but useful dogsbody. However, as the campaign progressed he proved himself an irritant and potential liability. He'd visited a witness in the case and asked her to sign his 'Free the Taylor Two' petition; and he'd pestered Ann with numerous unnecessary phone calls in which he'd made various half-baked suggestions and observations. Only recently Ann had said to me: 'That Dick is really starting to do my head in.' Now she took me to one side. She said she was worried that Dick would emerge from the court to say something inappropriate to the press. She asked me if I'd have a word with him. I could understand her concern – one silly outburst might cast a shadow over everything we'd achieved. The Taylors were planning to criticise the press strongly for the way they'd reported the original trial; the press would be looking for someone gullible like Dick to provide material for a backlash. I walked over to him and said bluntly that when he got outside he was not to talk to any journalists. He looked puzzled. In case he hadn't properly registered what I'd said I repeated it more emphatically: 'Have you got me? If I catch you talking to any journalists I'm going to squeeze your head. D'you understand?' He looked hurt and bewildered. I suppose until that moment he'd assumed he was an asset to the campaign. Crestfallen, he nodded.

After a short while the studded door swung open. Michelle and Lisa walked out to more cheering and clapping. Michelle embraced her mother; Lisa her father. There was a flurry of other embraces before they gave a little speech of thanks. Michelle caught my eye and tugged at Lisa. The two of them came over to me. Michelle smiled warmly: 'Thanks for everything, Bernie.'

Lisa said: 'Yeh, we really appreciate everything you've done for us.'

Michelle asked me to keep an eye on Dick to make sure he didn't say anything to the press. I said: 'Don't worry about that. He won't be talking to anybody. I've already had a word.' Then Lisa took me by the arm and said she wanted me to meet somebody. She brought me over to a short Afro-Caribbean man whom she introduced as George. He was George Silcott, brother of the infamous Winston Silcott, a hate-figure for the tabloids since his conviction for the murder of PC Keith Blakelock during the riot on the Broadwater Farm Estate in Tottenham, north London, in October 1985. What had especially angered the tabloids was that Winston had been on bail for another murder charge at the time of the riot. He'd subsequently been convicted of that murder as well. He had constantly claimed he was innocent of both, and there had been a long-running campaign to free him. Lisa had told me she'd been writing regularly to Winston from her own prison cell. She'd described him as 'sweet' and said he'd helped her through her darker moments. She claimed that on his letters he always put the stamp upside-down, leaving the Queen's head topsy-turvy. It was a small act of rebellion, his way of punishing Her Majesty for having prosecuted him. George was a quiet, polite man. He said he'd attended the hearing to show support and to thank the Taylors for supporting his brother. George had a plastic carrier bag in his hand. From it he took two T- shirts and gave them to Lisa and Michelle. The T-shirts had printed on them a head-and-shoulders picture of his brother, along with the words, 'Hostage' and 'Winston Emmanuel Silcott'. The sisters said they would wear them when they went outside to face the media. I couldn't believe they were serious. I didn't know whether Winston was innocent or guilty of the two murders, but I did know that now was not the time for the Taylors to link themselves with him. As they walked off to change, and out of George's earshot, I said: 'Look, are you sure this is a good idea? You're worried about Dick saying the wrong thing to the press, then you and Lisa go out to face them wearing T-shirts supporting someone they hate. They'll fucking slaughter you.'

Michelle and Lisa said they didn't care: they wanted to show their support for Winston because they believed he was the victim of a miscarriage of justice as appalling as the one to which they'd been subjected. It was their decision, so I said no more.

When they had put on the T-shirts a court official told them that if they wanted to avoid the media they could leave by a back exit. They said they wanted to leave by the front. Perhaps ten yards away, well beyond the group of people who'd gathered to celebrate the Taylors' victory, I noticed two figures standing in a badly lit alcove. I realised with a start who they were: Detective Superintendent Chris Burke, the man who'd led the murder investigation, was talking to the mother of murdered Alison. Burke's face was etched with pain. He was moving his hands slowly as he talked. No doubt he was trying to explain to her how those he had assured her had murdered Alison were now deemed innocent. Alison's mother didn't seem to be listening. Her face was expressionless, as if she was in deep shock. At that moment I felt deeply sad for her. Her daughter was dead, and whoever had killed her was still free.

The Taylors were about to move out to face the waiting journalists. Lisa said: 'Come on, Bernie. Come with us.' I said it was probably best if I didn't: 'You don't want the press making too many links between us. You know what they're like.' Lisa nodded; Michelle shrugged her shoulders. Then the two of them turned to their family. The group started off towards the entrance. I lagged behind. Michelle and Lisa were laughing and joking as they walked.

Outside, the street seemed full of television crews and photographers. The audience greeted the sisters' arrival with a loud cheer, then fell silent as Michelle began to read from a prepared statement:

We have spent two years of our lives protesting our innocence and only now has the deliberate mistake by the police come to light. We will not say that by being released justice has been done, because we should not have been put in this position in the first place. We also want to thank our legal team for believing in us and working so hard to prove our innocence and also to thank the Lord who gave us strength.

I almost laughed. Surely this wasn't the same legal team that Michelle had angrily criticised in letters to me? I suppose the sisters were only being polite. As for the Lord, I hadn't remembered him cropping up much in conversations over the last 11 months. Winston Silcott's face grinned at the crowd from the sisters' T-shirts. I cringed. It was bad enough that Michelle and Lisa were wearing the T-shirts, but the photo on them made everything worse. I assumed Winston's supporters wanted to get away from the police mug-shot photos that made him look like a machete-wielding psychopath. But in their attempt to portray him as a normal fun-loving sort of guy they'd gone too far the other way. Now he grinned inanely like a buoyantly over-enthusiastic game-show host. The sisters held hands and raised them in a joint clenched-fist salute. Their supporters responded with a cheer.

It was time for me to go. I slipped away, unnoticed.

TWO

The Picture of Christ

If my brother Paul hadn't been charged with wounding and assault I wouldn't have become involved with the Taylor sisters.

Paul had fallen out with a friend, and it had resulted in violence. He'd been remanded in custody to Belmarsh Prison in south-east London after police told magistrates they feared he might try to interfere with witnesses. I wanted to help my brother escape the charge, and I had every intention of interfering with the witnesses he was now prevented from visiting. I had a long list of convictions myself, and had served two prison sentences for wounding, so I knew the system. I knew what level of proof the police would need to secure a conviction. I also knew precisely what evidence would be needed to derail their case. I didn't know whether Paul was guilty or innocent. I wasn't even going to ask him: it didn't bother me. My job as a nightclub doorman meant I had plenty of free time during the day to find ways of discrediting what the police alleged. For me, any work I could do to undermine the police was a labour of love. I didn't mind using illegal methods because, as far as I was concerned, so did the police. From my own experience I knew how they could lie and cheat and use all sorts of illegalities to fit people up. I knew their tricks, but I'd learnt several of my own to counter them. In short, I hated the bastards and would do anything in my power to defeat them.

Within a week or so I'd gathered together enough 'new evidence' to enable Paul to make a credible application for bail. He was given a date in July 1992 to have his application heard. The venue was the Old Bailey.

I decided to attend the hearing. Like most people reading newspapers at that time I'd been following the Taylor sisters' trial. Reports had frequently made their way onto the front pages, with lurid follow-ups inside. I was used to violence, but I still found the case disturbing. I'd come across violent women before, but I just couldn't believe that such young women could carry out such a vicious attack on another woman. I could just about imagine a woman defending herself in such a frenzied way against a potential rapist, for instance, and I could just about imagine a woman in an extreme moment sticking a knife several times into another woman or an unfaithful lover, but 54 times? No way. Only a man could do something like that: I'd certainly encountered quite a few men who had that capability. From the newspaper photos the alleged murderers looked like ordinary south London girls. I prided myself on my ability to size people up quickly – to a large extent my job as a doorman depended on it – and to me the Taylor sisters didn't look hardened or potentially violent. They looked like ordinary girls, the sort of girls I met in droves several nights a week on the door at the nightclub. Perhaps because of my instinctive feeling that they couldn't have done it, I felt uncomfortable with the coverage in the tabloids. Several of them seemed to report the story as if the sisters' guilt was obvious. Yet I hadn't read anything that convinced me they were. There certainly didn't seem to be any so-called 'smoking-gun' evidence. Everything seemed circumstantial – and highly questionable. At the same time, it was all academic to me. I didn't personally know anyone involved with the case, and there were more important things on my mind.

The fact that the trial was taking place at the Old Bailey hadn't really registered with me. So when I arrived there for Paul's bail hearing I was intrigued by the long queue of people for the public gallery. I'd gone there with my brother's case in mind, nobody else's.

An elderly woman was standing at the back of the queue clutching what looked like a lunch box of sandwiches. I asked her what the queue was for. My ignorance displeased her. She said with irritation: 'It's those Taylor girls. The murder.' I walked towards the entrance, down past the mumbling line of murder groupies. Some of them must have thought they'd spotted a queue-jumper. I heard a few shouts: 'Oi, you! Get to the back!' and 'We've been here hours!' I politely told them to fuck off and walked to the other smaller queue that had formed for security clearance. A guard asked me several prepared questions regarding recording equipment, bags and mobile phones. Satisfied I had nothing on his list, he waved me through. I went in search of the court usher to find out which court my brother would be appearing in. A man in a well-ironed black gown almost sighed with boredom when I asked him for information. He asked me my brother's name and began to flick through his sheaf of listings. Then he looked up and said: 'It's been adjourned for seven days.' I asked him why. He said he didn't know. I can't say I was surprised. I'd often felt with my own cases that the legal process was one long adjournment. All the same, I felt exasperated by my wasted journey. I didn't have anything else to do for the rest of the day, so I decided on a whim to sit in on the Taylor sisters' trial for a few hours. I had, after all, managed to jump the queue for the public gallery, although I'd neglected to bring sandwiches.

I followed some people from the queue who were being let in a few at a time. An usher stood guarding the open door of the courtroom. He looked behind him to check for vacant spaces inside before letting us in. I spotted a gap in the middle of a bench and squeezed past several pairs of bunched knees to secure my place in the packed courtroom. Before I sat down I noticed John Shaughnessy, the victim's husband, sitting directly behind me. I recognised him from the newspaper photos. Looking around I also spotted a few members of the Taylor family on a bench to my right. The proceedings had not yet started, but Michelle and Lisa were sitting in the dock. In the flesh they seemed even more unlikely as murderers. They just looked like nice ordinary girls, although there was one detail which, to my cynical eye, made Michelle seem a little more cunning and worldly than she might at first have appeared: she was holding a Bible, a picture of Jesus Christ and what looked like a chain with a small crucifix attached. Nice touch, I thought – a show of Christian piety for the benefit of the jurors. Seasoned criminals had over the years taught me several courtroom tactics for swaying gullible jurors

– using a walking stick for sympathy; dressing nerdishly to destroy the image of hardened criminality; crying 'No! No! No!' when the victim gave particularly damaging evidence. I assumed Michelle had received similar guidance while on remand.

As I sat waiting for the proceedings to begin I read the latest instalment of the story in a discarded copy of *The Sun*. It helped me clarify in my mind the essential details that had so far emerged. The one thing not in dispute was that Alison Shaughnessy had been stabbed to death. Alison worked at Barclays Bank in The Strand. Her husband John, eight years her senior, worked as assistant purchasing manager and gardener at the Churchill Clinic, a private hospital opposite the Imperial War Museum in Lambeth, south London. Michelle Taylor was also employed at the clinic as a part-time domestic assistant. She lived in the staff accommodation, as John had before his marriage. Lisa Taylor, a window cleaner, had frequently stayed at the clinic with her sister.

In his opening address the prosecutor had said Michelle Taylor had been John Shaughnessy's mistress both before and after his marriage to Alison. She'd also kept a secret diary in which she confided her hatred of the victim. Alison, London-born of Irish parents, had met Irishman John when she was 16. He'd been her first serious boyfriend and she never learned of his affair, although she'd become 'somewhat vexed' by her husband's friendship with Michelle. The prosecutor said: 'But, unworldly and immature, she did not suspect the true nature of their relationship or the true feeling Michelle harboured for Shaughnessy.' Michelle knew John would never leave his unsuspecting wife, said the prosecutor, and in her desperation to keep the affair going she pretended to be friends with Alison. She went on pub outings with her; she attended the couple's wedding. But the prosecutor alleged her friendliness was a sham: 'Her obsession for Shaughnessy and her true feelings of repressed jealousy and hatred for her rival were all in her diary. The notes, jottings and the stream of consciousness revealed the deep unhappiness.' Michelle and John would often make love on Monday nights after she'd helped him arrange flowers at the clinic. Michelle would then drive John home to Alison. The prosecutor said Michelle realised despite her infatuation that she could not have John for herself: 'She knew he would never leave Alison. He told her so.' So she hatched a plot to kill Alison; Lisa Taylor, who disliked the way her sister had been treated, went along to support her. They waited for Alison to return home from work, persuaded her to let them in on some pretext, then stabbed her to death at the top of the stairs. That night she helped John arrange flowers as usual, then drove him back to his flat. She went in with him and affected 'shock and horror when he found the body . . . While John tried to raise the alarm, Michelle ran into a nearby pub shouting hysterically, "Call the police, my friend has been killed".'

I could see how that account made for a good story, but cutting through the dramatic prose of the tabloids I felt something was lacking – evidence of guilt. As far as I could see, the prosecution so far had only provided evidence of possible motive. I knew from my own experience how barristers could select a few facts from a complicated story and distort them in a way that made you look like the most wicked person alive. I hoped I was about to hear hard evidence that would justify the sisters' appearance in the dock. I put the newspaper to one side as the proceedings began. Over the course of the day I found myself getting increasingly wound up by what was unfolding in front of me. The evidence seemed to centre on Michelle's personality and her feelings for Alison and John. I also felt that much of what the prosecution was saying was being left unchallenged. I assumed the Taylors' legal team had considered every aspect, but there were many ways of looking at and explaining the same thing. I felt the Taylors' team weren't doing enough to offer an alternative view. I kept a close eye on Michelle and Lisa. I just couldn't imagine them as murderers. If they were guilty, I felt sure they'd have cracked under police interrogation. To me, they radiated innocence. What was happening reminded me of the many times when I'd sat in the dock listening to prosecuting barristers trying to convince a jury to convict me on the basis of little more than the suggestion that I was a deeply unpleasant person. But at least I'd been spared the attentions of the press, whereas with this case almost everything said by the prosecution could be found in national newspapers the next day. In a way I felt the press had almost turned itself into an arm of the prosecution. I didn't have anything against the press. In the past I'd helped out several journalists with gangland stories: they knew I was friendly with the infamous Kray twins. In fact, through visiting Ronnie Kray in Broadmoor Special Hospital I'd recently started helping a journalist with a story about one of Ronnie's fellow patients – the Yorkshire Ripper. Like most ordinary decent criminals, I had an especial hatred of nonces – the sex murderers of women and children – and liked journalists to stick the boot into them. But Michelle and Lisa Taylor weren't nonces, and I was very far from being persuaded they were even murderers. On the train home that evening I decided to write to the sisters to point out the biased way I thought their trial was being conducted. It was a short letter, which read in part:

> I can only hope that your legal representatives are studying the text used by the tabloid press and considering your position in relation to it. They are all but saying that you are guilty – a view that I would not share. I do not normally put pen to paper to voice my views, but I feel that your treatment is bordering on criminal.

When I posted the letter I hadn't really expected Michelle to reply. I felt I'd said all I needed to say. If she took my advice, all well and good. If she didn't, that was a matter for her. So I was surprised when a few days later a letter from Michelle dropped on my mat. It was written from Holloway Prison. She didn't say much; she just thanked me for my views and suggested I write again. I wish now that our correspondence had ceased at that point, but I suppose I was flattered she'd replied so swiftly. I suppose, too, the fact that she and her sister were at the centre of so much media attention made me more interested than I might otherwise have been. I'd written similar letters in the past to non-celebrity prisoners whose cases had interested me, often after reading about them in local papers. I'd given a bit of advice, and the correspondence usually petered out after a few letters. Even when serving my own prison sentences I'd helped prepare my fellow inmates' parole applications and appeal papers, such was my dislike of the police and 'their' system. Partly because Michelle and Lisa seemed so vulnerable and innocent I immediately felt more engaged by this case and more willing to put myself out. I can't say I felt that way for purely unselfish reasons; it certainly crossed my mind that I might at some point make money out of my involvement with them. But, as with my dealings with the Kray twins, I knew that money could be made without having to deceive those concerned. Journalists were often more than willing to pay a third party for arranging interviews and the like. In this case I felt that if the prosecution couldn't produce anything better than what they'd so far produced, then the jury would have to acquit the sisters. And in the event of their walking free I'd be on hand to help them negotiate with the journalists who'd be falling over themselves to interview them. But the vague prospect of money certainly wasn't my primary motive. Indeed, as I learned more about the case, money soon became irrelevant.

I wrote back to Michelle and told her a bit about myself. I also said I'd try to attend the rest of the trial. I sent her a photo, so she'd recognise me. In the meantime my brother's case had been considered by a judge in chambers. Bail had been granted on the condition that he live in Wolverhampton with our younger brother, which he'd agreed to do. So now I was free to give the Taylor sisters my full attention.

The trial had entered its third week when I returned to the Old Bailey. Since my last visit I'd continued to follow the case in the papers. I'd also received another letter from Michelle and, after considering the evidence I'd read, wrote her a letter detailing my optimistic evaluation of their chances of freedom. I'd become more and more convinced there was little hard evidence against them, although I realise now that in my mind I'd already crossed over into their camp. The only evidence that properly registered was evidence that pointed to their innocence; I'd begun to close my mind to anything that pointed to their guilt. I'd developed a sort of selective blindness. All the same, some of what emerged still struck me as quite damning. Importantly, however, nothing was totally damning – and Michelle had an explanation for everything.

When Michelle went into the witness box she said she'd been a virgin when she met John. He had asked her to go on the pill. It was not until some months into the affair that he told her of his engagement to another woman. She agreed she'd been bitterly hurt when she found out. She refused to see him for a while, but their relationship resumed a few months before John's marriage. Indeed, she claimed they slept together on the night before the wedding; she accused John of lying when he denied this. She agreed that seven months before the murder she had feelings of hatred for Alison, as recorded in her diary: 'When I wrote all those things I was very upset. Things were going through my mind. At that time I couldn't be a friend to Alison because I was sleeping with her husband. As time went on it wasn't Alison I was jealous of, or hated, it was John.' The court heard she gradually became more friendly towards Alison as she realised John was using them both. She said she believed he loved neither of them. 'I wasn't jealous of Alison any more. I didn't have a hatred feeling towards Alison. In fact, she was very nice.' The prosecutor alleged that Michelle knew John and Alison were about to move to Ireland to start a family; she'd wanted to get rid of Alison because she feared she'd lose John for ever. Michelle denied this and replied vehemently: 'Me and my sister did not kill Alison.' She insisted her feelings towards Alison had grown into friendship long before the killing – they had several drinks and meals together – and that she'd stopped having sex with John months beforehand. She also told the court that three weeks after Alison's funeral John tried to renew their affair; she had refused, telling him he was disgusting. John claimed it was she who'd tried to start things up again.

Michelle's defence barrister said the case against her consisted of 'flights of fancy'. He said: 'The portrait is one of the jealous mistress when the truth is that at the time of the murder Michelle was neither the mistress nor was she jealous.' He said the case against her was pathetically thin: there was simply no evidence against her. He said she had no need to murder Alison: there were many other options open to her. She could have told Alison about the affair or put pressure on her lover to leave his wife by threatening to expose him as an adulterer or she could have tried to trap John by getting pregnant. In their closing speeches both defence barristers emphasised that the prosecution's case was weak and highly circumstantial. In particular, there was a complete lack of forensic evidence to put the sisters at or near the murder scene. Lisa's barrister, Ann Mallalieu QC, said the allegation against her client was 'totally absurd'; an intruder had most likely carried out the murder. She said: 'Where is the evidence they did this? There is none.' The prosecutor admitted in his closing speech that no direct evidence linked the sisters to the murder, but he submitted that the circumstantial evidence pointed to their having had both the opportunity and motive for the killing.

On the Thursday of that third week – the day the judge was due to sum up – I'd just come out of the toilet when a woman I recognised as the sisters' mother approached me as I began climbing the stairs to the public gallery. Ann Taylor asked: 'Are you Bernard?' I said I was. She thanked me for writing to her girls and asked me how I thought the case was going. We stood there talking for a few minutes about various aspects of it. We seemed to agree about everything. Derek Taylor came over; Ann introduced us. I liked Derek instantly: he was laughing and joking and came across as very practical, someone who would make the most of any situation. The usher announced that the court was about to begin. Del (as he preferred to be called) invited me to sit with him, Ann and other members of their family. As we made our way to our seats they told me that members of John Shaughnessy's group had been looking at them in a menacing manner. They feared some sort of incident outside if the jury found the girls guilty. I told them not to worry: I'd walk with them to their transport to make sure nothing happened. As we sat down I noticed that once again John Shaughnessy was sitting directly behind me. I'd seen him in the pub the day before giving interviews to journalists. I couldn't help feeling sorry for him: he'd been given a good going-over in the witness box and he wasn't getting very sympathetic coverage in the press either.

The judge began his summing-up, and I was soon impressed by his fairness. He said:

> There is no eyewitness account that either of these two defendants killed
> Alison. There is no eyewitness account that puts them at the flat at the

relevant time. There is no evidence that puts them in the street at the
relevant time. This is a case that depends on weighing individual pieces
of evidence and putting them together like a jigsaw puzzle.

As he went through the evidence he stressed its circumstantial nature. I
began to feel that the sisters had a better than average chance of getting
acquitted. When the judge touched on evidence that pointed to their
guilt I merely thought of ways in which it should have been more
adequately challenged. The judge warned the jurors not to make moral
judgements on the sisters. He said:

> Juries do not make moral judgements. Judges in my view should not
> make moral judgements. We are here to do a job. Inevitably all of us have
> got views about the morals of some of the witnesses we have heard in this
> case.

He told them to apply their minds only to whether Michelle and Lisa
were guilty of murder.

In the dock the sisters looked confident most of the time. At times
Lisa didn't even bother listening to the judge: she seemed more interested
in whispering to the prison officer beside her.

The day's proceedings came to an end. The judge said he'd finish his
summing-up in the morning. I walked outside with Ann and Del and a
man called Leon, who I later learned was Lisa's boyfriend. The group
with John Shaughnessy made for a nearby pub, while we made our way
to the train station. I told them I didn't believe the prosecution had
proved its case. I said my goodbyes after arranging to meet Ann and Del
at the court next day. On my train journey home I wrote again to
Michelle:

> I have just left the Old Bailey after listening to the judge sum up your
> case. I obviously haven't heard all of the trial but from what the judge
> remarked upon I think you've a 55 per cent chance of a true verdict and
> a 45 per cent chance of a wrongful guilty verdict.

I went through a few of the points I thought went against them, but also stressed several positive points in their favour.

> It's so hard to know what those on the jury make of it all – very little is clear because there is no evidence other than circumstantial as the judge rightly pointed out. You were looking okay up until the judge ordered that five-minute break. When you came back in you looked exhausted and very upset. It all will be over tomorrow one way or another so here's hoping the 12 listen to what they are told: 'If there is any doubt you must find the defendants not guilty.' I cannot see how there cannot be doubt, Michelle, every matter is either contradicted or in doubt. Lisa looks okay, she kept smiling about something to the screw. Hopefully you will not receive this letter because you will be home and dry by the time it gets through the system, but if not, don't ever worry about being left. I will stay with you throughout – no strings attached – just as a friend and to help when and if I can.

That night the more I thought about the evidence the more I thought the girls would soon be free. *Surely* the jury, good and true, would find them not guilty?

THREE

Guilty of Murder

When I arrived at court the next day I still felt confident the sisters would soon be walking to freedom. Their parents shared my confidence. They said they had a bottle of champagne on ice to be opened as soon as the girls got home. When the judge finished his summing-up, the court emptied. Most people headed outside to the July sunshine. The trial had lasted 15 days, but no one knew how long the jury would take. For the first few hours I stood in the street with the sisters' parents and a few other friends and relatives. We didn't talk much. A few supporters tried to reassure the parents that their girls would soon be free. Ann said: 'If there's any justice, they will be.' A few journalists introduced themselves, hoping to line up interviews for later. Around two I had the urge for a drink, so I headed across the road to the nearest pub. Inside, I saw John Shaughnessy and his group sitting at a table, huddled in conversation. I downed a pint quickly, then went back outside to Ann and Del. They were talking to a man I recognised as the sisters' solicitor. The parents introduced him to me as Michael Holmes. He said he'd been in to see the sisters; they were okay. Around four, for some unknown reason, I had a feeling the jury had reached their verdicts, and I said so to Del. He nodded, but seemed unconvinced by my apparent psychic powers. I went back across the road to the pub to use the toilet. On my way back through the bar someone shouted: 'The jury's back! The jury's back!' I looked across at John Shaughnessy, who was still at the same table. He didn't make to move; he just sat there, motionless save for the movement of lifting his drink to his lips. One of his friends said: 'Come on!' But he didn't move. He had the look of a man lost in his own thoughts. I realised how in many ways the verdicts were irrelevant to him: his wife was dead, and nothing was going to change that.

The jury, which had been out for six hours, was in place when I returned. I looked down on Michelle and Lisa: their faces gave nothing away, but I could imagine the churning of their stomachs. They were asked to stand. Dwarfed by prison officers on either side, they looked vulnerable. Michelle was clutching her picture of Christ and her chain with its silver crucifix. Now she looked anxious. Lisa just stared straight ahead. The judge asked the jury foreman if they'd reached a verdict on which they all agreed. The foreman said they had. There was total silence. The judge asked the foreman for their verdict on Michelle. 'Guilty,' he said. And Lisa? 'Guilty.' There were shouts of 'No! No! No!' Michelle stood rooted to the floor of the dock; Lisa put her head in her hands and wept. I turned to Ann and Del: they were dumbstruck. Some benches away I watched Alison's mother collapsing into the arms of her husband. The judge ordered silence. He thanked the jury, then turned to address the sisters. A female juror had started sobbing quietly.

The judge said: 'The jury have found you guilty of killing a young wife whose life was all before her, whose life is no more. There is only one sentence the law allows. Michelle Taylor, you will go to prison for life. Lisa Taylor, because of your age, you will be detained at Her Majesty's pleasure.' I looked again at Ann: she was staring at Michelle, stony-faced; Del was rubbing his face anxiously. The judge said a few more words, but they were drowned out by the conflicting sounds of sobbing and celebration. I watched the prison officers leading Michelle and Lisa through a wooden door to start their life sentences. I saw Lisa looking back over her shoulder, no doubt searching the sea of faces for her parents, but before she could find them a warder ushered her out the door.

I waited at the door of the court for Ann and Del: they still feared some sort of attack outside. As we walked down the stone steps to the ground floor I told Ann not to worry: 'It's not over yet. They can still appeal.' Ann didn't say anything, but I could see her look of stone turning to one of anger. Outside, we stood in the street, unsure of which way to turn. Journalists, photographers and camera crews buzzed around. Towering above us was the famous golden statue of Justice. I looked up and noticed an inscription: 'Defend the children of the poor and punish the wrongdoer.' How phoney, I thought, how typical of people in authority: wrongdoers were usually the children of the poor – and they did wrong because of their circumstances. A tabloid journalist asked Ann for her reaction. In tones of animated anger she tore into John Shaughnessy:

> My girls would never have been in the dock if it wasn't for him. John Shaughnessy is a bastard and I don't care if you print that. I will tell him to his face. That 'fatal attraction' stuff is a load of rubbish. The girls didn't murder Alison and I know that. They can't lie to me, their own mother. My Michelle has never even had a parking ticket. Michelle was young and impressionable and fell for him, but that's not a crime. John led my daughter along. He wanted the best of both worlds. He wanted to have a wife and my daughter as a girlfriend.
>
> He has caused all of this trouble. I think he's pathetic. The mere mention of him makes her feel ill. This whole thing has been a disgrace. I can't see what Michelle saw in John. Why do the women fall for him? I can't see anything great about him. I didn't like him but I was tolerant because he was Michelle's friend. My Michelle was used by him. He took advantage of her and she suffered because of it. She was completely devastated by Alison's death. How would you feel if you had found the body? It has been a year of hell for us all and I blame John Shaughnessy for that. My girls are very close. I remember when Lisa was ill and had to sleep downstairs. Michelle stayed with her all night because she didn't want to leave her alone. If we were not so close I don't think we would have got through this.

Ann and Del spoke to several other journalists. The crowd began to disperse. Still underneath the statue of Justice, we began to talk of a campaign to free the sisters. There was a group of around ten of us, and several people chipped in with their suggestions. We began walking slowly towards the station. On the other side of the road I noticed John Shaughnessy and his group. Lisa's boyfriend, Leon, saw them at the same time. He shouted at them and made as if to cross the road, but one of our group grabbed him by the arm and said: 'Leave it.' At the end of the road I said goodbye to Ann and Del, promised I'd be in touch soon to help get the campaign off the ground, then went to catch my train.

On the train I wrote again to Michelle:

> I have just left your Mom, Dad and friends outside the Old Bailey after what I can only describe as an extraordinary, yet farcical verdict by the jury. Nobody, not even the judge, could believe the foreman when he said 'guilty' and 'guilty' again for Lisa. Perhaps you were in shock but even the judge remarked to the jury, 'Your views may not be mine, but thank you.'

I wasn't entirely sure that the judge had said those exact words, but I thought he'd said something similar. I told her I'd heard all sorts of people expressing their disbelief.

> This is not the final thing, Michelle. You can go for a re-trial via the Court of Appeal. I spoke to your Mom, Dad and friends – you have some very special people supporting you. They did you both proud all around. At ten past four, just before we went in, I said to your Dad, 'I have got a feeling that they have reached a verdict.' It was uncanny. 'Life', as I'm sure you've been told, is not life inside. If all goes wrong, at your age you will probably do about seven years. Enough about the worst. Let us just think positive from here on in. I will do whatever I can for you as I don't think you should have got a guilty on such nonsense evidence.

That night I went to work at Raquels nightclub. I'd had to get up early to go to court, so I was tired. It was a quiet night – only a few fights amongst drunks – so I managed to get away early. I headed straight for bed. My partner Debra was already asleep. I got into bed beside her and collapsed into slumberland. Around nine that Saturday morning – not the time I planned to get up – Debra shouted upstairs to say there was a call for me. I was still tired, so shouted back: 'Tell them to call back later.' Debra said I ought to come down as it was important. Still half-asleep I felt my way downstairs and picked up the phone. I said to the caller: 'This had better be good.'

A female voice answered: 'It's me, Bernie. It's Michelle.'

I was astonished. I said: 'I thought you'd have been given plenty of liquid cosh [Largactil – a sedative used in prison] and been locked away on your own.' She laughed, and said she was okay. We started chatting. I was struck by how matter-of-fact she seemed, how devoid of emotion. I assumed she was still in shock. She said she'd like me to help with a campaign to prove their innocence. I said I'd already spoken to her parents about it and that I'd be more than willing to help where and when I could. We didn't discuss any details, because we couldn't talk for long. Michelle said she only had a few phone credits left, and she still had to ring her parents. We agreed to talk again soon, then said our goodbyes.

I felt pleased and flattered by the call. A strong sense of the injustice of what had happened also touched me. I felt suddenly determined to do whatever I could to help them; I was going to right this terrible wrong. They were ordinary girls from a working-class background, 'the children of the poor', yet the police and their system were going to destroy their lives. I had got the bit between my teeth. Unfortunately, as I only realised later, I'd also put on the blinkers: I could see straight ahead well enough, but I couldn't see what was happening on the sidelines. It was typical of me: it was all or nothing until I'd proved my point. I didn't give a thought to possible consequences.

I was wide awake now, my mind filled with thoughts of the campaign I could run. Even at that early stage I felt confident of victory: I could see the sisters walking to freedom and, most pleasing, I could see the dejected faces of the police. Like most criminals, I had a strong sense of outrage at how I'd been treated in the past by them. Given that I'd only ever been caught and punished for perhaps ten per cent of my crimes, I was probably less outraged than I might have been. It rarely occurred to me that in their attempts whenever possible to cause me grief the police might have been working in the interests of society. My feelings were a strange combination of self-pity and bitterness. I had my own sense of what justice was – and that tended to differ from what was enforced as law.

Later that morning, Saturday, 25 July 1992, I went to the shops and bought most of the papers. I was interested to see how they'd treated the story, although I didn't expect any surprises. As far as I was concerned, the press had tried, convicted and punished the sisters before the jury had been sent out. However, I still hoped that by immersing myself further in the details of the case I'd get ideas for fighting the sisters' campaign.

The sheer scale of the coverage astonished me. All the tabloids, and most of the broadsheets, carried the story on their front pages. And all the tabloids carried a further two to four pages inside. The general tone was best summarised by a detective's comment: 'Michelle was an obsessive woman who made *Fatal Attraction* look like a teddy bear's picnic.' She was described as a schemer who gave neighbours and workmates the impression of a sweet girl who wouldn't hurt a fly, yet had hatched a hideous plot to butcher Alison.

The *Daily Mail* devoted its centre pages to a feature headlined, 'LOVE, LUST AND A DEADLY OBSESSION'.

> It was a story of three women, a cheating husband and an affair that ended in savage murder.
>
> The young bride was home-loving, shy, devoted to her husband. The mistress was scheming, possessive and cruel. The man they both loved was an Irish charmer, weak, unable to control his emotions and incapable of ending an affair that spun horribly out of control.
>
> Into this deadly triangle came the mistress's sister, calculating, ruthless and driven by a warped sense of injustice . . .

I felt sorry for the sisters. They were really getting the full treatment.

The affair may have been an open secret at work. At home, with Alison, it was shrouded in lies and Irish blarney. However, illicit sex is one thing. Obsessive love is another. Michelle Taylor could not have the undivided attention of the man she loved. It led her to pay for her lover's stag night – a favour rewarded by Alison with an invitation to the wedding.

The two women had even become friends. Though it is hard to imagine the black thoughts that must have swarmed through Taylor's mind in those days running up to the wedding. Certainly those around them were aware of her slavish devotion to her rival's fiancé. 'She hung on everything John said – it was clear she saw herself as John's close friend. She would try to monopolise the conversation with John and she laughed louder than anyone else at his jokes.'

These perceptive remarks were from a family friend and Mr Shaughnessy's niece, Edel Slattery. Edel had shared a hotel room with Taylor at a hen night in the Irish city of Waterford.

'It seemed a bit funny but it's only looking back that it falls into place. We never really got beneath her character. I suppose we only saw her good side.'

Those comments seemed to me typical of the papers' general approach. They treated almost everything Michelle had ever done as sinister, suggestive of the evil to come. I didn't read a single 'fact' that I felt couldn't be challenged. In some papers Lisa was treated as being even more evil than Michelle:

Younger but more dominant and more self-assured, police believe she propelled Michelle's dream into terrifying reality. But even now, neither police nor social workers really know why. Michelle wore a locket around her neck with a picture of them both in it.

One detective said: 'Lisa is much harder and calculating than her sister and in the end probably said if you want to get rid of her let's just get on with it.'

John Shaughnessy received only marginally less sympathetic coverage. The *Daily Mirror* had the headline: SHE WAS THE PERFECT WIFE, HE WAS

THE PERFECT SHIT. However, my sympathy for him diminished when I read some of the things he'd been saying. He popped up all over the place saying he wanted to hang the sisters himself. He said:

> Loads of men have affairs and they don't finish up having their wives murdered. I never dreamed it could end up this way but I know she would have forgiven me for having the affair. We were devoted to each other.

He said he wished he'd never set eyes on Michelle. He said he should have told her to go away, but claimed she was like a leech:

> I should not have let the bitch get under my skin. I wasn't chasing Michelle, she was pestering me. But I know I should never have had anything to do with her. I wasn't an angel and it was my fault for not saying no, but I don't see why I should feel guilty because I was having an affair. I don't want people to feel sorry for me in any respect. But it's like I'm in the dock and I haven't committed a crime.

He described the night he found the body after Michelle had driven him home: 'When she drove me home that night she wanted to break my heart. She had killed my wife and was enjoying my pain.'

He told how he sat for hours in the mortuary with Alison's body:

> I was just holding her hand. I stroked her hair. I loved her hair even though it got in my face when we were in bed. While I was stroking her hair I could feel a bump on the back of her head where she had been hit. Finally the staff had to ask me to leave because they wanted to shut.

He said he'd contemplated suicide. He'd hoped a bus would run him over. He had reserved a plot next to his wife's in the graveyard where she was buried:

I would not like to marry again. Alison can never be replaced. I loved Alison and was totally devoted to her. I would never have left her for Michelle and the thought never crossed my mind. I never considered myself to be Michelle's boyfriend. I didn't know the full extent of her feelings. I just thought it was something casual. I am not the sort of bloke who likes to put it around. I would rather have a quiet drink at the bar or a cup of tea at home.

The way the papers tried to make the sisters' every action seem sinister was best shown in the stories about the aftermath of the murder.

The sisters even continued their charade after the murder. They sprinkled holy water over Alison's coffin in church and took holy communion with her family. Michelle sobbed throughout the service. She hugged Alison's relatives afterwards and told them: 'It's such a terrible shame.'

Alison's brother Robert Blackmore said last night: 'I cannot believe they had the nerve to do it. Michelle was crying her eyes out and everybody was looking at her. They had the cheek to queue up to sprinkle holy water over my sister's coffin at the altar. Afterwards Michelle came up to us and started sympathising. Her sister was with her. I just wish I could strangle both of the girls. They are evil.'

Of course, if the sisters were guilty, then their behaviour had been sick, but I was sure they were innocent. To me, they'd been genuinely grieving for Alison – and expressing their grief in the same way as the other mourners. In the *Daily Express* Alison's father described how he watched the sisters during one of two memorial services for his daughter.

'It was an astonishing act they put on. I didn't like them being there,' said Mr Blackmore. 'I had my eye on Michelle throughout the service, which was difficult, but I wanted to see how she would react.'

At the earlier service, Alison's mother recoiled when the killer tried to shake her hand. 'I knew Alison didn't like Michelle and there was no way I was going to like her,' she said.

I must have spent most of the afternoon reading those papers. I felt angry at the way the girls had been portrayed, but my anger filled me with resolve. Most importantly, some of the stories had given me ideas for the campaign. Everyone had heard of the Birmingham Six and the Guildford Four – some people even knew of the Cardiff Three – but to my mind this miscarriage of justice was as big as anything that had gone before. I wanted everyone to know of the Taylor Two.

'Free the Taylor Two' – that would be our cry. I vowed to make sure that everyone would hear it.

FOUR

Love Rat's Tart

I bought another pile of newspapers the next day. It was Sunday and I expected another splurge of lurid stories.

I wasn't disappointed. There were several bizarre tales concerning Michelle, John and various ex-lovers. In the *News of the World* (26 July 1992) I came across an article headlined ALISON KILLER HATED BEING LOVE RAT'S 'TART'. It was written by Gary Jones and Mark Christy. I knew Gary Jones as the paper's chief crime correspondent. He'd first contacted me around nine months earlier regarding some gangland stories. The article purported to be based on a letter Michelle had written to an unnamed friend:

> Murdering mistress Michelle Taylor has told how she came to hate her lover John Shaughnessy because he treated her like a tart.
>
> Michelle, 21, who got a life sentence this week for killing John's wife Alison, said she was just a 'bit on the side'.
>
> She told of her anger and confusion in a letter to a pal written during her 15-day trial at the Old Bailey.
>
> When John, 30, was told of the letter he smiled and said: 'Michelle may well have hated me. She proved it by murdering Alison. Maybe she feels she got her revenge.'

The rest of the article contained quotes from the letter in which she explained she didn't love John, that her feelings for him had changed in the year before the murder and that she didn't want to say what she now thought of him. As I read the article I began to feel uneasy: Michelle had expressed similar sentiments in a letter to me. Had Gary Jones somehow got hold of my letter? I certainly hadn't given it to him. I dug out her letter and compared the two. There were several differences. For instance, she hadn't referred to herself as Shaughnessy's 'bit on the side', nor that he'd treated her 'like a tart'. As for the similarities, I reasoned that as she was by her own admission replying to perhaps 30 letters a day, then inevitably she'd say similar things to different people. Besides, there was no major revelation in the letter: it didn't contain anything she hadn't said or implied at the trial. All the same, I was still worried she might think I'd betrayed her. I'd been paranoid for as long as I could remember. On several occasions, especially in nightclubs, this state of mind had saved me from a beating – or worse. The more I looked at the article, the more I convinced myself that Michelle would think I was responsible. I wouldn't have worked myself into such a state if I'd known then what Michelle only told me later, namely, that she and Lisa became so concerned that someone in prison was passing on details of their letters – and even phone calls – that they subsequently arranged for their mail to be specially sealed in the governor's office in their presence.

I decided I had to reassure Michelle I hadn't been the source of the story. I put all her letters in a large envelope: I was going to hand them in personally to the reception at Holloway Prison in north London. I assumed the newspaper's solicitors would have insisted on retaining any original letters in case of legal action. By giving mine back to Michelle she'd know I was innocent. Later that day I drove to the prison. I wrote Michelle a brief covering letter to explain what I was doing. The next day I tried ringing Gary Jones at the *News of the World*, but was told he wouldn't be in until Tuesday. When I finally got to speak to him I told him I'd been writing to Michelle and that the letter he'd used seemed similar to one she'd sent me. I asked him if it had my name on it. He said he didn't know – the name had been disguised. I asked him where he'd got it from. He laughed and said: 'Be fair, Bernie. I wouldn't tell anyone about the sources for my stories. You know it's not on.' I said Michelle knew I had contacts with journalists and I was concerned that, if she thought it was the letter she'd sent me, she might find me guilty by association. He laughed again and said it wasn't his problem. He added that I was a mug to have anything to do with the sisters: he thought the jury had delivered the right verdict. I told him I thought they'd been fitted up by the police, aided by the press. In the end we agreed to disagree. However, I still wanted something from him to prove I wasn't his source, so I asked if he would write me a letter to this effect which I could show to Michelle. He wasn't keen on the idea, but after I persisted he wrote:

> Whilst I understand your concern regarding the origin of the article, I am unable to supply any information. It is the *News of the World*'s policy not to identify informants. If Miss Taylor wishes to contact me I would be willing to allay her fears regarding your involvement.

What made things more irritating for me was that I was helping Gary Jones on a story about the Yorkshire Ripper. I'd been regularly visiting the former East End gangster Ronnie Kray in Broadmoor. I was also friends with his brother, Reggie. My friendship with the twins had developed some years earlier when I'd asked them to become involved in helping to raise money for a boy who needed a life-saving operation – an earlier campaign that had taken up more than a year of my time. I got on well with both of the Krays. In fact, just over two years earlier, I'd got my present nightclub job through an introduction made by Reggie.

One of Ronnie's fellow patients in Broadmoor was the Ripper, Peter Sutcliffe, who'd sometimes be sitting on a nearby table in the visitors' room. During one of my first conversations with Gary Jones he told me how he'd been attacked in a television programme for his methods in infiltrating and exposing a gang of paedophiles. I said I saw nothing wrong in using whatever means possible to cause pain – physical or mental – to paedophiles and other nonces like the Ripper. I told him how I often saw the Ripper when visiting Ronnie. This conversation must have stuck in his mind because a few months before the Taylors' trial Jones asked me to help him with a feature they were planning on the Ripper. He knew I wrote regularly to various prisoners: he wanted me to write to Sutcliffe to ask him his views on various subjects, including his crimes and motives. I'd never written to a prisoner other than to offer assistance, but Sutcliffe was a nonce, so I agreed. I decided the Ripper would be more likely to speak openly to a female, so I wrote to him using the name 'Belinda Cannon'. I told Ronnie what I was doing and he thought it was very funny – he loathed the Ripper and resented being confined in the same establishment as him. The Ripper responded at once. Over a few months he answered every question I asked him – from his favourite colour, to why he'd wanted to commit mass murder. The *News of the World* also provided a female journalist to take calls from him. I later told all this to Michelle: she wrote to me saying it didn't bother her. It was only much later, when we'd become bitter enemies, that she tried to suggest that my contacts with the Ripper were part of a pattern of deception of which she'd been unaware. Michelle and Lisa know I never had any intention of having them over.

In fact, one of the first things I did for them was to devise a way to ensure that no one had them over. After getting the letter of reassurance from Jones I underlined my good faith by composing an undertaking that they should ask everyone who had any dealings with them to sign. It read:

> I understand that on previous occasions individuals have pretended to befriend MICHELLE TAYLOR and LISA TAYLOR and have then sought to use their relationship with them and information obtained during the course of such a relationship for their personal gain.
>
> I confirm that I have no such ulterior motive in my relationship with MICHELLE TAYLOR or LISA TAYLOR. I realise that any information imparted to me during the course of this relationship must be treated as a confidence exchange between friends. I accept that I have no right to use such information for my personal gain or for any other purpose, without MICHELLE TAYLOR or LISA TAYLOR'S prior written authority. I agree not to divulge any such information to anyone else without such written authority.

I understand that I have no right to make any record, written or otherwise, of any conversations which I have with MICHELLE TAYLOR or LISA TAYLOR.

I was the first person to sign this undertaking. Then I sent it to Michelle along with Gary Jones's note and another covering letter to explain what I was doing:

I have sent an outline of the form which could prevent you and Lisa getting unnecessary grief and/or adverse publicity. You can consider it with your solicitor and let me know if I can assist you further. I have also enclosed ten cards for safe replies should you take up the idea. I shall discuss future ideas with you first, but for now I'll wait until I hear how your parents want me to help with the campaign. As I told you on the phone I know a few people through the Krays who may be able to help with the campaign. I learned a lot about the pros and cons for campaigns through Reggie, so hopefully I can apply them to yours and Lisa's. There is a method cons use in discrediting statements. Basically, you list all of the verbal evidence minus the embroidery and set about either disproving it or offering alternative meanings. It sounds like rubbish on paper, but if I could sit down and show you or your parents you would see its value.

The next day I got a call in the morning from Ann Taylor. She said Michelle had asked her to tell me that she'd received the package of letters and she now knew it wasn't me who'd sold her letter to the *News of the World*. Ann said that, before receiving my package, Michelle had sent me a 'funny' letter, but I was to ignore it. I told Ann not to worry about it. I arranged to meet her and her husband at their home in south London that evening. We agreed it was time to get the campaign moving.

It was the first time I'd been to the Taylors' home in Forest Hill. The street was more middle-class than I'd expected. I'd had an idea that they lived in a more working-class area than the quiet residential road I found myself in. Their house, too, was very pleasant — three-bedroomed and semi-detached. As I opened the gate I was confronted by a huge and lively Dobermann pinscher. I've never liked dogs – and they've never liked me, having bitten me twice in the past. There wasn't going to be a third time: I was just lining up my boot with the dog's head when Ann opened the front door. 'Hello, love,' she said. 'Don't worry about Duke. He's all bark and no bite.' By this time Duke was jumping all over me. He followed me into the house. Ann led me to the lounge, where Del was sitting. 'This is our hundred-thousand-pound house,' said Ann. 'That's what the papers called it, anyway. Bloody idiots.' I sat down, with Duke continuing to try to jump on me. Despite his size he was harmless, a bit of a nervous wreck, in fact. Ann said that on the morning the police had stormed into the house to arrest the sisters Duke had gone wild, barking and running around. The presence of so many uniformed strangers had scarred him psychologically. Since that day he'd developed a furious dislike of anything resembling a hat – even traffic cones. The family thought this was because several of the police officers had been wearing helmets and hats. Ann said that now, as a party trick, the family sometimes placed a traffic cone in the garden and roared with laughter as Duke attacked it. Their front room could have been called 'the brown room'. Brown carpet, brown curtains, brown-and-beige wallpaper, brown coverings on the big square armchairs. On the wall was a glass heart engraved 'To Mother'. Then my eyes caught something I'd hardly expected to see – a ceremonial dagger. It was on the wall above the settee.

'I'm not being funny, Del,' I said, 'but if journalists see that knife hanging up there, they'll have a field day.'

Del said it was harmless: 'They'll print a load of crap whatever we do, Bernie.' I also noticed that beside my seat was a pile of around 30 *True Crime* magazines. I felt like telling Del he ought to put them out of sight too, but I held my tongue. I remembered reading one story which claimed Michelle had studied former murder cases in her local library prior to Alison's murder in order to pick up tips on avoiding detection. The story was obviously false: looking at the array of reading material beside me I knew she wouldn't have had to leave her home to boost her knowledge. There had even been a story that she and Lisa had travelled to Southend to stab a stray dog to death in rehearsal for the murder. I couldn't believe that anyone brought up in a dog-loving family would do that. Besides, they wouldn't have had to travel all the way to Southend to find a mutt to murder – there were plenty of strays in and around south London.

Our little group was joined by the sisters' uncle, Norman Simpson. Over the course of the next six hours we discussed the possible ways forward. Ann and Uncle Norman were keen on getting a petition going. I was considerably less keen. I said no one had ever walked out of prison on the strength of a petition; it was a lot of hard work that generally ended up in the bin of the recipient. I believed the best way forward lay in challenging the police's evidence. After a lot of friendly discussion, and several pots of tea, we agreed to work on both. One group would work on the petition, the other would concentrate on the evidence. I stressed that under no circumstances should I be put forward as someone running the campaign. I said that several journalists knew about my criminal connections and convictions. If they thought I had control over anything it would be deemed tainted. Anything that might harm the sisters' cause, or image, had to be avoided. Everyone agreed. They decided to seek the first signatures for their petition the next evening at Forest Hill train station. They asked me if I wanted to come. I said no, and added that, regardless of the cause, the last thing people wanted on their way home from work was to be confronted with a petition. The Taylors disagreed and went off the next day to meet the evening commuters. I discovered later that the venture had been a disaster. They received lots of abuse and very few signatures. They decided in future only to ask people that they or their supporters either knew or lived near.

I talked about the areas of evidence on which we needed to focus. I'd read a piece in one of the newspapers about the time the sisters would have needed to get from the murder scene back to the clinic. The police alleged they'd made the journey in 11 minutes, which I found hard to believe. As the newspaper said: 'Had the journey taken minutes more the sisters would have been in the clear.' I said if we could prove the police timings were incorrect, then Michelle and Lisa couldn't have committed

the murder – and all the other evidence would become immaterial.
Later I put my ideas on paper to Michelle:

> I would personally think, without yet doing it, that at that time of day,
> the journey driven within legal speed limits would take more than the 11
> minutes which the police managed. What I have suggested to your
> parents is that we do the journey/route you would have usually taken in
> two cars. Videoing from the one behind we could record the speed of the
> vehicle and record the time it took. I've a video camera so it's no
> problem. The police probably 'tested' the route in a patrol car and
> everybody knows people give way to them, etc., so they would do it
> much quicker. It needs to be done at least ten times so an average can be
> found, taking into account getting caught up or getting through traffic
> lights, etc. I shall (when you mark out the exact route you gave police on
> the map I've given tonight to your parents) go along meticulously and
> mark out in advance every traffic light, pedestrian crossing, etc. and all
> of the speed limits. This could be a very important factor. I would not
> believe a word the police say. We must check every word of evidence.

I arranged to meet Del and Uncle Norman the following Monday to start
testing the timings. In the meantime I set myself the task of gathering
together all the stories that had been printed in six different newspapers
over the course of the trial. I told the family I'd try to use my contacts on
Fleet Street to get everything we needed. I spent a day travelling around
various newspaper offices. In the end I paid for the cuttings myself, then
handed them over to the sisters' legal team, who, even at that early stage,
knew that the sensationalist press coverage of the trial would form one of
the cornerstones of the sisters' appeal.

During the week I received the 'funny' letter from Michelle that Ann
had warned me was on its way. In it she accused me of being the one
who'd given her letter to the *News of the World*. I was pleased a few days
later to receive another letter from her withdrawing everything she'd said.
She told me she'd tried to get back the previous letter, but the mail had
already been on its way out of the prison. After she'd written the letter

she kept thinking she'd made a mistake. She'd decided that someone somewhere must have got hold of the letter and copied it. She now felt really bad for jumping to the conclusion that I'd given the letter to the paper. She said she knew she was wrong; she hadn't been thinking straight. She was sending my package back to me, along with the undertaking I'd signed, because she didn't want it: she trusted me. However, she said she'd keep the other undertakings to use them for anyone else who contacted her and she thanked me for drafting them for her.

Then she changed the subject. She said that one of her mates had just arrived back from court with a life sentence for murder. Michelle said her friend wasn't guilty; all she'd done was help get rid of a body because she was scared of her boyfriend. Michelle said there was no justice. What was wrong with the world? She said she wanted to fight not just for herself, but for all the other wrongly convicted people in prison. Her ambition was to change the whole legal system, because she wouldn't just be able to walk out of prison and put everything behind her. There were too many innocent people inside, and unless something was done then the system would never change.

I wrote back to tell her that the campaign would be getting properly under way on Monday when we would try to prove wrong the police timings.

FIVE

Timing is Everything

If I'd known how the campaign to free the sisters was going to take over my life I think I'd have just signed the petition and left it at that.

Instead, only ten days after the sisters had been sentenced, I found myself in the back seat of Michelle's white Ford Sierra Estate outside a pub near her former workplace, the Churchill Clinic. Del was driving and Uncle Norman was in the front passenger seat. I'd brought along a video camera to film the journey from the murder scene back to the clinic to prove the inaccuracy of the police timings.

The prosecution's case had depended upon a so-called 23-minute 'window of opportunity' in which the sisters had murdered Alison and returned to the clinic. The victim had definitely clocked off work at 5.02 p.m. The police said she'd gone straight home and would have arrived around 35 minutes later. Michelle had then been seen at the clinic around 6 p.m., so there were only around 23 minutes in which she and Lisa could have committed the murder, cleaned up and driven back. The police had allowed 11 minutes for the return trip. But I was convinced that, without a blue flashing light, no one could complete the journey in that time.

Del, Uncle Norman and I set off for Alison's former address in Vardens Road, Battersea. We parked a few hundred yards from the murder house, near the pub to which Michelle had run screaming after she and John Shaughnessy had discovered the body. On the dashboard, secured with a lump of Blu-Tack, we'd mounted a stopwatch. Uncle Norman stood outside the house. At my signal he began walking towards the car. At the same moment Del started the stopwatch and I began filming. Uncle Norman got in the car and we drove off. Throughout the journey back to the clinic I focused the camera on the speedometer, the stopwatch and the road ahead. We kept within the designated speed limits and obeyed all traffic signals and signs. However, much to our surprise, we covered the journey in much the same time as the police. We were all hugely disappointed; Del looked especially deflated. We drove back to Forest Hill and dropped off Norman. Del and I sat in the car talking. He was more upset than I'd first realised: he knew the significance of the timings. I told him not to be too downhearted because, as far as I was concerned, we'd only just done a dummy run. We needed to do the journey several times on several different Mondays to get the real picture. We talked for perhaps 15 minutes, both of us mouthing off about the police. Then I said we ought to beat the police at their own game: if the police could bend the rules – and Del needed no convincing that they had done – then so could we. I suggested we ought only to retain video footage of the runs that took a lot longer than 11 minutes. We could junk the rest.

'Fuck it,' I said. 'If the police can lie, then so can we.' Del looked at me and laughed. We had reached an understanding. For me, this was a turning point. It was the first time I'd talked about misrepresenting the facts. The term that we all started using was the one I'd first mentioned: beating the police at their own game. I believed then that Del and Ann were unlikely to disapprove of anything I did to help bring their daughters home. Over the next three months we did several more runs and developed various tricks to extend the journey time by several valuable minutes. For instance, we would gauge the changing of traffic lights in order to be caught at red. This helped us accumulate several tapes which proved the supposed impossibility of completing the journey in less than 15 minutes or so. We also investigated the possibility that there'd been roadworks on the route on the day of the murder. However, no matter what we did we still found we frequently managed to do the run comfortably within the 11-minute time-frame, sometimes in eight to nine minutes. We had to junk at least a third of the video footage. Uncle

Norman only came with us on a few of the runs. I noticed that the family were a little wary of him. They didn't like saying much about the case in front of him. I didn't know why – he seemed okay to me. Michelle gave a sort of explanation in one of her letters: she said they loved him loads, but he spoke a lot of rubbish – and it did her head in. She asked me not to say anything in his company.

I discovered that the defence team had not independently verified the victim's timings either. I offered to check them out. Did Alison's last journey home really only take around 35 minutes? If it took longer, then we could crack the so-called 23-minute 'window of opportunity'. At the trial the defence had also tried to smash that window by suggesting she hadn't got home until well after 6 p.m. An elderly neighbour had given a statement to that effect, and Alison's husband had recalled that in their last phone call that afternoon Alison had indicated she had some small task to do before going home. However, I thought everyone had ignored the obvious: I wanted to prove that her journey from work invariably took a lot longer than 35 minutes. That was how I found myself retracing her last steps. I stood outside Barclays Bank in The Strand. There was a television screen in the window tuned to the financial pages of Teletext. At 5.02 p.m. I started walking to the bus stop near Aldwych church and caught the first bus to Waterloo Station. I held my video camera at waist level, so nobody would notice me filming. At Waterloo I quickly filmed the arrivals and departures board to confirm the time and location, then boarded the first train to Clapham Junction. When I got off the train I walked up St John's Hill to Vardens Road. Then something happened for which I was unprepared – I got a feeling of great sadness. I suddenly felt for Alison in a way I hadn't felt before. Until then, she'd been little more than a photo, but now I was walking where she'd walked during her last minutes on earth. I was retracing her last footsteps, the ordinary steps of an ordinary young woman who'd been walking towards an extraordinary evil. I felt cold and awkward as I pictured the terrible fate that had awaited her. The people passing me – had they passed her? What had she been thinking? What was her mood? I reassured myself that by helping prove the Taylors' innocence I was bringing closer the day when the real murderer would be brought to justice. I felt sure the Taylors couldn't have murdered Alison. Or could they? With hindsight, buried in the back of my mind was the slightest of slight doubts. Most of the time over the next 11 months I managed to keep that doubt well buried, but occasionally it would emerge disturbingly from its grave. When I got to Alison's door I checked my stopwatch. Unfortunately for my theory, the journey had taken almost exactly 35 minutes, just as the police had claimed. I did the journey a few more times, but the police had been spot-on. I couldn't add any precious minutes to their calculations, so I gave up trying and moved on to other things. I speculated about the nature of the unknown minor task Alison might have done before going home. My brainwave was that she'd gone to pick up a parcel from Battersea sorting office. Another dead end, though: the office would have closed before Alison could have reached it.

While I concentrated on the evidence, Ann, Del and the other few members of our campaign team tried to galvanise the great British public. They wrote to MPs, put up fly posters and continued doggedly with the petition. I knew petitions had no effect on judges, but I also knew they helped lift prisoners' spirits. So I did my bit in this area too by asking people I knew in other prisons to send their signatures to the sisters to show support. One of the people I asked was called Jason. He was on remand at Chelmsford Prison after shooting two people at a nightclub. I wrote to Michelle to ask if she'd heard from him. I told her he wasn't a lunatic; he was only 21 and had done what he'd done in a moment of temper after being accused of pinching a girl's bottom.

I wrote letters to local papers to try to get them to put in appeals for information. In particular, I wanted information about a man who'd apparently been seen outside Alison's home around the time of the murder. I wrote to Michelle:

> I have sent the letter off to the *South London Press* regarding the man spotted leaving 41 Vardens Road. Basically, I have given the description given by the doctor and asked if anybody has seen the man in the past year acting suspiciously in south London. It may sound rubbish, but

what if two, three or four people say they have seen, and been concerned about, a man fitting the description? At least it will add to his authenticity and throw more doubt on an already shaky case. I've explained another reason to your mother and she can explain to your face next week.

The 'other' reason was that I was hoping some cranks would come forward to say they'd seen the man. I knew that in most high-profile cases, all sorts of nutters offered themselves to the police as witnesses – or even perpetrators – despite having absolutely no connection with the crime. I was usually careful about what I put in letters to the sisters, just as Ann and Del were careful about what they said on the phone. We were all anxious to avoid letting the authorities find out about our dodgier activities. Between us we kept the sisters abreast of our progress. The parents were even more paranoid than I was. They were sure the authorities were listening in to their calls, so they devised a sort of code to convey to the sisters news of developments. Unfortunately, the code was sometimes so elaborate that the sisters didn't know what they were talking about. Michelle told me in a letter that they often had to guess what Mum and Dad were trying to convey. Michelle often wrote to tell me I didn't have to wait to get permission from her and Lisa to do things. She said that as long as I cleared things with her parents, and they were happy, then she and Lisa would be happy too. However, she said she didn't want to give me the impression she wasn't interested in what I was doing; she stressed she was interested in everything. But even if I had the parents' permission, I always liked to give the sisters the final say in any planned action.

I visited the sisters in prison for the first time at the end of August 1992 – just over a month after their trial. The parents and their youngest daughter were with me. After handing in our visiting orders we took our places in the waiting-room. Ten minutes later a prison officer took us into the visiting-room where Michelle and Lisa sat at a table. The first thing that struck me was Michelle's size: she was much shorter than I'd expected. Prison had not done much for her complexion, which was pale and pasty. Lisa, however, looked well on it. She was radiantly pretty.

Michelle did most of the talking, but still seemed shy, although not as shy as Lisa, who seemed very distant, as if she'd detached herself from the situation. In fact, she was very child-like in her mannerisms, distractedly playing with her hair. We discussed the campaign and the evidence that needed to be challenged. I could tell Michelle and Lisa had a strong bond that went beyond their coming together in the extreme circumstances of prison. They could communicate together without words. When Lisa was asked something about the case she'd look quickly at her sister. Their eyes would meet and then, as if they'd agreed an answer telepathically, Lisa would turn back and answer her questioner, usually in a few syllables. I found their behaviour a little spooky at first. Michelle was certainly dominant, but not overpoweringly so. At heart I detected an equality in their relationship, albeit with a tinge of deference on Lisa's part. I suspected that, although Michelle was the public performer, Lisa had no problem making her voice heard in private – and her opinion would have had great weight with Michelle. The conversation turned to John Shaughnessy, who had allegedly turned up drunk at the prison the night they'd been convicted. Michelle said he and a few friends had shouted abuse up at the walls. The Taylors didn't even refer to him as 'John'. They called him 'the shit'. Michelle was dismissive of the way Alison had been portrayed in the press, with several papers referring to her as 'the perfect wife'. She said that when Alison and John had gone round to the Taylors' family home for tea Alison had acted like a snob. Ann Taylor nodded her head in agreement. Michelle then said that before the murder Alison had started wearing lots of short skirts and make-up. She added: 'It wouldn't surprise me if she was having an affair. That was probably how she was killed.' I was taken aback by the lack of sympathy for Alison around the table. In fact, it was more than lack of sympathy – it was outright animosity. But I hadn't known Alison, and I couldn't defend her. Perhaps sensing my discomfort, Michelle changed the subject. Before long, our time was up and the visit came to an end.

Over the following months Michelle and I exchanged scores of letters. It often seemed that not a day went by without my writing or receiving a letter. Most of the time we discussed various aspects of the case, but we also wrote about personal stuff – our backgrounds, our families, our relationships, things we'd done in the past, things we wanted to do in the future. We became friends and confidantes. In my line of work there were very few people I could trust and I found myself confiding things in Michelle which I wouldn't have told anyone else. In particular, I found myself telling Michelle about my relationship with my common-law wife, Debra, with whom I had two children. We had been living together for several years, but there were tensions in the relationship. Debra felt I didn't spend enough time with her and the children. She could tolerate absences caused by my paid work, but she'd started to become exasperated by the amount of time I spent on various causes for which I received no money. Before becoming involved in the Taylors' campaign I'd spent more than a year trying to raise money for a life-saving operation for a severely ill local boy. Once I'd become involved I'd found that the campaign ate up almost all my free time, but I couldn't help myself. In the end the boy died before he could have the operation. I then became free to spend more time with Debra and the children. But just as Debra started getting used to seeing more of me, I placed myself at the heart of the Taylors' campaign. Before long I was not only spending lots of time away from home on the campaign, but even when at home I was writing letters and making phone calls about it. I must have been talking about it incessantly too. Debra and I started having rows. She accused me of caring more about strangers than I did about my own family. I refused to see things from her point of view. I started criticising Debra in my letters to Michelle. I said a lot of hurtful and unfair things about her to my new friend. In time I would come to regret my cruel indiscretions.

Michelle reciprocated my openness; she seemed to talk about herself frankly and honestly in her letters. She came across as such a caring person that I simply couldn't imagine her plunging a blade 54 times into a harmless young woman. In one letter she wrote that she'd never be able to hurt someone violently, either physically or mentally. She didn't deny she was capable of violence, but she said she'd only fight people who hurt either her family or those she was close to. She said when she was younger she used to hit first and ask questions later, but as she'd grown older she knew that was the wrong attitude, and she'd changed. She said violence was not a solution to anything. She loved children – on the day of the verdict, as she and Lisa had sat in their cell confidently anticipating freedom, they'd talked about what they'd do with the bit of money they might make from selling their stories. They agreed that first they'd pay off any debts their parents had, then they'd take their family on holiday, then they'd pay for a coach to take all the local kiddies to the seaside for a day. If there was any money left, they were going to give it to charity. However, getting convicted had ruined their plans, and this made her bitter – bitter because all the kiddies had lost out. Their trip to the seaside would have to be postponed indefinitely. The thought of these disappointed children made her take a swipe at John Shaughnessy, whom she blamed for everything. She said he was evil and that no word in the English language could describe his personality. She said he had no feelings. Even thinking about him made her feel sick.

One of the things that strengthened my bond with Michelle was our mutual loathing of the police. I was pleased that she seemed to despise them as much as I did. During the campaign I found myself being investigated by the police for two separate violent assaults connected with my work as a doorman. Both men involved had ended up in hospital, one of them missing an ear, the other so badly beaten that his daughter couldn't recognise him for two weeks. Because of the warped world in which I was living I felt I'd done no wrong. In my eyes both men had been punished for their own bad behaviour. So I resented the police becoming involved. As far as I was concerned, the cases were now closed. The police, however, didn't share my view that Bernie's law superseded the rule of law. They seemed determined to drag me into court to convict me, which made me loathe them even more. I kept Michelle informed of what was happening. One of the cases involved a court appearance, the other an ID parade, although in the end I wasn't convicted of either assault. Michelle was very sympathetic about how the police were wasting my time. In several letters she described the police variously as 'low-lifes with criminal minds', 'the scum of the earth', 'nobodies' and 'bastards'. She asked me to excuse her language, but said that what had happened to her had really turned her against them. She said they had nothing better to do than go around setting up innocent people; the world was a crazy place with so many untrustworthy people running it. She hoped I wouldn't end up in prison, because that would mean yet another innocent person inside. She wondered what the police would do if they did ever actually manage to arrest a real criminal, someone who was genuinely guilty of a crime. She thought they'd probably let them go. She told me I was worth ten policemen and reminded me to keep laughing and smiling inside when I sat in the dock. She even said she'd prayed for me. But I didn't need her prayers. In my experience the intimidation of witnesses tended to produce better results than a reliance on the Lord.

There was one prosecution witness in the Taylors' trial whose evidence had caused them a lot of damage. Her name was Jeanette Tapp, known to everyone as 'JJ'. I knew that if we could get her to change her evidence we'd greatly boost the sisters' chances of freedom. JJ had been a friend and work colleague of Michelle and Lisa's at the Churchill Clinic. In the early days following the murder she'd made two statements giving the sisters a crucial alibi: she said they'd been watching television with her in her room at the clinic at the time the police believed Alison was murdered. However, after the police arrested her on the same morning they arrested the sisters, she changed her story. She said she hadn't actually seen the sisters until much later that evening. Most importantly, she claimed she'd only said she'd seen them earlier because they'd asked her to. She'd complied with their request because she didn't think for a moment they'd had anything to do with the killing. JJ was also linked to another crucial bit of evidence. Michelle and Lisa claimed they'd been shopping in Bromley for a few hours in the mid-afternoon before heading back to JJ's room. However, Michelle's cashpoint card had been used to withdraw ten pounds from a branch close to the clinic at a time she was supposedly shopping in Bromley several miles away. At the trial Michelle denied making the withdrawal. She said that JJ, who knew her

PIN number, must have stolen the card and used it. JJ categorically denied this – and was supported by the fact that she'd made a cash withdrawal from her own bank several miles away only 24 minutes later. Out of all the evidence against Michelle and Lisa I found the cashpoint stuff the most difficult to explain away. However, I'd convinced myself that the sisters were innocent, so I knew there had to be an innocent explanation. In time I would find one, I was sure. The most pressing problem, though, was to find a way of neutralising the main thrust of JJ's evidence regarding the alibi. I had no doubt that the police had bullied JJ into telling lies. She'd only changed her story after they'd threatened to charge her with conspiracy to murder. I wanted to get her to go back to telling the truth. If we could get her to make a fourth statement, then at the very least she'd be shown to be totally unreliable; she'd be of no use to either side, prosecution or defence. I felt we needed to put her under pressure. Someone at the Churchill Clinic managed to get hold of JJ's new number. With Michelle and Lisa's knowledge, a few members of the campaign team started making silent phone calls to JJ. Then, by coincidence, one group of campaign supporters ran into JJ as they put up 'Free the Taylor Two' posters near her home. The supporters spotted JJ at the same time she spotted them. In her panic to get away, she rushed across the road – and came close to being splattered by an oncoming car. Ann told her daughters this story on one of the prison visits I attended. Everyone laughed. I didn't want to spoil the party atmosphere, but I didn't think fly-posting around JJ's home was a good idea. It could have been seen as threatening. At that stage I wanted JJ to be put under pressure, but not the sort of pressure that might have made her run to the police – the very people who'd polluted her mind in the first place. I was sure that by approaching JJ in the right way she'd come round to telling the truth. I expressed my views later to Ann and Del, then put them in a letter to Michelle.

I decided to ring JJ myself to try to strike up a friendship, but she put the phone down. I rang again and told her I wasn't a journalist, just someone who wanted to help her and the sisters. I didn't say I was running the campaign to free them. She was suspicious, but I kept talking to her calmly and gently. I gave her my name and telephone number, which seemed to reassure her. We chatted for a little while. She said she was pregnant, but had been so scared by recent pressure that she'd almost lost the child. She knew the sisters were planning to appeal against their convictions and was worried she might have to appear in court again. She asked me what I wanted. I said I wanted to meet up with her – she could bring along her boyfriend too – because there were things I needed to ask her about what she'd said in court. I told her there was no need to be frightened; I could understand how the police had bullied her into telling lies. I wanted to give her the chance to get everything off her chest in a way which would help both her and the sisters. She said she hadn't lied in court: Michelle and Lisa hadn't been with her at the time of the murder, and she hadn't stolen Michelle's cashpoint card. I told her that I felt she was mistaken. The tone of her voice changed. I could detect fear and anxiety. She insisted again that she'd been telling the truth.

'I'm not going to lie for them any more,' she said. I kept on suggesting she'd been mistaken, and became more aggressive, even sneering. Suddenly her voice broke and she started crying. Full sobs reverberated down the line into my ear. I kept up the pressure, suggesting that the police had so played with her mind that she'd lost sight of the truth. She sobbed uncontrollably, yet in the midst of her tears she remained adamant that she hadn't lied in court. She said she wouldn't meet me. She suggested I write to her via the clinic's matron. In the letter I could set out in detail what I wanted to discuss. The call ended. I tried not to feel guilty about making her cry. I told myself she was a spineless dupe who'd allowed the police to use her weakness to fit up two innocent girls. And yet our conversation had disturbed me. Over the following days the more I thought about it the more uncomfortable I felt. JJ had stuck firmly to her story under my persistent questioning, so she wasn't that weak and malleable. What if she was telling the truth? I experienced another flicker of doubt. But if she was telling the truth, then the sisters were lying – and I was a fool. I stifled my doubt. My blinkers were firmly in place: there had to be another explanation. I did write to her, but she never replied. When I tried ringing her again, her number was unobtainable.

On my next visit to the Taylors in prison we discussed ways of winning back JJ. I suggested Michelle should send her a Christmas card with a simple inscription, such as 'From your friend Michelle'. Such a card couldn't have been interpreted as sinister if it fell into the police's hands. The aim would have been to give JJ the impression that there were no hard feelings. In fact, there were a lot of hard feelings. Michelle loathed JJ and spoke of her with contempt. Both Michelle and Lisa had taken great joy in the knowledge that JJ had been bombarded with silent phone calls before I'd spoken to her. Del Taylor didn't like the Christmas card idea. He didn't want Michelle involved so obviously. Instead we agreed that Michelle would write me a back-dated letter, supposedly written just after the trial. In it she would describe her sympathy for JJ and her understanding of her plight. I would then call on JJ and show her the letter. This would reassure her that the sisters had no grudge against her and that they simply wanted her to do what was best for everyone. It was important that the letter was not sent out in the normal way as it would have been given a prison date-stamp. Instead, on my next visit Michelle secretly passed it to me when the prison officers weren't looking. I quickly hid it inside my shirt. However, I never ended up showing JJ the letter: we couldn't find her new address. Del and I scoured the Kennington area looking for her. I called on a few addresses while he waited up the road, but no one knew where she'd gone. Or, if they did know, they weren't going to tell me.

A few months after the trial I read an article that offered the possiblity – as I told Michelle in a letter – of a 'blinding breakthrough'. The article concerned phantom withdrawals from cashpoints. A solicitor in Liverpool, Dennis Whalley, had gathered together 400 instances where people claimed that money had been withdrawn from their accounts at cashpoints without their knowledge or permission. I'd been seriously troubled by the fact that money had been withdrawn from Michelle's account at the time she was supposedly shopping in Bromley. Although Michelle had blamed JJ for the withdrawal, at the trial the prosecution had claimed the cashpoint records were 'infallible'. Yet here was a way of showing that neither Michelle nor JJ had been responsible. I believed that if Mr Whalley could prove the machines were not 100 per cent accurate then we could have this evidence ruled inadmissable. I telephoned Mr Whalley who suggested I pop in and see him sometime. Within a few days I drove to his office in Liverpool. Foolishly, I didn't make an appointment, so I couldn't see him personally, but his staff kindly gave me countless copies of newspaper cuttings on the subject. When I returned to London I informed the sisters' solicitor about this line of inquiry. He was very interested and agreed it was worth pursuing. I wanted to build on Mr Whalley's work. I wanted to gather together lots more instances of disputed cash withdrawals – at least 1,000 if possible. I wrote to more than 40 major regional newspapers throughout the United Kingdom asking them to print an appeal to their readers. I kept Michelle informed by letter: 'I really feel excited about this, 'Chelle. I had gone over and over that poxy card issue trying to think of an acceptable way to explain it and then it suddenly appears in the press!'

I visited the sisters in prison at least once every two months. My visits became more frequent when they were moved from Holloway to Bullwood Hall near Southend, which wasn't too far from my home in Basildon. On balance, Michelle was pleased to get away from Holloway. She'd made some good friends there, but she'd been worried by the number of junkies around the place. She said she hadn't taken her eyes off Lisa for more than a minute because of all the dodgy people around. Although we could talk reasonably freely on the visits, there was usually a prison officer somewhere in the background. Michelle, who had an almost obsessive fear of being snooped on, applied to have my visits treated as 'legal' visits, so that I could have the special privilege enjoyed by a solicitor visiting his client, namely, the right to total privacy. However, I had to apply for security clearance and, being an ex-convict, this wasn't forthcoming. Lisa found prison life hardest to cope with. Her problems were magnified by her stormy relationship with her boyfriend Leon. She would speak to him on the phone regularly, but their conversations usually left her miserable. She had been particularly exasperated when he himself had been sent to prison for a month for a relatively minor offence – and had then started writing her whingeing letters about how he couldn't cope with life inside. She thought his moaning was insensitive, if not pathetic, when she herself was facing a life sentence. Things eventually came to a head. Michelle wrote to tell me that Lisa had come off the phone to Leon in tears every night for a week – and had finally decided to dump him. I wrote back quickly to stress that Lisa needed to let Leon down gently. I said he could do a lot of damage to the campaign if, bitter at being brutally dumped, he took revenge by running to the newpapers with his story.

The campaign became my obsession. In some periods I was working between 12 to 18 hours a day to free the Taylor Two. Michelle often acknowledged this in her letters, telling me to slow down and try to get some sleep. I was pursuing all sorts of lines of inquiry. There had been two other vicious murders of women in that general area, those of Penny Bell and Rachel Nickell. Both had received a lot of publicity, and we tried to find links to suggest a madman was on the loose. Michelle was particularly struck by this idea, especially as Penny, Rachel and Alison had all been killed in the summer. In one letter Michelle wondered whether a madman was out there who only attacked in summertime. She developed this idea on one of my visits: she said that, as the murders had all been committed around the time of the Wimbledon tennis championship, the murderer might be some deranged foreign tennis fan who only visited London for the tournament. Ann Taylor spoke to Penny Bell's husband on a few occasions, but we couldn't make any convincing links between the cases.

I also wrote to women's magazines asking if their readers could supply extracts from their own feveredly romantic teenage diaries to put into context the extracts from Michelle's diary that had been used against her. We wanted to show that her sometimes-hostile observations about Alison were nothing abnormal for a young woman disappointed in love. I also placed an advertisement in a Bromley newspaper asking if anybody could recall seeing two girls fitting Michelle and Lisa's description shopping in Bromley on the day of the murder. It was a long shot, but I hoped some crank might come forward. The sisters had only been able to give the police one name of a person they'd met in Bromley that day, but he hadn't been terribly helpful.

There was another piece of evidence which had initially caused me some concern. In their first statements the sisters had both denied that Lisa had ever visited Alison's flat. Lisa had said she didn't even know where it was. However, as the inquiry progressed, the results of fingerprint tests came back – and Lisa's fingerprints had been found on Alison's front door. At the trial, as was her right, Lisa didn't go into the witness box to explain herself. She left that task to Michelle, who explained that some weeks before the murder she and Lisa had popped around to Alison's flat to clean the windows. Apparently, John had suggested they do so because they had the equipment from their father's cleaning business. This was how Lisa's prints had come to be on the door. Michelle said she'd lied about Lisa's ever being there in order to avoid having her sister dragged into the nightmare of the police investigation. This was the story they both told me in prison. They said it was a silly lie, and they both regretted not telling the truth, but they had nothing to hide. In fact, they were surprised that more of Lisa's prints hadn't been found. I knew from my own dealings with them that Michelle was very protective of Lisa, so after speaking to them I had no difficulty in believing them. I thought that once again the police had made something out of nothing. In a letter I even doubted if the police had genuinely found Lisa's prints. I asked Michelle if anybody had independently checked the police's claim: 'They also claimed there were 40 sets of prints in the flat. Have names been put to them all or are there unknown ones? Did the police discontinue matching prints when they found Lisa's?'

Another witness I tried to contact was Dr Unsworth-White. He lived in Alison's road and had told police that on the day of the murder he'd seen two young white women coming down the steps of the murder house. However, he'd failed to positively identify either Michelle or Lisa at identity parades. I wanted to find out if the police had leaned on him in any way to make his evidence more convincing. I was hoping also that

I might be able to encourage him to alter his evidence in some slight way. We got his address from the electoral roll in the library, and I knocked on his door one night. There was no reply. I returned there on another evening with Del. Again there was no reply. I put a note under his door asking him to contact me, but he never responded. I noticed that at the same address was a bell-push with the name 'Burke' on it. I speculated with the Taylors that this could be a relative of Detective Superintendent Chris Burke who'd led the investigation. Michelle, in particular, found this coincidence especially sinister. She wrote to say it was very interesting: the bits of the puzzle were starting to come together. Ann started referring to the doctor as 'Dr Whites'. Apparently, this was the name of a brand of tampons she remembered from her youth. Everyone found the joke very amusing.

By the end of 1992 we all felt we were making good progress in the campaign. As the date approached for the hearing to decide whether the sisters would be granted leave to appeal, Michelle wrote to say she thought they needed to go back into the public eye. She said many things needed to come out for the public to see how the police had set them up. I agreed with her. I knew that publicity would form a crucial part of the next stage of the campaign.

I was sure we could find honest journalists who'd be willing to broadcast the truth.

SIX

A Dollop of Vomit

People always asked: 'If they didn't do it, who did?'

I told the Taylors that a good way of getting journalists to look at the case afresh would be to uncover credible new suspects. I'd read an article about one of John Shaughnessy's brothers, Tom, whose wife had poured boiling wax over his genitals, severely injuring him. This domestic dispute had occurred some months before Alison's murder. I began to construct a far-fetched theory that I intended feeding to journalists. It consisted of a heap of sinister insinuations bolstered by a few facts. Using the fact of John's affair with Michelle, I imagined that he'd been unhappy with Alison and had wanted a divorce. However, as a good Catholic girl, Alison would not grant him his wish. So, in this fantastical scenario, he'd joined forces with his *brother* to get rid of his wife. John had played on his brother's bitterness at his own wife's behaviour and had got him to agree to help murder Alison. I theorised that John could have met his brother at lunchtime to give him a set of keys to the flat. The brother could then have lain in wait inside. This was important because the way Alison had picked up the mail and carried it upstairs with her keys and bag indicated there hadn't been a struggle with a stranger at the front door. The prosecution claimed this proved Alison had known her attacker or attackers – and had let them in to the flat. But my theory enabled us to show how the murderer was already waiting inside. In my mind I weaved together various thin strands to try to corroborate this nonsense. For instance, a witness claimed to have seen John out walking at lunchtime. Then, at the time the murder was committed, John's rock-solid alibi was that he'd been buying flowers from the stall at Waterloo Station run by Buster Edwards, a former member of the Great Train Robbery gang. John regularly bought flowers from Buster for the clinic. However, on that day he forgot his chequebook and even asked Buster the time. I concluded that John had been deliberately trying to establish an alibi: he'd wanted Buster to remember him and the time he'd been there. Buster had given evidence for the prosecution at the trial, but I thought that with his criminal background he might be willing, with a little encouragement, to change his story to suit our needs. Del Taylor and I paid him a visit. At first we chatted generally: Buster remembered Michelle for having once baked him a cake. He said he didn't think the sisters were guilty. He added that, shortly after the murder, a policeman had told him they suspected some blacks of having done it. I told Buster we were running a campaign to free the sisters. I asked him if he'd give us 'a leg up', that is, whether he'd be prepared to help us. I explained about John. I asked Buster if he'd be willing to say anything that might point the finger away from the sisters. For instance, that another man had waited for John or that John had appeared nervous. Buster cut me short. He said he didn't want anything more to do with the case. Our conversation ended with Buster saying he disliked John for stating in the press that he'd like to hang Michelle and Lisa himself. Buster said he'd 'pull him' for it if he ever saw him again. All the same, he couldn't help us. We told Michelle and Lisa what had happened. Lisa called Buster 'a fucking grass'; Michelle was surprised he knew she'd once baked him a cake. At the time of baking it she hadn't known who it was for; she'd only found out afterwards.

I abandoned the scenario of John and Tom Shaughnessy colluding to murder Alison. There were insurmountable problems with the theory, not least the fact that Tom, too, had a cast-iron alibi. I could see that even the most hopeless journalist would rapidly tear my theory to shreds. However, trawling through the unused evidence from the investigation – the family had given me access to everything – I soon found a more promising suspect. He was a homeless man. Around the time of Alison's murder the police had been tipped off that this derelict, about whom no one knew much, had told someone in a homeless shelter that he'd stabbed a woman. Over the coming months I'd try to turn 'the homeless man' into something I soon realised he wasn't – Alison's murderer. In this process several journalists would unwittingly help me give substance to this fantasy.

In the meantime I got into the papers myself. In October my correspondence with the Yorkshire Ripper was printed in one of the Sunday tabloids. I'd written to Sutcliffe posing as a blonde barmaid – and he'd responded passionately with letters signed 'with big juicy hugs'. The paper joked that 'the mad mass murderer's "sweetheart" is really a beefy nightclub bouncer called Bernard!' I wrote to Michelle to explain how I'd come to write to the Ripper. I didn't want her to think that, because I'd had over a nonce, there was any hidden agenda in my dealings with her. She phoned to tell me not to worry about it and even wrote to say that whatever stuff papers said about me meant 'nish' to her. During my correspondence with Sutcliffe I'd also been writing to another nonce. In August 1991 the country had been horrified by the sex murder of a seven-year-old boy who'd been snatched while riding his BMX bike. The child had been sexually assaulted and strangled before being thrown down a ravine. A local man, Richard Blenkey, had been charged with the murder. The *News of the World*'s crime reporter Gary Jones, who'd suggested I write to the Ripper, told me a few facts about Blenkey that the jury wouldn't get to hear. He said that 14 years earlier Blenkey had tried to snatch another boy, but the youngster had managed to fight him off. Detectives also knew that Blenkey had been in the vicinity of another abduction. The victim in that case – another young boy – had never been found. I'd been having a lot of success with the Ripper, so I reasoned I might get something incriminating out of Blenkey. I got Jones to find out which prison was holding Blenkey on remand and I started writing to him. I wrote to him for about three months. Initially, he denied having anything to do with the murder and said he intended pleading not guilty. Then, remarkably, three weeks before his trial he confessed to me in a letter that he had indeed murdered the boy. I gave the letters to

Gary Jones. The prosecution produced them at the trial – and Blenkey immediately pleaded guilty. He got a life sentence with a recommendation that he serve at least 20 years. The father of the victim publicly thanked me for having saved the family the ordeal of a trial from which the murderer might easily have walked to freedom. As a criminal I felt uneasy about effectively informing on Blenkey to the police, but as a father I came to feel proud of what I'd done. Although I didn't have to attend the trial I was named in national newspapers as the person who'd 'forced a child killer to confess'. Again, my thoughts turned to Michelle: I was worried she'd read something sinister into my actions. I wrote to her to give her the option of ceasing contact with me, but she wouldn't have it. She wrote back swiftly on 11 November to say that what I'd done was right. She asked me to imagine how many other children Blenkey might have hurt if he'd been set free. She said I'd done nothing wrong: okay, I'd had to go to the cops, which was against my principles, but Blenkey wasn't a normal person, so I'd done the right thing and wasn't to have second thoughts about it. Our only worry was that, because of the publicity, the prison authorities might try to intervene to stop me writing to her. So she wrote a letter to me at my mother's address, using a pseudonym for me – 'Patrick Lawson'. With the Taylors' knowledge, I occasionally used another name too – Bernard King – so journalists wouldn't link me with the campaign. A few years earlier I'd changed my surname by deed poll to 'King' – the surname of my partner and the mother of two of my children. I'd done this for the children's sake, because we weren't married – and I knew how cruel other children could be. However, in the twilight world of my work it was also useful to have another name. One of my local papers, the *Standard Recorder*, did one of the first big articles about the 'Justice for Lisa and Michelle Taylor' campaign. I was quoted throughout as 'Bernard King'. The journalist spoke to Ann and Del: '"Bernard has been absolutely wonderful," says Michelle's mother Ann. "Terrific," adds her husband Derek.'

We didn't have to work hard to find eager journalists keen to expose yet another miscarriage of justice. In most cases they came to us, particularly after the sisters were granted leave to appeal in November.

Every time I called round to the Taylors' family home there seemed to be a well-spoken journalist sitting in the front room, notebook in hand, nodding sympathetically as Ann and Del (usually Ann), explained why their daughters were innocent. On the television side, Carlton Television's *London Tonight*, the BBC's regional news programme, *Newsnight, Channel Four News, Sky News* – and even ITV's *This Morning* with Richard and Judy – all showed great interest in the campaign. On the newspaper side the interest came from the broadsheets – *The Guardian, The Independent,* and *The Observer.* Their journalists were particularly keen on the angle that the tabloids' coverage had prejudiced the original trial. I tried to get some of the tabloids' crime reporters interested in the story, but they all – with varying degrees of politeness – told me to fuck off. They all thought the sisters were guilty. I put this down to their being too close to the police – and too frightened of having their own shabby behaviour exposed. Features on the case started appearing first on television news programmes. After one of the first features in December, Michelle wrote to ask me if I'd seen it. She hadn't seen half of what the papers had written about her, so she'd been a bit upset when confronted with some of the material for the first time. After that first programme she'd sat in her cell and had wanted to cry. Lisa had passed by on the way to the toilet and had spoken to her through the hatch. Lisa had started crying – and Michelle had ended up getting annoyed. She said she had to hide her emotions from Lisa, because if her sister ever saw her upset she'd think she'd given up. The programme had made her re-read her diary. She said the newspapers had printed complete shit; she'd never realised how someone could take a sentence or a word and change the meaning completely. She said her parents didn't know half the things she'd gone through with John – and she'd make sure they never knew because they'd be too hurt by the knowledge. She said John used to make her life hell – that was why she'd had to escape from him. She added that life had dealt her some nasty cards: you escaped one hell only to be put into the next.

In December the king and queen of daytime television, Richard Madeley and Judy Finnigan, invited Ann Taylor onto their show. Ann thought she'd be given an easy ride on a show not famed for the sharpness of its investigative journalism. But Richard Madeley gave her a hard time over Michelle's diary extracts. And in other areas he was a lot more critical and inquisitive than many of the so-called 'top-notch' investigative journalists who'd been wearing out the Taylors' front-room carpet. When I next spoke to Ann she called Richard a 'cheeky ponce' and made a sneering remark about his acquittal for allegedly shoplifting alcohol a few years earlier. She had a lot more time for the journalists from the BBC's prestigious late-night current-affairs programme, *Newsnight*, although, she said, sometimes even they managed to ask unwelcome questions.

Michelle wrote to me to say she was unhappy with my insistence that I wanted no money from the proceeds of a book I'd suggested we could write. We'd agreed that the case was so complicated, with so many twists and turns, that only a book would enable the public to come to know what had really happened. I said I'd help them write the book, but only on condition that all the money went to them. I didn't want to make a penny out of their suffering. My only agenda was to expose the rottenness of the system that had convicted them. The working title of the book was *The Dream Solution* – we were going to use that phrase from her diary to show that the *real* dream solution had been the police's work in fitting them up. Lisa had suggested the title *Beyond All Reasonable Doubt*, but that had been turned down. In the rest of her letter Michelle wrote about what she was going to do when she got out. She wasn't sure what exactly, but wanted to do something that related to the law in some way, because the legal system and coppers were totally fucked up. She didn't see herself getting married: she said her life never went like that.

The sisters spent their days working in the prison factory putting together light fittings. Michelle complained to the governor about a man at the factory who kept making snide remarks. She asked for a transfer and was eventually given a new job as a cleaner. In a letter she told me how things had got so bad with that man that she'd reached the point where she thought her mouth would no longer be doing the talking. As well as a factory, the prison also had a hairdresser's. Michelle once had a gripe about her cut and perm – the hairdresser had cut her hair too short. The sisters also socialised. They became friendly with an equally notorious prisoner called Linda Calvey, known to the tabloids as 'the Black Widow' (a reference to the spider that kills its partner after mating). Calvey had recruited her lover to kill her gangland husband, but had shot her hubby herself when the lover lost his nerve – or so it had been told in court. Calvey, naturally, regarded her life sentence for murder as yet another miscarriage of justice. Michelle and Lisa spoke of Linda in tones of awe.

The inmates also amused themselves by putting on shows. Michelle told me how she'd helped write two 'comedy' court cases. They'd used mop heads for barristers' and judges' wigs, black bin-liners for gowns. The cases had involved 20 'exhibits'. They'd shown ingenuity in assembling these props too: an orange had doubled as a brain cell, a piece of toast as a weapon, and they'd mixed together a goo of shampoo, coffee, powdered milk and tomato sauce to look like a dollop of vomit.

We examined exhaustively all the evidence of the sisters' case and pursued every possible way of throwing doubt upon the convictions. I noticed in John Shaughnessy's statement that he thought a gold bracelet his wife usually wore on her wrist was missing. There was also another bracelet he couldn't find, but he thought it might have gone missing some time before the murder. Missing jewellery? Evidence of burglary, surely? However, John also said in his statement that nothing else in the flat had been disturbed. Moreover, his wife's handbag lay untouched at her side when she was killed. I concentrated on the supposedly missing jewellery. I got Del to visit pawnbrokers in the area to see if anyone had pawned a couple of bangles or bracelets in the days following the murder. I told Michelle that all we needed was an entry to that effect in a pawnbroker's log book to have another little piece of doubt to add to our jigsaw. But Del couldn't get anything significant from the pawnbrokers. I thought the 'missing jewellery' line was still worth trying to develop, though. I knew that at the very least we'd be able to feed it to journalists who'd realise the implication that a mad burglar might have done the deed.

The New Year of 1993 got off to a brilliant start with the broadcast of the *Newsnight* programme in early January. The film gave the impression of having been thoroughly and independently researched. We were gratified, however, that they pursued so many of the lines of inquiry we'd suggested. The film mentioned most of the significant evidence against the sisters. Fortunately, nothing damaging was allowed to linger in the air for too long without being countered by the defence's arguments. The film was in the finest BBC tradition of fair and impartial reporting. The first interviewee was Ann Taylor who said that her daughters, especially Michelle, had been convicted on their morals – and nothing else. She meant the negative portrayal by newspapers of Michelle's personal life. One of the most useful interviewees, from my point of view, was the Home Office pathologist who said he'd never come across a case where a woman had stabbed anyone more than 12 times. He didn't say it was impossible that Michelle had done it, just that it would be surprising if she had. It also focused on the timings. The commentator said:

> But there's another point, and that's the timings. Police say they did the journey from the scene of the murder in Vardens Road to the Churchill Clinic in eleven and a half minutes, arguing Michelle and Lisa could have done it in that time, but the defence has always argued that the test drive was unfair, that the police were advanced drivers in a high-performance Rover, while Michelle, an ordinary driver in a ten-year-old Ford Sierra, could not realistically have driven it in less than 15 minutes. It's since emerged there were road works on the route at the time of the murder, reducing traffic to one lane, which might well have made the journey even slower.

The film got even better. They'd managed to get an interview with the elderly neighbour who was sure she'd seen Alison arriving home after six. I was impressed, especially as the old dear had been too ill to give her evidence at the trial, where she'd have been cross-examined on it. The film stressed the circumstantial nature of all the evidence and the lack of forensics. It mentioned the fact that some of Alison's jewellery was missing and that unidentified fingerprints had been found in the flat. It also gave prominence to our view that once the police found Michelle's diaries they made her the prime suspect – and dismissed other possibilities. The film ended poignantly with the Taylors' youngest daughter, 14-year-old Tracey, reading a poem that Lisa had sent from prison. In the poem Lisa spoke of the barbed wire and fences surrounding her – and looked forward to the day when the judges at the High Court would realise the truth and set them free. It was a great ending. Just what television is good at – weepy emotion. We were all delighted by the film, because we felt that no reasonable viewer could have watched it without coming away believing there was, at the very least, a huge question mark over the sisters' guilt.

The film gave us all a tremendous boost. Although the programme didn't have a mass audience, it carried a lot of prestige, especially among journalists. Interest intensified. Journalists told us that, following on from the Birmingham Six and the Guildford Four, the Taylor Two would be the next huge miscarriage-of-justice story. In fact there was a thriving network of co-operation between the many people working to expose alleged miscarriages of justice. One of the focal points of this network was a group called 'Justice for All': it had a very good database of all the experts who could be called upon to challenge any aspect of the prosecution's case. 'Justice for All' put us in touch with a speech expert who analysed the contents of JJ Tapp's police interviews. Helpfully, the expert concluded that JJ was weak and suggestible and seemed at times to be 'an accomplished liar'. We intended feeding that snippet to a trustworthy journalist at some point closer to the appeal hearing. Although Ann and Del were obviously convinced of their own daughters' innocence, they had a more sceptical view of some of the other miscarriage of justice 'victims' with whose campaigners we had dealings. Del, who had a good sense of humour, would sometimes say ironically that there'd never been a miscarriage-of-justice programme about a guilty person who'd escaped justice – only the innocent made it to the screen.

Our campaign was given another boost when the distinguished miscarriage-of-justice campaigning journalist, Bob Woffinden, started looking at the case too. Bob had turned the cause of the wrongfully convicted into his life's work. He'd been involved in many major campaigns and had even written a book called *Miscarriages of Justice*. Prisoners who might otherwise have rotted in jail could thank Bob for having helped set them free. We were flattered that he wanted to do a major article on the case for *The Independent*. We took him along on one of our visits to the sisters. We didn't want him to be privy to everything we needed to discuss, though. Halfway through the visit Michelle tapped Lisa's leg under the table. This was a pre-arranged signal for Lisa to ask Bob if he wouldn't mind leaving us. Bob, polite and courteous, got up and left. In her next letter Michelle said she'd been dreading the visit for a week. What had made it worse was that she'd had to sit next to 'that geezer Bob'. She said it was nothing to do with him personally; it was just that she now felt extremely uncomfortable sitting next to any man she didn't know.

While Bob was researching his feature, and without his knowledge, we decided to try to stitch up another *Independent* journalist. Her name was Rachel Borrill. During the trial she'd written an article about the ageing of fingerprints. The defence planned to argue that her article was one of those which may have misled jurors. We decided we'd invite Rachel around to the Taylors' house on the pretext of giving her an exclusive story. Then we'd secretly record her while we questioned her about her original article. Our hope was that she'd concede that the article might have misled people. Rachel, sniffing an exclusive, agreed to call around. We were very friendly to her and she in turn was most apologetic for any inadvertent offence the article may have caused. However, the conversation didn't really go anywhere and we never used the tape in the end. Michelle, though, wrote to say she'd be talking to her legal team to see if the tape could be used. In that same letter she criticised that legal team. She thought they hated having to visit her in prison because she used to give them such grief. But, she said, half the time they asked for it. She said she'd remind her mother to set up a meeting between me and her barrister, Richard Ferguson QC. She thought it wouldn't hurt the barristers and QCs to hear what I had to say because, even though they thought they knew it all, she personally thought they were all a bit stupid. I thought she was being a bit unfair.

Meanwhile, Bob Woffinden delighted us with his work. His four-page feature appeared in *The Independent*'s Saturday magazine on 27 February 1993. It was headlined, WRONG TIME, WRONG PLACE. It described the case as one of the most high-profile of recent times in which the tabloids – taking a break from their preoccupation with royal and ministerial romances – had 'concocted a heady cocktail of amorous adolescent adventures, infidelity, jealousy and murder'. Yet, he said, the evidence against the sisters had been, at best, circumstantial; and the girls were continuing to protest their innocence. The article didn't say much that hadn't already been said on *Newsnight*, but its prominence in such a prestigious forum added momentum to our campaign. Like *Newsnight* before him, Woffinden pointed out the importance that the police had attached to Michelle's diary. He misquoted Michelle's words about her 'dream solution' as her 'ideal solution', but he said that other favourable references to Alison had been ignored. We were pleased that he himself had ignored some of the diary's other words, such as 'I hate Alison, the unwashed bitch'. Those words had often been used against Michelle, so we were grateful to Woffinden for having omitted them. We felt that, if he'd left them in, his readers might have got the false impression that Michelle had felt murderous hatred towards Alison, rather than the occasional mild hostility that we, and now Woffinden, interpreted them as showing. He said the case against the Taylors was hardly overwhelming. He claimed it was almost impossible in practical terms for them to have killed Alison Shaughnessy. He mentioned the timings:

> Derek Taylor has since made the journey at least five times, with a video camera and a stopwatch, and says he has never managed it in less than 15 minutes, and that, in any case, on 3 June 1991 traffic in the area was particularly slow-moving because of road works.

I laughed as I imagined Del keeping a straight face as he told this porky. He knew as well as I did that we'd done the journey several times in eight to nine minutes. Woffinden said there were logical and innocuous explanations for all the apparently incriminating evidence on which the Crown relied. And for the first time he mentioned in passing the story of a homeless man who'd allegedly confessed to a social worker that he'd killed a woman. The next stage of our media campaign would involve expanding on this credible new suspect. Again, we were delighted. Again, as with the *Newsnight* coverage, we felt that no one could have read the story without concluding that a major miscarriage of justice had almost certainly occurred.

After the lynching their girls had received from the tabloids, Ann and Del were grateful there were still nice journalists around who could be relied upon to tell the truth.

Then into our lives came the nicest journalist of all.

SEVEN

A Nice Man from The Guardian

It was Ann Taylor who first told me about Nick Davies of *The Guardian*. She said he was a very nice man. He'd been in touch with her expressing interest in writing about the case. She said he'd covered miscarriages of justice before and seemed genuinely to believe that the sisters had been wrongfully convicted. She was normally very wary of journalists, but Davies seemed to penetrate her defences in a way that most others couldn't. She found him polite and charming, and she liked the fact that he wasn't pushy. For her, he seemed to embody the idea that broadsheet newspapers tended to attract a better class of journalist, while the tabloids seemed to employ only roughneck scumbags with neither conscience nor decency – the sort of people who'd accept without question any lies fed to them by the police, especially with regard to her daughters. When Davies first contacted Ann we already had several high-class journalists working diligently on the case. We didn't want to upset them by sharing our 'exclusive' snippets with too many of their rivals. But Ann thought that Davies might be useful to the campaign in the future, so she encouraged him to keep in touch. Her intuition was correct: he turned out to be extremely useful.

Trawling through the unused evidence from the investigation I'd found a very promising suspect to fit that vacancy for 'most likely murderer of Alison'. He was a homeless man called David Wylie. A few days after Alison's murder someone claiming to be a social worker among the homeless tipped off the police about some frightening allegations being made by Wylie. The informant said that Wylie sometimes slept rough in The Strand (where Alison had worked) and most recently had been seen at a squat in Battersea (where Alison had lived). The social worker said that Wylie, weird and unstable, carried a knife – and was claiming to have stabbed a woman to death. As far as I could tell, the police hadn't pursued this lead vigorously. In fact, it seemed at first glance that the police hadn't even tracked Wylie down to rule him out of their inquiries. Over the following months I'd construct a very tall tale from some very short facts. I'd turn Wylie into the person most likely to have murdered Alison. At first, I genuinely thought I might have stumbled across the real murderer, but in a short time I came to realise that Wylie couldn't actually have been the killer. But his innocence didn't matter – and his possible guilt did.

Wylie became a necessary fiction in the publicity battle to convince the public that the Taylors were the victims of a miscarriage of justice. Our aim was to change the climate of opinion before their appeal, to make the public, the legal profession and even the judges feel certain that an awful injustice had been done to two young women. And to do this we needed sympathetic journalists eager for fresh stories and startling new angles – and what could be more startling than a credible new suspect?

The police discovered that the person who'd made the call about Wylie wasn't a social worker as such. His name was Graham Baldwin. He'd been homeless himself in the past and had helped form a charitable organisation called Homeless Emergency London People (H.E.L.P.). My first task was to track him down. It was at this point that Nick Davies first showed his usefulness: he had contacts among the homeless and quickly got the address of one of Baldwin's friends, a man called Graham Guillou. Rather than involve the sisters' solicitor at this early stage, I agreed with Ann and Del that I'd visit Guillou alone to see what he had to say. One evening I called at a terraced house in Dulwich, south London. The door was answered by a middle-aged man, disabled but mobile. This was Graham Guillou. I told him I wanted to talk to him about David Wylie. He led me in to a sparsely furnished lounge and introduced me to his wife. She was younger than he, slim, with dark, shoulder-length hair. I could see immediately that what these people needed most was money. I told them I was writing a book about the murder of Alison Shaughnessy and that the book's thrust would be that the Taylor sisters were innocent. I said I believed that David Wylie had committed the crime. When the girls were released – and they would be soon – the press would pay good money for stories about the real murderer. Furthermore, anyone who helped me prove that Wylie was the murderer would receive payment from the proceeds of the book. Guillou nodded enthusiastically; he said he knew all about Wylie. He asked me if I knew about his friend Graham Baldwin's call to the police. I said I did. I asked Guillou to think of everything he could about Wylie over the next few days; then I'd return to put everything down on paper.

I returned as promised a few days later. As I sat with Guillou for a few hours I compiled a damning dossier on David Wylie. It wasn't that Guillou told me anything especially damning about him – at least not specifically in relation to his possible involvement in Alison's murder – it was more that I twisted everything to point to Wylie's guilt. I did this simply by asking questions like, 'Is it possible that Wylie may have done such and such? Was he capable of such and such? Is it possible that he went to such and such a place?' Guillou would usually just nod and say: 'I suppose so.' I soon realised I could lead Guillou up any path I chose to take him. At the end of our session I read back my notes to Guillou and got him to sign them. I asked if he could arrange for me to meet Graham Baldwin. He said he'd try to sort out a meeting as soon as possible.

As I was leaving, Guillou gripped my arm and said: 'Here, take this. Thanks very much. See you soon.' He'd given me a gift of a malt loaf. I walked to my car feeling a tinge of guilt. Guillou had given me the gift as thanks for what he saw as my potential to help him. But I knew he was unlikely to get anything but grief for helping me. I didn't feel good about myself, but I reasoned I was working to put right a greater injustice. Guillou was merely an unfortunate means towards that noble end. I tossed his malt loaf over a nearby hedge. I contacted the Taylors' solicitor, Michael Holmes, and told him I'd had a very useful meeting with Guillou. I said I'd write up the notes and post them to him. He said that when he received them he'd take a formal statement from Guillou. Holmes had no idea what I'd been up to: he thought everything I'd done was above board.

Within a week I'd sent Holmes a very full account of what Guillou had allegedly told me. It was full of lies, half-truths and speculation posing as fact, but it read very well. I could almost believe it myself. The key fabrications were that, first: Wylie had been behaving especially weirdly in the weeks leading up to Alison's murder – behaviour which reached its zenith of weirdness on the day before the killing; second: that on the day of the murder he left the squat early before the others had stirred and went missing for the whole day; third: that he had an unhealthy obsession with women and tried to get hold of the addresses of the charity's female volunteers; fourth: that he was sexually frustrated, getting his kicks from porn and making crude remarks to women in the street; fifth: that he was suspected of carrying out crimes in the area where Alison worked; sixth: that he used to buy his cannabis from the pub at the top of the road where Alison lived; seventh: that he'd earned up to sixty pounds by pawning jewellery on the day after the murder; eighth: that he'd stated he'd stabbed a girl on the day Alison was murdered; ninth: that when Guillou had seen him for the last time two days after the murder, Wylie was no longer wearing the black leather zip-up bomber jacket he always used to wear. He was also supposedly wearing normal shoes, unlike his usual trainers – and his denim jeans looked like they'd just been washed.

Now all I had to do was to get Graham Baldwin to put his name to the same crap. Guillou arranged for me to meet Baldwin at his home in Worthing. Guillou was supposed to accompany me, but for some reason he dropped out at the last moment. Instead, Del Taylor and I made the trip in Michelle's white Ford Sierra. I brought along a small bottle of whisky for Baldwin – his favourite tipple, according to

Guillou. I hoped it would loosen his tongue and make him more amenable. We met in a pub and I tried to get him drunk, but he was in no hurry to finish his drinks. He repeated what he'd told the police, namely, that Wylie had confessed to 'doing a girl', but he was vague about the timescale. He was, however, certain that Wylie had not said he'd killed a girl on the day Alison was murdered. He was pretty sure the crime of which Wylie had spoken had occurred some time before Alison's murder. He rejected all my attempts to embroider what he knew about Wylie. He would say things like: 'That's not true', or 'I couldn't really say that'. In fact, the best I could get him to say was that, in his opinion, Wylie was a bit of an oddball. However, before leaving, he agreed to speak to the Taylors' solicitor. I was disappointed, but not deterred. I felt that so long as Baldwin stuck to his basic version of events – that Wylie carried a knife and had talked of stabbing a girl – and didn't comment on Guillou's, then the story might still stand up for our purposes. If we made sure that the story only emerged shortly before the appeal, then the police and media wouldn't have time to destroy it. What ever happened after the appeal didn't matter.

Ann decided that Nick Davies was to be the journalist entrusted with this exclusive, partly to repay him for having got Guillou's address in the first place. Ann contacted Nick and indicated she had an exclusive for him. It was arranged for him to come on a visit to meet the sisters in prison. We'd already briefed Michelle and Lisa about the story, indicating its weaknesses, but stressing its potential usefulness as a means of creating doubt just before the appeal. Ann, Del, myself, Lisa, Michelle and Nick Davies were soon sitting around a table in the prison visiting-room. We tended not to bring journalists with us on visits, because Michelle had made plain that she didn't trust any of them and certainly didn't like having them up on visits. But we told her this was a special case. Once we'd introduced the sisters to Davies, we outlined the nature of the damning new testimony we'd acquired regarding the homeless man. Davies was cock-a-hoop. He said he wanted to find and confront David Wylie as soon as possible. He thought that, with so much evidence against him, he was bound to confess. The last thing I wanted was for Davies or any other journalist to find Wylie, I was sure he would be able to destroy my fabrications. My eyes met Lisa's, then Michelle's. We didn't need to say anything. I felt we were all thinking the same thing.

'You aren't going to look for anybody,' I said to Davies. He looked puzzled and asked why.

'Because I said so,' I replied.

Davies, sensing my threatening manner, said plaintively: 'But if I find him, I'm sure he'll confess.'

Raising my voice, I said: 'Look, don't fuck things up for us. I've told you not to fucking look for him, so don't fucking look for him. Or you won't be able to look for fucking anyone.'

There was an uncomfortable silence. Eventually Lisa asked me about something totally different. For the rest of the visit we didn't discuss the homeless man. I could tell that Ann was annoyed with me for having threatened Davies so crudely, but when I explained myself to her later she seemed okay about it. I thought I'd better write to Michelle too in case she was annoyed. On 5 April 1993 I wrote:

> How are you and how are things with you and Lisa? I guess I am as popular as Salman Rushdie is in Baghdad! I stand by what I said to that 'nice Mr Davies'. And I fail to see how anyone can disagree . . . If 'nice Mr Davies' tells the world how he unravelled the mystery of the homeless man then what will be your gain? I cannot think of one.

Michelle wrote back swiftly to say she hadn't liked the way my words had caused an atmosphere, but at the same time she felt that what I'd said had had to be said. She felt that her mother's trust in journalists was often misplaced. She added that she didn't want anything printed about Wylie until the time was right.

Despite Michelle's words of reassurance, I was still worried that my heavy-handed treatment of Davies would make him take a damagingly critical view of the Taylors' case. I considered contacting him to apologise and to try to explain in a gentler way why we didn't want him to contact Wylie. But I knew well that, if we had nothing to hide, there was no justifiable reason for not talking to Wylie before the appeal. The fact was that we did have something to hide: we didn't want Davies talking to Wylie for the simple reason that, with a few pertinent questions, he might unravel my embroidery of lies, half-truths and speculation. In the end I decided not to contact Davies in case I made things worse. I imagined tying myself up in knots trying to justify my request. Besides, even if he ignored my request, there was no guarantee he'd be able to track down Wylie in time for his article's deadline. I can't say I felt guilty about trying to dupe Davies. Again, for me, the end justified the means. All the same, I knew Davies was an honest journalist who would never knowingly print untruths. He was assuming our good faith. He wasn't to know the real nature of our bad faith.

Over the next couple of months Ann kept in contact with Davies. She told me he didn't seem angry about my behaviour towards him. I was worried he might be hiding his true feelings, which we'd only discover when he stitched us up in his article. But Ann said she trusted him; she said he was nice. She said his article was scheduled to appear on the Saturday before the sisters' appeal in the second week of June.

As the sisters' appeal hearing approached, Michelle told me of the ill-feeling at the prison towards her and Lisa. She said lots of girls were wishing them bad luck – you only had to look in their eyes. She knew they were jealous because everyone seemed to feel they were likely to be set free. She said some girls were trying hard to stir up trouble, and she was finding it hard not to hit back. Lisa was a complete wreck after visits from their parents. Things had got so bad that the warders had arranged for her and Lisa to have two half-hour gym sessions a week all by themselves.

In the week before the appeal Michelle wrote to say she was experiencing a mixture of emotions. However, she and Lisa were trusting in God, and this was helping them cope. In that same week they must have become even more convinced that God was on their side – their legal team informed them that they'd discovered a crucial document in the police files regarding the apparently contradictory evidence of a key prosecution witness. The doctor who'd said at their trial he'd seen two white girls coming out of Alison's home had earlier said one of them may have been black. This fact hadn't been disclosed to the defence. I felt sure it was the breakthrough that would set the sisters free.

Around this time *The Observer* also printed a significant article which focused largely on how newspaper photographs taken from a video of the Shaughnessys' wedding had been doctored to show Michelle kissing her lover far more intimately than was the case (in particular the one used in the notorious *Sun* front page, headlined CHEATS KISS). In other television news stories Ann and Del were filmed at the House of Commons at the launch of 'Presswatch' (described as a new support group for the victims of press abuse). They were also filmed at the Law Society in Chancery Lane, where they were part of the audience for an annual lecture dedicated to a man who had spent the last 30 years of his life exposing miscarriages of justice. Meanwhile the youngest daughter, Tracey, appeared in one television news story poignantly reading yet another poem from her sisters. In that same film the journalists even got agony aunt Virginia Ironside to say that too much emphasis might have been placed on the extracts from Michelle's diary. According to Ironside, people often expressed on paper the desire to kill others: diaries were merely a forum for expressing things you didn't mean at all. In another news piece Ann pointed out that shortly after Michelle had written the 'unwashed bitch' comments she had baked Alison a cake for her 21st birthday, thus showing her real feelings of friendliness towards the victim. I didn't think Ann should have mentioned the cake – I felt viewers might have interpreted it as evidence of Michelle's being two-faced.

In the excitement of those last days before the appeal I'd almost forgotten about Nick Davies's planned article. But when it came it merely added to our confidence that the sisters would soon be home. Davies's feature appeared on 5 June 1993, five days before the start of the appeal. It was the cover story in *The Guardian's Weekend* magazine, spread over four pages under the headline ROUGH JUSTICE. I started reading with trepidation, fearing a possible stitch-up, but I soon relaxed. The first page, and almost half the second, was taken up with the homeless man David Wylie – although Davies didn't give his real name, preferring to use the pseudonym 'Derek Williams'. To my relief, Davies had clearly not managed to track him down. Davies didn't use my wilder speculations, but I was pleased to see he'd stuck in the nonsense about Wylie's supposedly 'missing' black leather jacket and trainers. In a few well-written sentences Davies painted a dramatic portrait of a dangerous and unstable individual who clearly had a lot of questions to answer. On the last page he returned to the homeless man:

> Ann and Del Taylor do not claim to know that Derek Williams is guilty of murder. They can see that he may have been boasting to make people frightened of him or that the social worker and his colleague may have wanted to get him into trouble. Their lawyer has written repeatedly to the Crown Prosecution Service, asking for evidence that the police ever followed up the tip that was received that night by Sean Oxley in Bow Street police station. As far as the lawyer can establish, the police never succeeded in tracing Williams. That is the point which now worries Ann and Del Taylor.

Most of the third page was devoted to making JJ's evidence look extremely suspect. I was pleased that Davies avoided mentioning JJ's claim that the sisters had asked her to give them a false alibi and that she was frightened they might harm her if she declined. He concluded his summary of JJ by giving the sisters space to say that, although JJ had lied in court, they didn't blame her. In fact, they felt sorry for her. I had to laugh: they'd have been happy to see her under the wheels of a bus.

In the rest of the article Davies stressed there was no scientific evidence to link the sisters to the crime, but he didn't mention Lisa's fingerprints on the door. I was also relieved that he ignored the cashpoint evidence against Michelle. He also said that someone had seen them shopping in Bromley that day – that wasn't true, of course: in the witness box that person could only verify that he'd seen them in Bromley some time that year – he wasn't even sure of the month.

I thought the article was brilliant. Not only had Davies turned the homeless man into a very credible suspect (whom the police had supposedly ignored), but he'd also glided over the more damaging evidence against the sisters, making the case against them seem very weak. I'm sure Alison's family would have regarded it as a very partisan reworking of the defence's case. The overall effect would have been to leave the reader in no doubt that a major miscarriage of justice had occurred. We couldn't have hoped for a more sympathetic article – and in such a prestigious paper, too. The nice man from *The Guardian* had justified our faith in him. Everyone was delighted. I rang Ann and joked that if the appeal judges were *Guardian* readers then the girls were home and dry. Ann laughed. It was good to hear her laugh after all she'd been through over the last two years.

Television news programmes eagerly followed up the article. In the week of the appeal *Sky News*, *Channel Four News* and Carlton Television's regional news programme, *London Tonight*, all did helpful stories. And they all conveyed much the same information. The emphasis was on the credible new suspect ignored by the police (supported in a few of the films by guest appearances from Graham Guillou). The other elements included: JJ's lies; Ann's assertion that Michelle had been convicted on her morals; the impossibility of the prosecution's timings (bolstered in one case by an appearance from Del); the elderly neighbour who was certain Alison had arrived home after six; the jewellery allegedly stolen from the flat (suggestive of a mad burglar) and the Home Office pathologist popping up to say he'd never come across a case in which a woman had inflicted so many stab wounds. Each television news piece opened dramatically: 'Today *Sky News* can reveal vital new information of someone who confessed to stabbing a woman at about that time – a man who was never questioned.' *Channel Four News* started with the words:

> Campaigners working on behalf of two sisters jailed for murder say they've uncovered vital new evidence which will prove the girls' innocence . . . Lawyers acting for the sisters say that since last year's trial new evidence has emerged suggesting Alison was killed by a man.

And the 'exclusive report' on *London Tonight* said the same, though more colourfully:

> Life on the seedy side of The Strand, a twilight world that tourists pass by on the other side. And it's here that new claims have come to light that a down-and-outer became a killer, stalking and then murdering Alison Shaughnessy who worked close by at this bank.

Like almost everything that had appeared in newspapers and on television in the previous six months, these stories would have left viewers in little doubt that the sisters had been wrongfully convicted. Our media campaign had succeeded in a way that we couldn't have imagined when we'd first sat down less than a year earlier. However, our run of good fortune ended on the day before the start of the appeal. A headline in the *Daily Mail* (9 June 1993) declared: SISTERS SETBACK IN ALISON APPEAL. The article read:

> Evidence which could have helped free two sisters jailed for murder has been withdrawn.
>
> A witness was said to have told how he heard a tramp say he had killed a woman at the time of Alison Shaughnessy's murder two years ago. But he has refused to go to the Appeal Court tomorrow to speak for Michelle and Lisa Taylor after saying his story was misunderstood. The man, said to have been working in a soup kitchen when he heard 'the confession', gave police a sworn statement yesterday saying he did not believe the tramp had anything to do with the killing. He then went into hiding and is not being named.

Ann and Del were especially shaken by the story. The fact that it appeared in a 'scumbag tabloid' merely underlined how right we'd been to deal only with quality journalists. We'd all known that the 'homeless man' yarn would collapse under any serious prodding, but we'd prayed that the collapse wouldn't take place until after the appeal – by which time we hoped the sisters would be free. We checked the other papers and were relieved to discover that no one else had picked up on the story. We also watched the television news throughout the day, but again, no one bothered broadcasting the fact that they'd earlier run a story that didn't stand up. We were grateful for their decency in keeping this mistake out of the public eye. We discovered from the lawyers that Graham Baldwin had been the one who'd spoken to the police. He'd walked into a police station to make his statement after becoming concerned at the way the 'homeless man' story was being reported. Of course he had every right to be concerned, because I'd helped make sure that what had been so extensively aired bore little relation to the truth. Baldwin told the police he'd been prompted to approach them after reading that the 'suspect' David Wylie had made his confession after the murder of Alison. Baldwin stated categorically that Wylie had spoken to him of 'doing' a girl two to three weeks *before* Alison's murder; Wylie had also indicated that his actions stemmed from a love affair that went wrong. Baldwin added that he'd made this plain to the Taylors' solicitor, Michael Holmes. He also said that Graham Guillou had not even been present when Wylie had mentioned the stabbing. Then, to give the story a final kick in the head, the police had tracked down Wylie himself. He proved he was out of the country when Alison was murdered. The 'homeless man' story had been comprehensively rubbished.

In the end – to our great relief – it didn't matter. The *Mail* article appeared on Wednesday. By Friday the sisters were home and free. So those quality journalists whose stories had helped the campaign had no reason to feel they'd been hoodwinked. After all, the Court of Appeal had vindicated the main thrust of their stories, namely, that Michelle and Lisa's convictions were unsafe and unsatisfactory and should be quashed. The fact that one significant element of the media's earlier stories had turned out false was an irrelevant detail. Indeed, it was the sort of minor detail that soon became drowned out in the deafening blast of coverage that trumpeted this latest miscarriage of justice.

EIGHT

With Thanks to All

After I'd watched the sisters' walk to freedom I went for something to eat before driving to their house in south London. I felt delighted for Michelle and Lisa, although their wearing of the Winston Silcott T-shirts made me anxious about how the tabloids would treat them the next day. I was astonished by what we'd achieved in just 11 months. Very few people walk away from life sentences, and, of those that do, most have to spend several years in prison and endure several rejections by the Court of Appeal before their final release. This had to be the quickest success ever. I switched on the radio to catch the news bulletins. I zipped from station to station. The story was everywhere.

There were several journalists and a television crew outside the Taylors' semi. I drove past and parked a little way down the quiet residential street. I used my mobile to phone the house. Ann answered and told me to use the side-alley to avoid the press. Inside, I found the parents with their two other children and a few close friends. The family's huge Dobermann pinscher, Duke, jumped up to greet me. I asked where Michelle and Lisa were. Ann said they'd gone up to Lisa's bedroom to be alone together for a little while. I was surprised – I'd expected to find them dancing around the front room, champagne glasses in hand. In the garden was another television crew from ITV's regional news programme, *London Tonight.* Ann said the sisters had agreed to give them a live interview on their main evening show as thanks for the helpful stories they'd done on the case. I sat down in the front room where I'd so often sat over the last 11 months. The atmosphere was strangely subdued. After about 20 minutes Lisa walked in. She saw me sitting on an armchair in the corner and came straight over to embrace me.

'Thanks for all you've done,' she said. I felt warmed by her gesture and truly happy she was free. I knew she'd been finding prison life especially tough. I was sure it would have destroyed her if she'd had to serve her full term. Michelle followed Lisa into the room. She too came over and embraced me. I told her I couldn't stay long because I was working that night. She expressed disappointment.

'Can't you come back here when you're finished?' she said. I told her I would if I could. She bent down, kissed me on the forehead and said: 'Thanks. Make sure you do.' The two of them then walked out to do their interview. I needed to leave. As I walked down the hallway to pick up my coat from the kitchen, Ann Taylor stopped me. She said: 'Don't you ever hurt her – or you'll have me to deal with.' I felt a little unnerved by her words. She was talking as if I'd just married her daughter. I thought she was reading a little too much into Michelle's quick peck on my forehead, which I hadn't registered as anything other than a platonic friend's affection. I was already living with Debra, my partner of many years, and our two young children. Admittedly, my relationship with Debra had been put under strain by my obsessive devotion to the Taylor sisters' cause, but it was still there all the same, and I wanted it to continue. I laughed to hide my embarrassment and said: 'I'll see you later, Mrs T.' I was going to say something, but decided on balance that, after everything that had happened, she was just being understandably over-protective of her daughter. Through the verandah doors I could see Michelle and Lisa sitting in the garden waiting for their interview to begin. Ann and Del went out to join them. I picked up my coat, but changed my mind about leaving. It would have been silly not to stay another few minutes to watch them live on television. I went back into the front room, where everyone was intently eyeing the screen. It was the top story. Before long, the camera went live to Forest Hill. Michelle and Lisa were relatively restrained in what they said, although they still criticised the police and media with righteous anger.

Del called the police wicked and evil. The room filled with murmurs of approval. The sisters said that religion had been very important to them during their ordeal. In fact, the first thing they'd done after leaving the Court of Appeal was to head for their local church to give thanks to God. I couldn't blame them: they'd certainly got a result. The interviewer asked Ann if she thought at all about Alison's parents. Ann said: 'Yes, very much so. They have no answers as far as their daughter's death is concerned. We've said all along, and we still say now, our girls did not commit this crime, but whoever did is still out there, and if the police had done their job in the first place maybe they wouldn't be suffering now, as they probably are.'

When it was over, Michelle and Lisa trooped back into the front room. I said my goodbyes once again. I walked out the front door to find Ann at the gate talking to a tabloid journalist. She was telling him the girls had been offered twenty-five thousand pounds for their story and she wanted to know if he could better it. I nodded at her and walked up the street to my car. I had to smile – only minutes earlier her daughters had been in the back garden slagging off the tabloid press and now she was in the front garden trying to do a deal with them.

I drove home to Basildon and Debra. She was in the kitchen doing the washing-up. She'd already fed the children and put them to bed.

'So they're out then?' she said.

I said they were. We chatted about how the day had gone. She was genuinely pleased I'd achieved my aim, but I could tell she was relieved that at last I could forget about the Taylor sisters. Over the last 11 months we'd had countless rows about the time I was spending on the campaign. She was always accusing me of putting strangers before my own family. We'd had similar rows in the past when I'd led another campaign to raise money for the local boy who'd been horribly injured in the road accident. But then, at least, I'd been around a lot to help with our own children. It wasn't that she'd minded my trying to help the poor boy in that case, it was just that my commitment to him had seemed open-ended. In her eyes, once I'd done my bit, I should have stopped and let someone else take over, whereas I had wanted to keep on going. In the early days of my involvement with the Taylors I'd tried to explain to Debra what was driving me, but it was hard to put it into words. I often felt surprised myself at the obsessive hold the case had over me. Debra broke off from the washing-up to make me something to eat. There was silence for a little while. Then she asked me what the sisters were going to do now. I said they were going to finish writing the book they'd started in prison. She didn't know I'd been writing it with them. More silence. She asked me if I was planning to have something to do with it. I knew I was about to trigger a row, but I wasn't going to lie.

'I'm writing it with them,' I said.

I could see Debra's jaw dropping. 'You have got to be joking,' she said, in a tone of final-straw exasperation.

I said I wasn't. She tried to reason with me. I had achieved my aim and now I should get back to looking after my own family.

'They're out now, Bernie. You've done what you set out to do. Now move on.'

I didn't try either to justify my intentions or to make them in any way more palatable to her. I had decided, and that was that. I soon realised I'd pushed her beyond her threshold of toleration. She'd had enough. She said if I did the book, then our relationship was over: 'You forget them – or you go.' Pig-stubborn and self-righteous, I wasn't going to argue with her. I just left. I suppose I didn't honestly think our relationship was over. I was angry; she was angry. In my heart I thought we would probably get back together again. But I wanted to make her understand that I had no intention of compromising my plans to write the book. With hindsight, I find my total insensitivity towards Debra astonishing.

I went to do my night's shift at Raquels. Violence was the club's distinctive offering to the world. I'd been there for just over three years, and in my early days I was usually involved in at least two fights a night. These weren't usually gentle scuffles with harmless drunks. Our valued customers didn't tend to observe the Queensberry rules when fighting. If they hadn't brought along their own weapons – knives, machetes, knuckledusters, coshes, bottles of 'squirt' (liquid ammonia) and even hand-guns – they'd use whatever came to hand: heavy ashtrays, bottles, glasses, chairs and tables. The dance floor was as often the venue for pitched battles as it was for dancing. Fractured skulls, broken bones and comas were what customers often took away from the club; ears, eyes and parts of noses were what they sometimes left behind. Bouncing trouble-makers down the stairs and throwing them out the doors didn't always end the trouble. The aggrieved revellers, especially if they were part of a gang, would often call for reinforcements and try to storm the place. One time the doors were petrol bombed. Over three years, under my leadership, the security team had ruthlessly established a rough sort of order over the once-prevailing anarchy. My attitude was that violent people should be dealt with violently. We, the doormen, had a stash of our own weapons which we were not reluctant to use. People used to joke that there were three ways of leaving Raquels: on foot, by taxi or in an ambulance. There was a fourth, actually: out the back, head-first down the concrete stairs, although we reserved this exit for the most badly-behaved customers. Some nights there seemed to be more ambulances outside the entrance than taxis.

That night, however, was quiet. I didn't finish work until the early hours. I drove to south London, where I also had a flat. I considered dropping in on the Taylors, but decided I couldn't face them. I spent what remained of the night in my own flat. The next day I called on the Taylors. Michelle was pleased to see me. I told her what had happened with Debra and she was very sympathetic. She said she didn't like the idea of my being all alone and miserable in my own flat. She suggested I spend that night at her house. I didn't see any harm in it; we were just friends and we'd be staying under the same roof as her parents.

I had a few things to do during the day, but I went back to see them in the evening. We stayed in talking until late, discussing some of the things that had appeared in that day's newspapers. The sisters had made it onto several front pages, but the coverage, at least in the tabloids, had been very begrudging. Several seemed to imply that the sisters were guilty and had got off on a technicality. A comment piece in the *Daily Mail* had the headline, IS NO ONE GUILTY ANY MORE?, and asked the question: 'Is anyone concerned that when a wrong is corrected, another wrong remains, a crime goes undetected and unpunished?' The writer wondered if there would be many expressions of grief for the murdered woman. One thing that united the tabloids was their fury at effectively being blamed by the Court of Appeal for prejudicing the sisters' trial. An editorial in *The Sun* thundered: 'Justice would be better served if there were fewer judges from Brasenose College, Oxford, and more *Sun* readers from the University of Life on the bench.' The only thing that surprised me was that the tabloids hadn't commented on the Winston Silcott T-shirts, beyond stating the simple fact that the sisters had worn them (although the next day, Sunday, the *News of the World* slagged them off for doing so). Michelle and Lisa didn't seem particularly bothered by anything in the papers. The general attitude of the tabloids did, however, make them decide not to take up any of the lucrative money deals on offer for their stories. They said they'd been inundated with requests for interviews. The only story that Michelle commented on was a report that John Shaughnessy had said he was 'totally disgusted' that the sisters were free.

'As if I care what that slag says,' she said.

The police announced they wouldn't be reopening the case and they weren't looking for anyone else in connection with the murder. That was their petty way of saying they still thought the Taylors were guilty. I said it was typical police behaviour: merciless in victory, graceless in defeat.

Around one in the morning Michelle and Lisa asked me if I'd take them out for a drive. I was happy to oblige. Before they got in I warned them that the car was stolen and had false number plates. I said: 'It might be a bit embarrassing if we're stopped by the Old Bill.' Both laughed and said they didn't mind, so long as I didn't tell their parents about the car's origins. We set off in high spirits. There were hardly any other cars on the road as we drove around south London and on to the West End. I went wherever they told me to go. Michelle said she wanted to see the Churchill Clinic where she and John Shaughnessy had worked and met. As we passed it she said: 'It seems so long ago that I was here.' We laughed and joked and talked about nothing in particular, although Lisa did most of the laughing. Michelle was the more serious of the two. It was hard to believe there were only a few years between them. At times they seemed to come from different generations. They were saying what most people say when they come out of prison: 'Oh, doesn't everything seem fast! Doesn't everything seem so large!' Being locked in a cramped cell for months or years tends to have that effect on you. We drove past the Nat West cash machine where Michelle's card was used on the day of the murder. I asked her jokingly if she wanted to make a withdrawal. Lisa laughed, but Michelle told me to fuck off. Then, later, we drove along The Strand towards the Barclay's Bank where Alison had worked. As we passed it Michelle looked away. I said: 'Familiar?'

This time Michelle didn't swear at me. She just said 'I want to go home.' On the way back I drove along the main road from which you could see the back of the flat in which the murder had taken place. Again, I noticed that Michelle made a point of looking away.

When we arrived home Michelle told me I was sleeping in the back bedroom, so I said goodnight and made my way up the stairs. I opened the door and switched on the light, but quickly switched it off again when I saw that 14-year-old Tracey was already sleeping alone in the one double bed. Michelle had come up the stairs behind me.

'Tracey's already in there,' I whispered.

She laughed and said: 'Don't worry. She won't bite you.'

I was still unsure about what was expected of me.

'Eh, would you like me to sleep on the floor?' Michelle told me not to be silly: the bed was big enough for two, three even. I felt uneasy, but didn't want to make a fuss about something that no one else seemed fussed about. I took my bag into the bathroom and undressed. I put on a shirt and football shorts before returning to the bedroom. In the darkness I carefully got into bed on the opposite side to Tracey. About ten minutes later the door opened and Michelle came in. She climbed over Tracey and got into bed between us. I didn't say a word, neither did Michelle. Nothing happened, and we both fell asleep.

I didn't sleep very well. As the daylight came through the curtains I felt a little panicky. What if Michelle's parents got the wrong idea? I needn't have worried, because around 8 a.m. Ann popped her head around the door and told Michelle the time. Moments later both she and Tracey got up. Michelle called my name, but I pretended to be asleep. They went downstairs without me. I followed shortly afterwards. Downstairs nobody said a word about who had slept where. I reasoned that if nobody thought there was anything odd about the sleeping arrangements, then maybe it was just me who had the problem with it. But no matter how I tried to shrug off my uncomfortable feelings, I still felt uneasy about what had happened.

On the Saturday week after their release the sisters threw a party at a church hall in Forest Hill to thank all those who'd helped them. I arranged for one of the club's DJs to play for free. I didn't plan to go, because I was working that night. But Michelle rang me several times during the evening and asked me to drop in after work. In the end I agreed. I soon regretted it.

There were about 100 people there, mostly friends and family, with a sprinkling of friendly journalists. Ann kept telling me to dance with Michelle. I'd never danced with anyone in my life and I had no intention of breaking that pattern. However, Ann wouldn't leave me alone. I started to feel extremely awkward. She kept saying: 'Go on, have a dance with her. Shall I leave you two alone?' I smiled through my embarrassment, but remained firmly in my seat. Her ham-fisted attempts to get me on the dance floor did, however, make me realise with a jolt that Michelle had intentions towards me; intentions that were sufficiently serious for her to have already discussed them with her mother. The party was quite flat; there were only about ten people dancing. I'd already missed the evening's high point – a visit from the vicar and a local MP. Now the only entertainment was being provided by a man who was a little unsteady on his feet. I hadn't met him before, but I was told he'd campaigned to free three people convicted of murder, the so-called Cardiff Three. He'd kindly helped out at the party by bringing along various utensils for serving the food. When I finally spoke to Michelle on her own almost the first thing she said was: 'That fool's really beginning to annoy me.' She asked me to have a word with him. I walked over and took him to one side. He was swaying slightly.

'Leave now or you'll be leaving in a fucking body bag,' I said.

He didn't need to be told a second time. He just turned and headed off towards the exit, leaving behind his carrier bag of utensils. I walked back to Michelle. 'He's forgotten his bag,' she said.

She picked it up, then, laughing, she deliberately bent several of the forks and spoons. I bent most of the rest. As a final gesture of thanks and goodwill, Michelle ladled into the bag a few mounds of trifle. She said: 'He might be hungry later.' I threw in a few mangled sandwiches, then grabbed the bag and ran out after him. He hadn't got far. When I caught up I handed over the bag.

'Cheers, mate,' I said. 'Here's your stuff – and a little extra for your help.' He didn't look in the bag. He just took it, turned and staggered into the night.

NINE

Animal in the Zoo

In the first few weeks after their release they experienced a mixed response from the public. They were invited to appear on stage at a public meeting organised by the Socialist Workers' Party. One of the party's leading lights was the campaigning journalist Paul Foot, who'd exposed several miscarriages of justice. Lisa told me excitedly how they'd raised their fists in support of other unjustly imprisoned people – and the audience of revolutionary socialists had given them a standing ovation. For a short while after their release Michelle and Lisa would read the party's newspaper, *Socialist Worker*, but they soon became bored by it ('It's too political,' said Lisa). The sisters also received a lot of hate mail, including a parcel which, when opened, covered them in flour. The attached note warned them that the next parcel would be a bomb. It was signed 'Kilburn IRA'.

They began talking about moving away from Forest Hill: too many people knew where they lived, and they feared they might be attacked. I felt, however, that they were also keen to get out of the family home. They both loved their mother dearly, but I could tell she overpowered them. Critical and inquisitive, she wanted to know what they were doing at all times and who they were doing it with. Moreover, she was continually telling them what they could and couldn't do.

Uncle Norman offered them the use of a flat above a television repair shop he owned in nearby Brockley. I was keen to get the book finished. We agreed it would be in everyone's interest if we moved in together for a short time. I could get the book written by having their undivided attention, and they would feel more relaxed and secure by having me around in case someone did try to attack them. However, a few days before the move, Lisa changed her mind. She'd recently started another relationship with a man called Garth. Like her previous boyfriend, he was black. This led Del to mutter in my ear behind her back. Del wasn't racist, but I suppose like many people of his age and background he wasn't entirely comfortable with the idea of his daughter's going out with people from other cultures. I liked Del a lot, but by and large he did seem to spend most of his time muttering things under his breath. I suppose he had learnt to keep quiet and do as he was told. I got the impression he was a bit worn down by his wife. She didn't have a high opinion of men and was always having digs at them. One of her sayings was: 'Men are only good for one thing – and they're not very good at that.'

Lisa decided she wanted to move into Garth's flat instead. Michelle didn't mind: she said I could still move in with her, while Lisa could come round during the day to help with the book. The flat was small and basic, but was fine for our needs. There was just one bedroom in which there were two single beds. As I helped Michelle move into the flat I noticed among her possessions a small box of oddities – a plastic rose, menu cards from restaurants, till receipts, bus tickets, birthday cards and Valentine cards. I asked her what the junk signified.

'It's John's stuff,' she said.

'What? John Shaughnessy?' I asked.

She nodded. She'd kept everything he'd ever sent her – and anything else that betokened the times they'd spent together. Unlike me, she didn't regard as strange the idea of preserving these relics of a relationship with a man who believed she'd murdered his wife and who'd testified against her. For the first few weeks we slept chastely in our separate beds. I guessed that Michelle wanted me to make a pass at her, but I had no desire to do so. I knew things would just become too complicated if I did. And with the collapse of my relationship with Debra I was in no mood to start up something new with someone I didn't fancy. I wanted to keep a friendly distance: anything else would have interfered with work on the book. Meanwhile, Lisa's relationship with Garth seemed to follow the pattern of her previous relationship: lots of rows and tears. Lisa would often telephone Michelle, crying down the line about Garth's latest bad behaviour. Michelle would come off the phone in a fury. She said Garth was treating her sister like a skivvy, expecting her to clean his flat and wait on him hand and foot. She'd be really troubled by it. I told her she had to let Lisa live her own life and that she shouldn't let herself be drawn into other people's crap. But Michelle seemed to put everyone else's worries before her own. One of her secondary worries was her inability to get a job. She applied for lots of posts, but kept getting rejected. No one, it seemed, wanted to give her a fresh start. She went for several interviews, but never got the job. She said that the interviewers always knew about her background; she felt that a lot of the time, they'd simply called her in out of macabre curiosity to have a look at her. She said she often felt like an animal at the zoo. We used to discuss what she could do. She surprised me one day by saying she'd once applied to join the police. In fact, her application was being processed at the time she was arrested for murder. I told her that that was one career option which might now be closed to her. She laughed, but I could tell she was beginning to get depressed. She started saying quite often that she'd sooner be back in prison. Things were less complicated in there. I'd tell her not to be silly. I knew from my own experience that it usually took a few months to settle back into the real world. I told her that things would be all right soon.

Michelle and Lisa were both protective of Tracey, who'd been distraught at their imprisonment. Her upset had been heightened by playground taunts, the sort of childish stuff you might expect in the circumstances – 'Your sisters are murderers', and the like. However, Ann and Del had been so worried about the psychological effect the whole experience was having on Tracey that they'd arranged for her to have counselling. After her sisters' release the taunting had continued. A particular group of girls kept saying: 'Your sisters did do it. They're guilty.' Tracey often came home in tears. One afternoon Lisa, Michelle and I were sitting talking in

Michelle's bedroom. The subject turned to Tracey's latest stories of verbal abuse. I told Michelle and Lisa – without being too dismissive of Tracey's stories – that they shouldn't get too wound up about them. My words didn't have much effect. They discussed the taunts as if they were death threats. They got more and more wound up. Finally, they said they were going to sort out the girls responsible.

'Nobody messes with our sister,' Michelle said. I could tell from her expression that she wasn't just planning to chat to them. She clearly intended using violence or, at least, the threat of violence. I told her she was mad; if the press got hold of such a story they'd really make a thing of it. Michelle said she didn't care. She repeated coldly: 'I told you nobody messes with our sister.'

In the bedroom they kept a rounders bat and an ornamental wooden truncheon, the latter being a holiday souvenir inscribed with the name of the resort. Michelle picked up the former; Lisa the latter. They said they were going to find the culprits. I told them again they were mad, but they'd made up their minds. I had some things to do at my own flat, so I left. When I saw them later they were laughing about their confrontation with the girls. They said they'd really frightened them, but had not actually used any violence. I didn't join in their laughter – I couldn't see the funny side of threatening children with weapons.

Another juvenile who fell foul of Lisa and Michelle was a pizza-delivery boy who fancied Tracey. Teenagers used to congregate in and around a fried-chicken shop in Forest Hill. There was a pizza parlour nearby. Tracey's admirer worked there, delivering pizzas on his moped. Michelle pointed him out to me a few times as we drove past. He had the build of a sparrow and can't have been more than 16. Michelle said he'd started talking to Tracey and giving her little gifts. But they were never 'going out', as such. To me, it all seemed very innocent. If anything, I thought it was good for Tracey. However, Michelle and Lisa didn't like what was going on. To them, Tracey was too young to have a boyfriend, especially an older boyfriend who might take advantage of her. They got especially worried when Tracey started occasionally wearing one of his T-shirts and his jumper. They assumed he was ingratiating himself with her in order to make an assault upon her innocence. If he was there in the street when I was driving past with Michelle she'd say, 'There's the bastard.' She and Lisa kept discussing what they ought to do about him. I kept telling them not to do anything – it was all part of growing up. I said they should, by all means, keep an eye on things, but not interfere without good reason. I usually tried to make a joke of it: I said they ought to encourage the relationship in order to secure free pizzas. They wouldn't listen to me. After much debate they decided to confront the boy and put a stop to his game. At first they thought of ordering a pizza in the hope he'd deliver it. That way they could 'get hold of him' when he called. They abandoned that idea when they decided there were too many other pizza-delivery boys working at the same place – the sisters might have had to spend a fortune on unwanted pizzas before Romeo arrived on his moped. The boy began to obsess Michelle; she kept talking about him. She said she was terrified a man would treat her sister like John Shaughnessy had treated her. She wanted to protect Tracey from bastards like him. I told her she was being over-protective, but she said she didn't care. Eventually, Michelle and Lisa approached the boy outside the pizza parlour and told him forcefully to stop bothering their sister. Wisely, in my opinion, he chose to seek love elsewhere.

We worked hard on the book. I'd assumed she'd want to use it partly to criticise John Shaughnessy for his treatment of her. I was wrong. She did often say negative things about him, could even be contemptuous of him, but when we came to put things down on paper she was extremely protective of him and most reluctant to let me write anything too critical. Her protectiveness extended even to the pettiest details of how he looked and what he wore. She wouldn't let me put him down in any way whatsoever. The impression of him she wanted the book to convey was of an Irish charmer-cum-playboy. I asked her once what had most upset her during the trial. She said the worst moment had been when the prosecution described how she and John had had sex in the gardener's shed in the clinic's grounds. For her, this presented to the world a sordid image of their relationship. Perhaps, also, it confirmed that John had just used her as his bit on the side. I was surprised when she said she'd like to meet up with him again to ask him why he said what he'd said at the trial.

She seemed willing to tell me everything about her relationship with John. She said he was her first proper boyfriend, the first man she'd ever slept with. By this stage I'd read John's statement to the police. I didn't bring up the fact that in that statement he vigorously denied being her first lover. He alleged she was already on the pill when he met her. Michelle described the evening when John first ended their relationship – and revealed he'd also been seeing Alison. She'd just come back from a wonderful holiday with her family. She was looking forward to seeing the man she loved. When they next spoke he told her he wanted to take her out for a meal, because he had something important to say. Her heart had fluttered with excitement; she thought he might be planning to ask her to marry him. She spent hours dressing herself up in preparation for the joyous occasion. John picked her up at home. She'd hoped he might be taking her to a posh restaurant in town. Instead, he took her down the road to a Harvester. They both had a starter, then tucked in to the steak and chips of their main course. Michelle was half-way through her fillet steak when John said: 'I'm getting engaged.' She had beamed at him warmly, expecting his next words would be: 'And you're the lucky woman.' Sadly, that was not to be. He told her he was going to marry someone called Alison. Michelle told me she was too distraught to finish her meal. She'd burst into tears, then fled the restaurant, leaving John, and her half-eaten steak, at the table. She said she hadn't known there was anyone else in John's life (although by that stage he'd been going out with Alison for more than two years). The shock of losing the man she loved had made her ill. She was even off work sick for a while. Throughout the engagement and the marriage Michelle had continued to sleep with John. I asked her if she felt guilty about this. She would say she felt sorry for Alison: 'How could John tell her he loved her when he was with someone else?'

She usually managed to avoid saying anything too critical of Alison, but occasionally she would surprise me with her odd interpretations of Alison's behaviour. For instance, once when we were going through the press cuttings I commented on how attractive Alison looked in the professional photos she'd had taken of herself. Michelle snapped: 'Attractive? Look at her. Who does she think she is, posing like that?' She then laughed mockingly. In other conversations Michelle would describe Alison's flat as a tip because everything was in boxes. But I knew from reading John's statement that the couple had not long moved into Vardens Road. Most bizarre, though, was Michelle's conviction that Alison had been having extra marital affairs in the months leading up to her murder. She'd mentioned this before, but I hadn't picked her up on it. I asked her why she thought so. She said Alison had taken to wearing short skirts and lots of make-up. I said that surely the short skirts had been more to do with the onset of summer. As for the make-up, I said that most normal girls wore make-up. I pointed out teasingly that even she used it sparingly. Also, I said, the police had gone through every aspect of Alison's life and had not found even a hint that she was anything other than a devoted and faithful wife. Again, Michelle just shrugged her shoulders. Those sort of comments of hers made me feel uneasy, but at the time they didn't really register as significant. For me, the book was all about exposing the failings of the justice system; I wasn't going to get bogged down in Michelle's unprovable theories about Alison.

One evening, after a fruitless day's work on the book, she said she wanted to get away from everything for a few days, because it was all getting her down. I said it would be a good idea because, in her current state of mind, working on the book was pointless. She asked me if I'd go with her. I agreed and, for some reason, we decided on north Wales as our destination. Shortly before then, the police had discovered the stolen Sierra outside my flat. They towed it away one Sunday afternoon. I assumed someone had grassed me up. The police called at my flat and asked me if I knew who owned the car. I said I didn't. They couldn't pin anything on me, so I wasn't arrested. I had to hire a car to take us to Wales. For some reason we ended up at Colwyn Bay, where we found a cheap hotel near the seafront. When the receptionist asked us our names I looked at Michelle and she looked at me. For a joke I said: 'White. Unsworth-White' – the name of the doctor whose apparently unreliable evidence had helped secure the sisters' freedom. On the way up the stairs to our room we both laughed. Michelle said: 'That's twice he's come to my rescue.'

We'd chosen a room with two single beds. Michelle chose the one near the window; I put my bag on the other. It was early afternoon, so we decided to go for a walk around the town. Michelle was a different person. She seemed really happy to be away from London and her various troubles. We had a bargain meal in a café, then headed for a pub. We couldn't be bothered trying to find Colwyn Bay's finest, so we settled for some barely tolerable dive. There were only about six people inside. No one paid us any attention as we settled in for a drinking session. Michelle talked about prison. She told me she'd cracked up when, before the trial, Lisa had been granted bail. Michelle said she'd barricaded herself in the prison chapel and refused to come out. The staff had finally coaxed her out. She was sent to the prison psychiatrist, because she couldn't sleep and felt she was on the verge of a complete breakdown. The psychiatrist had given her a tape to listen to at bedtime. It had on it a song by The Temptations titled, 'Just My Imagination (Running Away With Me)'. I laughed. She asked me what was so funny. I said that her imagination running away with her had been what had got her into trouble in the first place – if she hadn't transferred her negative thoughts about Alison into the diary found by the police, the case against her would have been even weaker. She smiled, but didn't join me in laughter. She said she'd never keep a diary again. The afternoon swayed into the evening and, before long, they were ringing the bell for last orders. We were both very drunk when we ambled back to the hotel. That night we slept together for the first time.

I woke up before Michelle the next morning. As she lay beside me, snoring fitfully, fanning her beery breath towards me, I felt like a condemned man waiting for the sun to rise. I knew I'd crossed a line, and I just wished I hadn't. I told myself it wasn't going to happen again. I'd tell Michelle that we had to be friends, and friends only. But I didn't. When she awoke, she oozed happiness, almost skipping out of bed into the bathroom. If she'd shown just one sign that she was feeling even a smidgeon of regret then perhaps I'd have had the courage to tell her my true feelings. But I'd never seen her so happy – she was almost cooing with delight. Most worryingly, from almost her first sentence that morning she was talking as if we were a married couple of long standing. I couldn't face breakfast. I had an urge to get out of the hotel. We went for a walk down the town. All the time I wanted to tell her that what had happened was nothing serious and that we should forget about it, but she was so happy I didn't have the heart. I was, however, determined not to spend any longer than I absolutely had to in the situation I was in. Around midday I told her, after she'd returned from the toilet, that I'd phoned a work colleague while she'd been away. Something had cropped up at Raquels which meant I had to get back. I could tell she was disappointed, but she didn't make a fuss.

On the drive back to London I thought only of ways to ensure things wouldn't become more complicated. I didn't want to get into the habit of sleeping with her and, although I knew she'd expect me to share the one bedroom, I also knew that the late nights caused by my job would give me an excuse to avoid getting too intimate. I thought that, in time, things between us would just wind down naturally.

It didn't take long for me to realise how wrong I was.

TEN

A Girl Needs Romance

From Wednesday nights through to the early hours of Monday mornings I tended to see little of Michelle, which displeased her, to say the least. On week nights I'd be working at Raquels and at weekends I'd be at Epping Country Club in Essex, the Ministry of Sound or the nearby Elephant and Castle pub, both in south London. So for five days a week I spent most of my time at the flat either sleeping or getting changed to go out. For the other two days I'd try to sit down with Michelle to work on the book, but the atmosphere caused by her accumulating resentment at my frequent absences created a difficult working environment. Inevitably, despite my resolve after Colwyn Bay never to sleep with her again, it did happen occasionally. Many relationships have a honeymoon period before they decline into bitterness and arguments. Michelle and I bypassed the former to zip straight to the latter. I always regretted sleeping with her, because no sooner was the act over than she'd demand to know what I felt about her. Did I care for her? Did I love her? Did I even want to be with her? Whatever answer I gave was the wrong answer.

If I said I cared for her, but stopped short of saying I loved her, she'd subject me to screaming abuse: 'I fucking knew it. You're only using me. You're no better than John.' If I let her browbeat me into making an untruthful declaration of love I also got a mouthful of abuse: 'You're a liar. You're just saying that. If you did, you wouldn't stay out all the time.' I couldn't tell her the truth, because it wasn't what she wanted to hear, and anything she didn't want to hear was a lie. No matter how honest I intended to be, I always ended up playing games with words – never entirely dismissing her barkingly deluded fantasies about 'The Relationship', but never being so honest that the ramshackle structure of our togetherness collapsed in a mushroom cloud of dust and debris. I knew I was being a bastard. I knew she wasn't being entirely unreasonable in expecting more than I was willing to give. In a sexual sense she was right: I was only using her and I was only leading her on. I knew we could never be an item, because I didn't want us to be an item. All the same, I did feel sorry for her. She'd been through a traumatic time and I wanted to be a friend to her. But a caring friend was different from a committed partner – and the latter was what she craved. I tried to distance myself from her gently, but this only made her cling on tighter. She became maddeningly possessive, which is only ever a way of trying to control people, to bend them to your will – and I'd always resisted anyone's attempt to bend me to their will. If I went to work she'd telephone to check I was there. If someone rang me on my mobile I could sense she was straining to hear who. Then, if she couldn't work out for herself she'd ask me outright when the call ended. Often I'd tell her to mind her own business, but occasionally I couldn't face the argument, so I'd give her the name. Then she'd want to know what they'd wanted and where I knew them from. Whatever my stance, she bombarded me with questions.

I'm not saying Michelle wanted the whole romantic package – the flowers, the chocolates, the scented love-letters – but she wanted more than I could ever give her. The only thing I'd ever given my girlfriends was a hard time. I couldn't stand all that lovey-dovey, holdy-handy, kissy-pissy crap. One ex-girlfriend once told me that if romance ever died, I'd be taken in for questioning. So at a fundamental level, as a relationship counsellor might say, we were incompatible. But Michelle just closed her eyes to it.

On top of everything she continued to carry the troubles of her family on her shoulders. Anyone else's problems became her problems. Garth and Lisa's relationship, especially, seemed to occupy her mind. It was as if she was part of a love triangle with them; she might as well have been. She'd go on and on about their latest petty falling out, as if she were the victim. She'd ignore my suggestion that she should mind her own business. Often, their rows would cause our rows, and as the weeks passed things got so bad that to escape both Lisa's love-life and Michelle's questions I'd tell her I wanted nothing more to do with her. I'd leave and go to my own flat. After one such row she wrote me a letter in which she said she knew it was too late to say sorry to me now, because I'd already decided the relationship should end. But she wasn't sure she could move from loving me to becoming my friend so swiftly because I'd changed her life so much, yet now I'd hurt her so much that she couldn't handle the pain. She said she loved me. I felt trapped. I began to realise that things between us could only end badly.

However, we were still working on the book and I'd often have to call around to see her. After a row Michelle would be at her most sweet and charming. She'd apologise sincerely; she'd promise not to involve herself in Garth and Lisa's relationship; she'd assure me she was going to let Lisa learn from her own mistakes. I told her their relationship was hardly likely to last, anyway. And I was right.

Lisa became convinced that Garth was sleeping with one of her friends. She decided to leave him. One day Michelle, Lisa and I were all at the family home in the company of Ann and Del when the subject of Garth came up. Lisa had never introduced him to her parents. The only times they'd seen him were in the early days when he'd pull up outside the house at all hours, sound his horn and expect Lisa to come running, which she did. Lisa's anger about the way she'd been treated soon became apparent, and to cheer her up we all talked light-heartedly of revenge. I suggested burning his beloved car, a BMW. Lisa said it was 'always garaged'. I said we could overcome that problem by putting a piece of cardboard under the garage door, raising the cardboard and pouring petrol down our makeshift funnel. Once enough of it had flowed into the garage and under Garth's car, we could light it. Lisa perked up, but then said disappointedly that she wasn't sure which garage was Garth's. I said we could always look for it. The conversation got more sinister. I suggested Lisa get another key cut for Garth's flat before returning the one she had. We could then wait a few weeks, enter the flat when he was out and douse the lounge floor in a flammable liquid. With the carpet saturated, we could then place a lighted candle in a saucer behind the door just inside the lounge. When Garth entered he'd knock over the candle, igniting the liquid and engulfing himself in flames. We all screamed with laughter at the thought. I said, almost through tears: 'It's always nice to come home to a warm fire.' I didn't think anyone was serious. However, when I drove Lisa home she said: 'I'll show you where those garages are.' We drove to an estate of high-rise flats with blocks of garages at the front. We looked at the ones nearest Garth's flat. Lisa said: 'I'm not sure. They all look the same.' Shortly afterwards she moved out of his flat and into ours. Fortunately for Garth, Lisa quickly forgot him and we didn't pursue our ideas for revenge.

I was grateful for Lisa's arrival. She was company for Michelle and, initially, her presence seemed to ease Michelle's possessiveness. She also gave me a good excuse for not sleeping with Michelle. The two of them would sleep in the same room, while I slept on the settee in the front room or at my own flat. However, Lisa wasn't always there and I still slept occasionally with Michelle. I tried to get her to see we were simply friends, but she refused to accept such a casual state of affairs. For her it was all or nothing. I tried to get her to go out more, so she didn't have to sit at home festering and stewing, working herself into a frenzy about the state of 'The Relationship'. But she was reluctant to go out; she was always aware of people looking at her and pointing at her and talking about her. Most of the time it was an effort just to get her to go to the local pub. After a while I stopped trying too hard, because whenever we went further afield the evenings usually ended in some sort of unpleasantness.

One night I decided to take Michelle and Lisa to the Limelight Club in London's West End. A promoter I knew from Raquels had invited the three of us to come to his opening night at the venue. Michelle and Lisa said they'd never been to a West End club. I said I'd drive us to the nearest station to get a train into town. I now had a new Ford Granada. As we set off for our evening's entertainment something bothered Michelle. She'd no sooner sat in the front seat than she jumped up and got out. 'I'm not getting in that. It's bugged,' she said. I asked her what the fuck she was on about. 'The car's bugged. I saw the microphone in the roof at the front.'

I started to laugh. I said: 'That's a microphone for a hands-free telephone, not a bugging device, you idiot.'

She still refused to get in, so I told her to pull it out if it would make her feel better. She went back indoors and returned with a pair of scissors. She leant into the car and cut off the microphone. Then, holding it as if handling a turd, she threw it across the road. I didn't say any more about it. I knew the police had secretly taped the Taylors in the police station before their arrest, although the sisters hadn't said anything incriminating, so I reasoned that Michelle had an excuse for being so paranoid. All the same, her behaviour struck me as odd. What would an innocent person have to hide from a would-be eavesdropper?

In the West End we went around various pubs in Soho and Tottenham Court Road before going on to the club. People frequently recognised the sisters. Nobody actually said anything to them. It was just a case of people nudging one another, or whispering to friends while looking in our direction. As soon as Michelle felt she was being watched she wanted to leave. Lisa was more cocky and carefree. She'd laugh at people's reactions and mimic them while saying to me: 'Stick with me and I'll make you famous.'

Michelle was not amused. She looked at the two of us as if we were naughty children. Hardly anyone turned up for the promoter's launch party, so we left the club after an hour. We'd missed the last train, so we stood on a corner while deciding how we were going to get home. A greasy-looking man hurriedly pushed his mobile hot-dog stand towards us as if rushing for the best pitch. He shouted at us to get out of the way. We didn't jump at his command, so he looked at me and said: 'Oi, you, move.'

'Who the fuck is "Oi"?' I said, 'And who the fuck are you talking to?'

He came over to stand in front of me.

'You,' he said to me, 'And you,' he said to Michelle and Lisa. I saw little point in talking to the ignorant git, so I head-butted him. He fell backwards and crashed to the ground. I picked up one of his half-cooked hot-dogs and threw it so it bounced off his head. I looked at the sisters: 'It's time to go,' I said. Passers-by went to the man's aid as we walked off briskly, laughing.

Michelle was – on the surface, at least – the sort of woman a vicar might describe as 'clean-living'. She talked of the church, she talked of God, and at times she'd talk with the high-minded prudishness of a Victorian dame. She smoked and drank moderately, but she'd have died rather than take drugs, and she was quick to describe as 'whores' any women who seemed too generous with their sexual favours or who wore revealing clothes.

During our frequent rows Michelle started to accuse me of having affairs with other women. She felt that the sort of clubs at which I worked held many moral dangers for me in that regard. I tried to reassure her by telling her she could visit me at both Raquels and the Ministry of Sound whenever she wanted. I soon wished I hadn't. At that time in 1993 the Ministry of Sound was the venue in London for ravers who'd been pushed back into the legal clubs from which they'd earlier tried to escape with their illegal raves in fields. I'd usually be there on a Saturday night. I used to enjoy it, partly because there was little trouble. Very few of the ravers drank that liquid aggression known as alcohol – they tended to save their money for drugs; Ecstasy primarily. Then they'd flail and bounce on the spot all night in their own happily hermetic little worlds. If you had to have a word with any of them, they usually ended up hugging you. Any threats of violence usually came from your fellow doormen. The music would go on until nine or ten in the morning. Then the hard-core ravers would all head off round the corner to the Elephant and Castle pub, which opened at ten, and continued to rave until around three in the afternoon. Despite the best efforts of the management of these clubs to prevent drugs being taken on the premises, they weren't hard to get hold of. I tended to avoid them myself, but some of the other doormen and their friends would be on cocaine or speed.

Michelle didn't really fancy the idea of spending a whole night at the Ministry of Sound, so I told her to meet me at the end of my shift at the Elephant and Castle for the wind-down session. She said she would. I invited Lisa, too. I don't know quite what Michelle was expecting, but I could tell as soon as she entered the pub that she wasn't happy with the human wreckage she encountered. Lisa, however, seemed to be enjoying it. Michelle hadn't been there long when she asked me if there was anywhere else we could go. I knew that a group of doormen and their friends were having a drink at another pub around the corner. I decided to take Michelle and Lisa there. When we got to the pub, I spotted the group of about ten sitting at a table at the far end. They were all shit-faced in that unmistakeable druggy way, giggling and on the verge of hysterical laughter. I brought Michelle and Lisa over to them. They sat down and I introduced them to the group. None of the group said anything. They just looked at Michelle and Lisa, looked at each other, then burst into mad laughter. It had nothing to do with the sisters. It was just end-of-night druggy nuttiness. Without saying anything, Michelle got up and walked out. Lisa followed her. This caused more hilarity. I didn't bother following them. When I next saw Michelle she didn't refer to it.

Michelle seemed over-keen to go to Raquels. She insisted she wanted a night out, but I felt she just wanted to monitor my every move, because by that stage she'd begun seriously to suspect me of infidelity. I didn't really want her there, but she kept on and on at me. In the end I arranged for her and Lisa to come one night, more for Lisa's benefit than for Michelle's. I felt that Lisa needed her spirits lifting after her split from Garth. On that first trip to Raquels I introduced them to my best friend at the time, a fellow doorman called Ray Buck. I'd inherited him from the old regime. Several people had advised me to get rid of him, because they considered him unreliable in times of danger. However, I got on really well with him – he was a good laugh – and I decided to ignore the warnings of others. I might have liked him personally, but I didn't like the way he dished out unnecessary whacks to harmless drunks rather than leading them peacefully out of the club as he could have done. And, in contrast to his use of violence against the incapable, I began to notice how he always managed to absent himself when serious trouble with capable people looked likely. He always had a good excuse, though, and because I enjoyed his company I tended to give him the benefit of the doubt. Ray was in his twenties, about 5 ft 10 in., and beginning to turn to fat. He came from the Basildon area and was engaged to a local woman called Clair, who I liked a lot. He lived with her at her mother's house, but things there had been under strain. He had all sorts of financial problems caused by debts he'd run up. Nothing too serious, but serious enough for bailiffs to be continually calling at the house. Ray told me that Clair's mother was getting tired of dealing with his creditors and their representatives. He felt she would probably boot him out before long. Also, the social security people had added to his financial troubles by starting an investigation into his cash-in-hand security work at Raquels. He'd been forced to sign off the dole, causing a shortfall in his income.

I hadn't expected to play Cupid, but on that first night Ray and Lisa took a real shine to each other. Within a week they were an item. Ray, perhaps lacking the spirit of the true English gentleman, didn't regard his engagement to Clair as an impediment to his pursuit of Lisa. I can't say his behaviour surprised me; he'd frequently been unfaithful to his fiancée with women he'd met at the club. What surprised me was that he told Lisa of Clair's existence. Perhaps he'd been afraid I'd let that fact slip to Michelle who'd have passed it on to her sister. Whatever – by the end of the week Lisa knew about Clair, but still wanted Ray. In fact, he told me she'd asked him to leave Clair. Ray said he would, but asked for a little time to arrange the move out of Clair's – and into Lisa's. Ray's honesty didn't extend to his dealings with Clair. He didn't tell her what was going on. She had to find out for herself from friends.

Now Michelle and Lisa both had boyfriends who were doormen at Raquels. So they started coming along regularly. One night Clair came to the club's front door and asked me if Ray was working. He was upstairs in the main bar with Michelle and Lisa, so rather than let her walk in and find them I told her to wait while I fetched him. I told Ray that Clair was downstairs looking for him.

'Don't let her in,' he said nervously. 'Tell her she's barred or something.'

I said there was no way I was going to tell her she was barred. I told him to go down and sort it out with her – or I'd let her in. Lisa and Michelle glared at Ray, but he just sat where he was.

'She'll go away eventually,' he said.

I went back downstairs and told Clair that Ray knew she was there and, if he wasn't down in a few minutes, she could go up. Ray obviously wasn't coming down, so I let her in. I followed her upstairs in case something happened. She went to one of the smaller bars and bought herself a drink. Michelle, Lisa and Ray hadn't seen her walk in. I went over to them and said that Clair was now in the club. Ray shrugged his shoulders, but Michelle and Lisa started getting really mouthy and aggressive. Lisa said: 'She'd better leave or we're going to do something.'

I told them that Clair had done no wrong and that it was up to Ray to sort things out. I said: 'You two keep out of it.'

I'd shamed Ray into doing something. He got up and walked over to where Clair was standing. He spoke to her briefly. I was surprised to see her suddenly turn and leave without drinking her drink. Ray walked back over to us, smiling.

'What the fuck did you say to her?' I said.

He just laughed and said: 'Not a lot.' A few minutes later another doorman approached me to say there was a woman downstairs who wanted to talk to me. When I got there I found Clair standing outside the entrance, trembling. I asked her what was wrong. She said that Ray had just told her she ought to leave the club quickly, because Michelle and Lisa were out of their heads on drugs and were going to 'stab her up'. I told her Ray was talking bollocks: Michelle and Lisa never took drugs and they certainly weren't going to stab her. However, I said I couldn't be sure that nothing would happen to her if she stayed in the club.

'If you're asking my advice, I think you should go home now.' Clair looked hurt. She began to cry. I said: 'You'll be all right.' She nodded, then walked off into the night, sobbing. I felt sorry for her. She was a decent girl and she'd done Ray no wrong.

Later on that night Michelle and Lisa asked me what Ray had said to Clair. When I told them, they went beserk. They asked Ray if it was true. I think he was taken aback by their obvious anger. He tried to laugh it off, saying: 'At least it got rid of her.' Obviously Ray couldn't return to Clair's, so that night he moved into the flat with us. I was pleased, because it gave me an excuse to stay at my flat without too many questions being asked by Michelle.

When I went round the next day Michelle motioned me into the kitchen. She asked me again what Ray had said to Clair. I told her. She kept saying, 'He's a liar. We never said anything like that.' She didn't need to convince me. I knew Ray had lied. But Michelle was really upset by it. Something had touched a nerve.

Ray regularly found himself financially embarrassed, so I said I'd try to find him additional work. He knew I did other 'jobs', usually set up for me by an intermediary – Fatman from Wickford. 'Fatman' was an adjective as much as a nickname – he weighed about 22 stone. These jobs involved debt-recovery, threatening people, beating them up or destroying their property. The victims had usually fallen out with people over business, money, love or the siting of the garden fence. Whatever the reason, they'd annoyed someone sufficiently for that person to pay good money to have his (or her) revenge. Customers would arrange the deal with Fatman. They never knew who I was or how to contact me. This protected me from being grassed up if the police became involved, as they sometimes did. If customers unwisely gave them Fatman's name, he would say he'd sold the debt on. We did work all over the country, even once in Switzerland. Our clients ranged from solicitors to drug-dealers, with all sorts in between: market-traders in Manchester, property developers in Bristol, Smithfield Meat Market people in London. On busy days I'd have up to 20 jobs to do, and I did this work three to four days a week in addition to my nightclub shifts.

One day Fatman told me that, as the result of a neighbours' dispute, one of the neighbours wanted the other 'taught some manners'. I asked him what exactly was required. Fatman said I needed to inflict a medium-hard beating that would require the victim to seek hospital treatment, without necessitating a lengthy stay on the wards. The job was worth one thousand pounds – two hundred for Fatman and eight hundred for me. In order to do the job properly I needed a partner, so I asked Ray if he'd like to join me for two hundred pounds. Ray agreed enthusiastically, although I didn't tell him I was only giving him a quarter of the fee.

I'd been told that the best time to get the man was when he walked his dogs at six in the morning. I decided to attack him the next day. Early next morning Ray and I set off from the flat armed with a shampoo bottle full of industrial ammonia, a knuckleduster and the Taylor sisters' souvenir truncheon. On the journey I discussed with Ray the plan of action. I'd squirt the ammonia in the man's face, Ray would then hit him with the truncheon and I'd finish him off with the knuckleduster. Ray said: 'Okay', but I could tell he wasn't looking forward to the task. Neither was I. It was just business. It was a misty morning, so we were able to park quite close to the man's house without worrying about nosy neighbours taking our registration number. It was a very exclusive area of Essex: tree-lined streets hid roomy bungalows set in spacious grounds with neat front gardens and wrought-iron fences. An expensive car sat in each driveway. We sat in the car watching the bungalow until a light came on.

A side-door opened and a man emerged with two poodles on leads. As he started to walk down the gravel drive I said to Ray: 'Must be him. Let's go.' Ray looked pale and nervous. We got out of the car and walked towards the man.

'Good morning,' I said to him.

'Good morning,' he replied. I asked him if he knew where Mr Smith lived. He said: 'Yes, that's me.' Before he could say anything else I squirted him in the face with the ammonia. He screamed and clutched his burning eyes. Ray didn't do anything. I shouted: 'Fucking hit him!

Hit him!' But the truncheon remained in his hand by his side. The dogs had started yapping madly and jumping up and down. Their leads threatened to tangle us all up. I hit the man in the head with the knuckleduster. He fell to his knees, still screaming and clutching his face.

I shouted again at Ray: 'For fuck's sake, *hit* him!' This time Ray started waving his truncheon about without bringing it down on the man.

'I can't get him! I can't get him!' Ray said.

I hit the man once more in the head with the duster. He fell forward, still screaming. Ray and I ran to the car and drove off. As we made our escape through the country lanes we passed a police car speeding towards the victim. I was furious at Ray. His cowardice could easily have got us arrested. I asked him why he hadn't hit the man. He said, sheepishly, that he couldn't get at him. I didn't say anything. I knew he'd bottled out of it. And Ray knew it. And Ray knew that I knew.

We drove back to the flat. Michelle had known I was going on an early-morning job to bash someone with Ray. Later that day, when we were alone together, she sensed something was troubling me. She asked me what the problem was. I told her what had happened that morning and how Ray had let me down, almost getting us arrested. She just raised her eyebrows and smirked, as if to say, 'What do you expect of him?' She'd never particularly liked Ray; indeed, since the incident with Clair she'd started actively to dislike him. She was almost pleased I'd seen through him too. She indicated by some snide remarks that she didn't think he was man enough to look after Lisa. Michelle suggested I refuse to give him his payment. I thought about it, but as I was already only giving him a quarter of the total I decided to give him his unearned cash. It would be his last from me.

ELEVEN

Prisoner: Cell Block H

I thought Michelle's clinging neediness might have been just a temporary reaction to the trauma she'd experienced. I hoped that as she readjusted herself to life on the outside she'd come to realise that I was not the man she needed. I was wrong. She became more and more possessive. In the early days after her release she'd often said how she'd never again allow herself to fall for someone in the way she'd fallen for John Shaughnessy. But she was lying to herself, because as soon as we'd slept together she'd returned herself to that same emotional landscape of unrequited devotion. And it wasn't a passive state of pining. It was an active state of aggression: I'd done the deed and now I was going to pay the price. With hindsight I can see why she must have felt I was giving her mixed signals, but at the time I felt I was giving her a consistent message, namely, that our relationship could only ever be temporary. I didn't attach the unifying importance to sex that Michelle did. I had a casual attitude towards it, which Michelle certainly didn't share. Each time I slept with her I regretted it, because I knew by her behaviour afterwards that she felt something important had taken place. It was as if my sleeping with her gave her proprietorial rights over me. I kept telling her we should slow down a bit and just be more relaxed about things. But she wouldn't have it.

When I was leaving for work she'd ask me to telephone her when I got there. I'd say 'Yeah, OK', but I hardly ever bothered. I couldn't see the point in ringing someone I'd spoken to only 30 minutes earlier. If I did ring, Michelle would ask, 'Who's that talking in the background?', and if she could hear no one in the background she'd say, 'You aren't at work, are you?' It used to fuck my head right up. So in the end I never called. Then when I got home I'd find her pacing up and down the flat, slamming doors and stamping her feet. Before long she'd start shouting: 'You said you'd call. Why didn't you? Who have you been with?' The ranting would go on until I shouted back. Then matters would deteriorate until we were just trading insults.

Sometimes I'd come home in the early hours to a dark and quiet flat. I'd assume she was in the bedroom asleep, but as I tiptoed into the front room a voice would hiss from the darkness: 'Where the fuck have you been?' She certainly knew how to make me jump. Then she'd start: 'You told me you would ring. I've been sitting up all night waiting for your call.' I couldn't understand how anyone could lose a night's sleep waiting for a call about nothing. But there was much about Michelle's behaviour I was coming to find hard to understand.

When she'd been in prison our relationship had developed at arm's length. That situation was considerably different from the reality of living with her. Her cranky behaviour started grinding me down. I found myself growing more resentful of her by the day. If her only aim was to draw me closer to her, then she couldn't have chosen a worse way to try to bring it about. She was driving me away, and on bad days I even began to wonder whether I'd be able to stick with her in the flat long enough to finish the book. The book had become increasingly important to me, not because I saw it as a way of making money (I'd already put in writing to Michelle that I didn't want and wouldn't accept any money for it) but because I saw it as a way of highlighting the injustices of the case and of the legal system in general. Now the book had become the symbol of what had torn me from Debra and the children. In my heart I knew I was wrong to have chosen to continue pursuing the Taylors' cause after their release. To try to justify my stupidity I had to finish the book. But my arrogant stubbornness was driving me deeper and deeper into the mire. I should have gone home to Debra and said: 'Sorry. You were right. Stuff the book.' Unfortunately, I lacked the capacity for that sort of humility. I wanted to finish the book to prove I'd been right, even though I knew I was wrong.

I missed Debra and the children; I wanted to be back with them. Without Michelle's knowledge, I began to have family days out with them. Things between Debra and me started improving, although not to the point where I was unfaithful to Michelle. This made me feel guilty. I began staying away from the flat more regularly. I'd stay either at my own flat or at a friend's. This made Michelle even worse. She became convinced I'd returned to Debra, and, unknown to me, she began telephoning her using an assumed name.

One day Debra said to me: 'Has a girl called Sharon got hold of you?' I said I didn't know anyone called Sharon. Debra said: 'Well, someone calling herself Sharon keeps ringing here asking if you're here. Then she asks when's the last time I saw you and when am I seeing you again.'

I thought it might be someone connected with the police. I told Debra not to say anything to the caller. In fact, Debra herself realised before I did that 'Sharon' was Michelle. The next time she called, Debra shouted down the phone at her not to ring her again. Michelle's frustration led to more rows. Thankfully, though, despite everything, I managed to complete a draft manuscript of the book, although it still needed a lot of work. I sent that draft to a publisher, Hamish Hamilton, who'd expressed interest. That interest, I hoped, would get me out of the mess I was in. If Hamish Hamilton, or another publisher, agreed to take on the book, then Michelle would have something else to occupy her mind. In time, surely, she would come to accept my views about the relationship and we might return to just being friends.

Michelle told me she'd got on very well with several of the prison warders at her last jail. She said they'd been 'very supportive' of her and Lisa. Indeed, some of them even threw a party for the sisters at a pub near the prison some weeks after their release. I wasn't invited, although I don't think I'd have gone even if I had been. I found the idea of socialising with your former jailers a little unusual, although – if only from observation – I knew that the atmosphere at women's prisons seemed different from that at men's. When I'd visited Michelle and Lisa both at Holloway Prison and at Bullwood Hall I'd felt there was less of a 'them-and-us' attitude between warders and prisoners. Bullwood Hall, in particular, seemed more like a care home run by enlightened social workers than a prison. I knew that one of the warders had kept in regular contact with Michelle by letters and phone calls. I didn't make anything of it until one day Michelle said: 'She's really beginning to freak me out.' I asked her why. She said the woman appeared to want to be her best friend, whereas Michelle would have been happy for all contact to dwindle, then cease. Michelle said I might get a chance to meet the warder when she called around to the family home later that week. I asked Michelle why she didn't arrange to meet her at our flat. Michelle said: 'I'd rather meet her at my mum's.'

I happened to be at the house on the afternoon the warder called. Michelle answered the door and I heard the sounds of greetings. Then a hulking woman wearing patched jeans and monkey boots stomped into the front room. Her bulky face, undecorated by make-up, was framed with a Cliff Richard haircut. I know it's wrong to jump to conclusions about people on the basis of how they look, but her appearance conformed to the stereotype of the butch lesbian. I'd worked with more feminine-looking doormen. In fact, if she'd wanted a job on the frontline at Raquels repelling the Basildon bad boys I'd have signed her up on premium wages. Someone made her a cup of tea. Michelle, Lisa and the warder began exchanging stilted banalities. For some reason I felt uncomfortable. I didn't join in the conversation. As the warder sat there smoking roll-up cigarettes while holding a cup in one of her spade-like hands, I couldn't help feeling she was eyeing me as a rival. I tried to give the impression I was just visiting, because I didn't want a fist-fight I knew I couldn't win. After about an hour she said she had to go. When she had left I said jokingly to Michelle: 'I think she wants more than friendship from you.' Michelle told me not to be silly. I said: 'I hope you didn't fall by the wayside in there. You know, *Prisoner: Cell Block H*' (a reference to the Australian women's prison drama supposedly popular with lesbians). Michelle looked at me frostily and told me to fuck off.

BOVE: Alison Shaughnessy on holiday in Piltown, County
Kilkenny, Ireland, where she was married – and buried.
© Bobby and Breda Blackmore

OPPOSITE PAGE: Alison Shaughnessy at home.

ABOVE: John Shaughnessy (far right) listens to Alison's parents, Bobby and Breda Blackmore, as they talk to journalists outside the Old Bailey after the murder trial in 1992. © PA News

RIGHT: Former Detective Superintedent Chris Burke, who led the murder investigation. © C. Burke

Author Bernard O'Mahoney on his
way to court. © B. O'Mahoney

Author Bernard O'Mahoney with Lisa (left) and Michelle Taylor in the flat they shared. © B. O'Mahoney

Michelle (left) and Lisa Taylor sit on the sofa where Michelle was later to make her confession. © B. O'Mahoney

Ray Buck, future husband of Lisa Taylor, on the door at Raquels nightclub, Basildon, Essex. © B. O'Mahoney

Michelle (left) and Lisa Taylor celebrate their release with a joint clenched-fist salute on the steps of the Royal Courts of Justice in June 1993. © PA News

If I hadn't been under so much pressure at work, I might have been more tolerant of Michelle's behaviour. But I'd been having a lot of trouble at Raquels where rarely a night went by without serious violence. A few months earlier I'd taken control of the door, but by September 1993 I felt that to bolster my position I needed to form an alliance with a strong 'firm'. That was how I ended up going into a partnership that would ultimately have a profound effect on my life. The person I shook hands with was Tony Tucker, who ran a large and well-respected door firm. He used his control of security at clubs to give dealers, at a price, exclusive rights to sell drugs on the premises.

Not long after I'd started my new partnership Michelle and Lisa came up to Raquels to see me and Ray. At the end of the evening as the four of us were about to get into my car for the drive home I found myself being verbally abused by a dissatisfied customer. The man was standing near a burger van outside the club. I told him to shut up, but he wouldn't. So I punched him in the face as Michelle, Lisa and Ray looked on. The man fell back, his head hitting the pavement with a thud. Michelle, Lisa, Ray and I then got into the car.

'I know I've fucking hurt him,' I said. 'Did you hear his head when it hit the floor?'

By the burger van I could see the man's friends trying to revive him. Someone was shouting: 'Call an ambulance!' A lot of people had witnessed my punch, so I hoped he wasn't badly hurt in case I was arrested for it.

'Get out of here,' Michelle said. 'Worry about it later.' As we drove off, Michelle, Lisa and Ray kept looking behind to check for police activity. I knew if the police stopped us they'd arrest everyone in the car. I imagined what a dream story that would be for the tabloids, even though the Taylors hadn't done anything wrong. The man recovered from his injuries, but the story made the front page of the local paper when the police appealed for witnesses. They described the man responsible for the 'unprovoked attack' as being aged around 40, heavily built, with a Birmingham accent. I was outraged. I was only 33 at the time.

Within a day or so I was arrested. The police were amused by the number of callers who'd given my name. I told them I'd been attacked first and had only struck out in self-defence. As always, I was able to provide lots of witnesses from the club. However, to make sure the case never went to court, the injured man was approached in a pub by someone I knew. Following this meeting, the injured man suddenly remembered that the incident was entirely his fault . . . The case against me was dropped.

One Friday in October I went into work at Raquels as normal. During the night our esteemed customers caused a bit of trouble; by the time everything had been sorted out I felt it was too late for me to drive back to London. I decided to stay at a fellow doorman's house. The next day I went to Michelle's flat. I was hoping she'd be out, but she was in. She was obviously annoyed that I'd been out all night without phoning her, but she didn't say anything. Instead, as usual, she expressed her disapproval by slamming cupboard doors and stomping about the place. I couldn't be bothered with her nonsense, so I just left her a note explaining that there'd been trouble, and left. I thought she might phone me at the club that evening, but she didn't. After work I didn't fancy returning to an atmosphere of angry silence, so again I stayed the night at my friend's. On Sunday morning I returned to the flat, but Michelle wasn't there. However she'd left a letter for me. In it she said she'd stayed up the whole of Friday night worrying about me. Why hadn't I phoned, especially as I'd said I would? She said she hadn't stayed up all night for the fun of it; then, to make things worse, I'd stayed out all night Saturday as well. She said she didn't ask for fuck all from me; all she wanted was for me to spend some of my free time with her. She said she wasn't sure about her feelings for me: when we weren't together she missed me, and when we were together she was happy inside. But right now she was 'hurting'. She said that when she and Lisa had been arrested and stuck inside, she'd hurt real bad; then when Lisa had got bail she'd hurt even more. These experiences had taught her to shut her feelings away. So she'd changed by the time Lisa returned to join her in prison after the trial. Lisa would then accuse her of not loving her, because she never showed her love; but Michelle said she'd found it hard to show love because she'd locked away her emotions. She said that in prison she also used to say she'd never love anyone outside her family, but since meeting me she knew that what she used to say wasn't true. She loved me – and she wanted to know if I loved her. She begged me to tell her the truth, because she didn't want to make a mug of herself by loving me when I didn't love her. She said she was going to stay at her mum's because she didn't want to be by herself. The overwrought tone of her letter turned my stomach. I felt exasperated by the workings of a mind that could create such a romantic fantasy out of the dull reality of our relationship. We might have been sharing the same flat, but we were living on different planets. Or, as far as I was concerned, I was living on earth; Michelle was somewhere else. I stayed at the flat on my own that Sunday evening. The next morning Michelle came round. To my surprise, we were able to have a quiet discussion about things. She went over what she'd written in the letter. She spoke calmly, but to my ears her tone just made what she was saying sound madder. She had a real sense of grievance: it wasn't just that I wasn't giving her what she needed; it was more like I wasn't giving her what she was *owed.* She used the language of obligation. The more she spoke, the more trapped I felt. Most of the time I just listened to her, but in the end I told her she was taking things far too seriously and that we ought to be just good friends. She looked at me sternly, then said sharply that she could never just be friends. I left it at that. That night we slept together, but nothing sexual occurred, although Michelle tried to arouse me. I made plain I wasn't interested. She huffed, and turned over.

In the morning we got up together. Michelle said she had to go somewhere – I can't remember where. I stayed behind to do more work on the book. Michelle's behaviour had at least had the effect of making me very diligent in my work on the book: I knew that the sooner I finished it the sooner I'd be free of the trap I'd helped fashion for myself. I sat on the floor in the front room and began to work my way through a box of case papers marked 'UNUSED'. I'd flicked through a lot of unused stuff before and I wasn't expecting to come across anything of use, so I wasn't totally engaged by what I was reading. All the same, I was moving through the documents methodically, if not with any great interest. Then, in the space of perhaps 20 seconds, I read a document that changed my life. If a fist had come up from the box and punched me in the face I couldn't have been more shocked. What I discovered was a letter from a solicitor's firm, dated from the early days of the case, not long after the sisters' arrest. The letter referred to Michelle's having made 'certain admissions' in the light of which Lisa was being advised to give evidence on behalf of the prosecution. The letter may have been couched in legal phraseology, but I knew instantly what it meant. Michelle had murdered Alison.

I'd received many shocks in my life, but they were usually shocks caused by violence. Yet I can't liken the shock caused by that letter to anything fists, knives, bottles and baseball bats had done to my flesh. Its effect was more instantly devastating. I felt suddenly chilled, as if my heart were now pumping iced water round my body. I didn't even need to reread the letter. I'd understood it completely at first glance. Michelle had told her legal representative that she was guilty of murdering Alison Shaughnessy.

For a few minutes I just sat there, barely moving. The activity was all in my mind. I felt everything – shock, anger, embarrassment and disbelief. However, what truly devastated me was the knowledge that I'd been conned. Michelle had just written me a letter pleading with me not to make a mug of her in love. Yet from the very beginning she'd made me the biggest mug of all. I thought of all the time and money I'd spent on the Taylors; all the risks I'd undertaken on their behalf, all the misery I'd inflicted on Debra and my own children. And throughout that time Michelle and Lisa must have been secretly laughing at me.

I don't know how long I sat there thinking like that. Suddenly, I heard a key in the front door. It had to be Michelle's. I heard the door close behind her. I heard her footsteps. With the legal letter in my hand, I got up off the floor and sat on the settee. I'd begun to shake with temper.

I was ready to confront the murderer.

TWELVE

Up Close and Personal

Michelle walked into the front room. I was sitting on the settee, perhaps three yards from her, holding the letter like a weapon. My face must have looked fearsome, because she stopped walking as soon as she saw it. I waved the letter at her and said sarcastically: 'You'd better get rid of this, hadn't you?'

She looked puzzled.

'Go on, explain it. *Explain it,*' I said. I handed her the letter. She looked at it quickly, but didn't read it properly. I could tell she didn't need to. Her face grimaced with recognition. It was her turn to look shocked. She screwed up the letter and threw it on the floor. All the time I kept saying things like: 'Come on, then. Let's hear it. *Explain it,* Michelle.'

She was silent momentarily, then anger erupted from within her. She started screaming abuse at me, calling me a bastard and other names.

'You've never believed in our innocence!' she screamed.

'Oh, yes I did.' I said, 'Until now I fucking did.'

She strode past me towards the door at the other side of the room, screaming at me all the time. She practically goose-stepped out the door into the hallway leading to the bedroom. Then she shouted, 'You fucking bastard', at the top of her voice before slamming the door furiously behind her.

There was silence for perhaps 30 seconds, then suddenly the lounge door flew open with a loud bang, as if she'd kicked it. She stormed back into the room and shouted: 'John Shaughnessy is twice the man you are.'

I suppose this was meant to hurt me, but at that moment I couldn't have cared less what she said about me or John. I gave a sarcastic laugh and knelt over to pluck the screwed-up letter from the floor. In a voice loud enough to be heard over her shouting, I said: 'Yes, but explain this. Go on, explain it.'

Her face was red with the effort of hurling abuse at me, but then she did something I'd never seen her do before – she started crying. Full sobs replaced her shouts. She sat down on the settee, but I didn't want her near me, so I stood up.

Still sobbing, and wiping away the tears that had begun to stream from her eyes, she said: 'It wasn't my fucking fault. It was Alison's.'

I didn't say anything.

She continued, her voice quieter, but distorted by the sobs. She said that Alison had told her that she and John planned to move to Ireland to live; they were going to have a baby and start afresh. Michelle said she'd questioned John about it; he told her he had no plans either to return to Ireland or to start a family. She indicated that in her mind Alison had therefore been lying to her in order to hurt her. From my own recent experience of Michelle I thought if John had ever said those words, or anything like them, he would have done so in empty pillow talk or under duress caused by the sort of persistent and remorseless questioning to which Michelle had so often subjected me. I knew myself that with her on your case you'd say whatever you thought she wanted to hear to get her to drop the subject.

Michelle said the situation with John and Alison had begun to make her ill. She'd lost weight and had difficulty sleeping. She said that on the Monday of the killing she'd told Lisa she was going to have it out with Alison. Lisa had said she'd go with her. Michelle, without Lisa's knowledge, had taken from among her father's tools a steel ruler, one end of which had been sharpened to a knife-point. Michelle said they'd driven to Vardens Road and parked near the Roundhouse Pub, which coincidentally was where her father, her uncle and I had parked when reconstructing the journey from Alison's flat to the clinic to prove the police had got their timings wrong. I knew that spot was a vantage point from which you could have a clear view of the pavement on the side of the road where Alison lived. Anyone parked there would be able to see people walking up the road from the direction that Alison always came.

Michelle interspersed her story with lots of swearing and interjections like: 'I couldn't fucking stand it no more.' Michelle said that when they saw Alison walking up the road, they got out of the car and went to meet her. When they reached her Michelle told her that John had sent her to collect some plant pots for the clinic which were too heavy for him to take on the train. Alison opened the main front door and then opened the door to the flat. Lisa had stood at that second door and held it open as Michelle walked into the flat behind Alison. She said she'd then followed Alison as she walked up the stairs. Michelle had been crying throughout the story, but at this point she became distraught, sobbing violently and wiping tears frantically from her face. She kept saying: 'I only meant to scare her. I only meant to scare her.'

'Well, what happened?' I said.

'I don't know what happened,' Michelle said. 'I grabbed her from behind, I stabbed her, and everything else is a blur.'

Michelle hadn't been looking at me; she'd kept her eyes focused on the floor. She said they'd put 'all our stuff' (by which I understood her to mean any bloodstained clothes and the murder weapon) into a bag and run from the flat to their car. Then they'd driven back to the clinic. She stopped talking and, with her head in her hands, just sobbed. I looked at her for a few seconds in silence, then swore at her and walked out of the flat, leaving the letter behind.

I got in my car, almost light-headed with astonishment at what I'd heard. There was only thing I wanted to do at that moment – to rip to pieces the manuscript I'd written proclaiming their innocence. To me, the only fact that that document now proclaimed was my own stupidity. So strong was my compulsion to destroy the manuscript that I crunched the car into gear and headed off to the South Kensington office of the publisher to whom we had sent the book.

As I drove like a madman through the busy afternoon traffic I tried to digest Michelle's confession. In fact, it wasn't a confession, because the word 'confession' suggests remorse and Michelle had shown no remorse whatsoever. In her self-pitying eyes she'd been the victim: wicked Alison had hurt her and poor Michelle had struck out to punish the evil-doer. Michelle had at least accepted full responsibility for what she'd done. She'd been at pains to minimise Lisa's role, emphasising that Lisa had not known she'd taken a weapon with her.

When I got to South Kensington I found a parking space on a meter. I stuck the minimum amount of money in the slot; I didn't plan to stay long. In the offices of the publisher, Hamish Hamilton, I asked to see Kate Jones, the editor I'd been dealing with. I'd met her before when I'd taken Michelle and Lisa down to discuss the book. I didn't waste time in getting to the point. I said I wanted her to give me back the manuscript as I no longer wanted it published. Kate didn't ask any questions. She could see I was agitated. She said she would need a letter of consent from the Taylor sisters before she could hand it over to me. In Kate's presence I telephoned Michelle from the office and told her to tell Kate to give me the book. Michelle, who'd stopped crying by this point, was distant and hostile. She refused. I couldn't understand why she wanted to stop me getting the manuscript. It wasn't as if she could get it published without me – it was my work, after all – and all I wanted to do was destroy it. I told Michelle that fact, but she still refused. I put the phone down. Kate looked a bit embarrassed. She said that the in-house lawyers would have to decide who actually owned the book before she could hand it over to anyone. I agreed, and left.

That night I stayed at my own flat. I didn't sleep much. I wish I could say that as I lay there in the dark I thought only of murdered Alison and the grief of the poor woman's family. But I didn't. I thought only of the way I'd been conned. I, supreme cynic and cunning manipulator, had let myself be led by the nose by Michelle, God-fearing Michelle. There was nothing I could do about it. In truth, there was nothing I wanted to do about it, apart from destroying the manuscript, cutting all links with the Taylors and getting on with my life. I felt grateful that, in the end, the 'new evidence' I'd thrown up to prove their innocence hadn't contributed in any significant way to their eventual release. But they were free, none the less, and they couldn't be tried again for the murder. As far as I was concerned, that was the end of the matter. I wanted nothing more to do with them. I certainly had no intention of telling anyone, except perhaps Debra, how they'd made a mug of me. I could hardly go to the police – I had, after all, attempted to pervert the course of justice on the sisters' behalf. In a way, I felt as guilty as they were.

The next day I went back to Michelle's flat to clear out my stuff. I hoped Michelle wasn't going to be there. She wasn't, but Lisa was. She was sitting on the settee when I walked in. I didn't greet her. I didn't know what she knew, so I told her what had happened – that I'd found the incriminating letter. She said she knew and that Michelle had asked her to talk to me. She said Michelle had not meant what she had said about John. Then she handed me an envelope. I opened it and found two letters from Michelle. I was used to getting letters from her after arguments. I stood there and started reading them. In the first letter she said she'd felt so close to me when we'd slept together the other night; she'd felt heavenly when cuddling me. She was missing me and had felt really sad when I'd left because she'd felt like we were saying goodbye forever. She said we used to be really great together at one time and that Wales would be her most precious memory of our time together. Wales? I gave a snort of sarcastic laughter, although Lisa wouldn't have understood why. *Wales?* What had we done in Wales that had left in her mind a golden memory of romantic perfection? We'd had egg and chips in a café, got pissed in a piss-hole pub and staggered back to a cheap hotel for a drunken fumble in the dark. If I'd needed further evidence of the bizarre workings of her peculiar mind then her nostalgia for Colwyn Bay provided it. She said she wasn't sure when things between us had started going wrong. She thought it might have been when I'd stopped phoning and had gone away for a day or so without telling her where I was going. She recognised, however, that that was the way I was and that if I hadn't been like that then the two of us might never have ended up together. She said that, on her part, she'd been too paranoid; her immediate reaction to my not being there had been to assume I was with someone else. If she'd trusted me, she said, then we would not be apart now, but trusting someone completely was really hard for her because of what 'that slag' John Shaughnessy had done by two-timing her. I gave another snort of sarcastic laughter. It did not seem to register with Michelle that John Shaughnessy had been married to Alison. If he'd been two-timing anyone, it had been his wife. She said that John had put her through hell for four years and, because of what he'd done, she was still suffering now. But God would punish him. God? The sanctimonious bitch was involving God again! She said she was sorry for making me suffer because of what John had done. She'd never stop loving me or caring for me and would always be there when I needed her. She said she truly hated John, who wasn't even good enough to be a piece of shit on my shoe. In fact, she hated him more than ever now; because of him she'd pushed away and hurt the best thing she'd ever had: me.

John Shaughnessy had not made Michelle kill Alison, nor could his behaviour towards her, however distasteful, justify her committing that crime. The only truth in her ramblings was that her murder of Alison, and her subsequent admission of her guilt to me, had pushed me away and hurt me. She finished the letter by saying that she didn't know what else to say and that she wished she had the power to right all the wrong because she truly didn't want to lose me. It was sick and it made me feel sick. How could Michelle right all the wrong? Alison was dead. No one could right that wrong. Her next letter was briefer. She said she'd been out that afternoon and had thought about things. If I still wanted her, then she still wanted me. In fact, she didn't ever want to lose me. She recognised that things were hard at the moment, but said we were strong together and could get through it. She was going to do her best to change herself, to stop letting the past destroy her life. All she asked from me was for me to be honest with her always – as she would be honest with me. She said again that I was too precious for her to lose. She didn't ever want to lose me.

I gave Lisa a look of total incredulity. What I found most incredible about Michelle's letters was that she only seemed concerned about the way she might have insulted me by comparing me unfavourably to John. Michelle wasn't stupid enough to put explicitly in writing to me that she'd admitted murdering Alison. But in trying to win me back she had to refer to it implicitly – how she'd let John and what he'd done to her push me away and hurt me; how she wished she had the power to right all the wrong; how she'd do her best to stop letting the past destroy her life. Her words chilled me. She knew well that the fact that our relationship was over wouldn't 'hurt' me. In letters to me she'd confirmed that I wanted to end the relationship and just be friends. However, she was right in one respect: I now knew all her 'faults'. The only thing she didn't seem to realise was that I'd never again soil my hands by touching her.

Perhaps she genuinely thought that the little matter of the vicious butchering of a 21-year-old woman wouldn't concern me. Perhaps – having on several occasions witnessed the way I dished out violence so casually and viciously – she thought I was so morally degraded that her little crime would be as nothing to me. Perhaps she felt I had so much blood on my own hands that I'd look with tolerance on her one-off misdemeanour. Of course, I did have a lot of blood on my hands. Over the years I'd put a lot of people in hospital – and some of them I'd almost killed – but only ever almost. I'd never actually killed anyone. At times, admittedly, I had planned to kill, but my intended targets had only ever been men who almost always had either used or were hoping to use maximum violence on me. Michelle had butchered an innocent girl simply because she was jealous of her happiness.

I told Lisa I wanted nothing more to do with Michelle. I said I didn't feel that way because Michelle had said John was a better man than me. I said I couldn't care less about John. The reason I wanted Michelle out of my life was because I'd been mugged off, conned into believing they were innocent of murder when I now knew they were guilty.

'Forget it,' Lisa said. 'It's not important. I could admit it to you today, then in six months' time say I was only joking. You would never know if I was telling the truth.'

I told Lisa she was insulting my intelligence. I said if she had any sense she would distance herself from her sister and live her own life, because Michelle was fucked up. Lisa didn't reply. As I collected my belongings

Lisa gave me a photo of herself. On the back of it she'd inscribed: 'To my best friend always.' I looked at it, but didn't thank her. In silence I finished collecting my bits and pieces together, then I left the flat without saying goodbye.

That night Lisa's boyfriend, Ray, telephoned me at my flat. He wanted to know if my falling out with the Taylors would affect his job at Raquels. I asked him if he knew exactly what had happened; had Lisa told him about the letter? He said she had. I told him that they had made a mug of me and, if he stuck with them, he had no job with me. Ray sounded taken-aback by my intransigence. He said that whatever had happened between me and them was none of his business and shouldn't affect his connection with me. I told him that, as Lisa now liked to join him at the club most nights he was working, if I kept him on while he kept her on I'd effectively be inviting her and her murdering sister back into my life; and, as far as I was concerned, I didn't want to talk to them, see them or have anything to do with them ever again. Also, I didn't want to employ someone whose income would contribute to their household. Ray started getting stroppy – not something he'd have done if he'd been standing in front of me. He asked me why I'd suddenly turned on him. I said it was nothing to do with my turning on him, it was to do with my being made a mug of.

I reminded him that he had a choice: 'Nobody's making you do anything, Ray.' I added that, as I'd already paid him a weekend's money in advance, I wanted the money back if he did decide to seek alternative employment. He said okay. I discovered later that as soon as he'd put the phone down he'd jumped in his car and driven to Tucker's house to ask for his wages. Tucker, knowing nothing of what was going on, paid him. When Tucker rang me that evening he mentioned that Ray had been round to collect his money. I was furious. Ray had now been paid for four nights he hadn't worked. I was determined to get back the money – or get him. The next morning I drove to the Taylors' flat and banged on the door. No one answered. Before driving off I put a note through the letterbox for Ray. It read: 'You have not even got the bollocks to face it like a man. See you soon.'

It may seem callous of me, but at that time I hardly thought at all about Alison's family or how I had in my own small way contributed to their desperate pain by working to free their daughter's murderer. At that time the only family I thought about was my own. I could hardly believe that, for the benefit of the Taylors, I'd caused such damage to my own family life. I felt intensely angry at Michelle and Lisa, but most of all I felt angry at myself. I vowed to make it up to Debra and the children. I wanted to move back in with them. I just hoped that Debra would give me a second chance. That same day I went to see Debra at what had once been our family home. I told her everything that had happened. She listened to me, astonished, her face darkened in disbelief. Initially, she was angry too that I had let the bogus cause of the Taylors create such havoc in our own life together. But so total was my renunciation of the Taylors and all their doings that her anger eased. I asked her if she'd let me move back home. She was reluctant at first, but in the end I think the sincerity of my contrition convinced her to give me another chance. I moved back home.

A few days later a parcel arrived for me. Hamish Hamilton had sent back the manuscript. A note inside said that the firm had also sent a copy to Michelle. I didn't even bother flicking through it one last time. For me, those hundreds of handwritten pages symbolised the waste of more than a year of my life. Now I would do something symbolic of my own. As Debra watched, I took a large pair of scissors from a kitchen drawer. Then, with great pleasure, I cut the manuscript to pieces and deposited the scraps in the bin where they belonged. I smiled at Debra and said: 'I feel better now.' And I did: I felt like I'd dumped a skip-full of trash from my life. Now I could start again properly. The Taylors were history.

Unfortunately, history doesn't always stay in the past. On a Tuesday morning, about two weeks after I'd moved back home, the telephone rang. Debra answered it on the extension upstairs. Only much later did she tell me what was said. A female was on the line.

'Hello, this is Sharon.' Debra knew immediately who it was.

She told me later that she'd said: 'I know it's you, Michelle. I told you not to call anymore.'

The caller denied being Michelle: 'My name's Sharon, honestly.'

Debra got angry and insisted she knew exactly who was calling.

Eventually 'Sharon' admitted she was indeed Michelle. She said: 'I've got to talk to you.' Debra asked her what she wanted. Michelle wanted to know if I'd moved back home. When Debra said I had, Michelle proceeded to tell her every tiny detail about our relationship – and added several hurtful lies for good measure. Michelle's words stabbed into Debra, each detail, half-truth or outright lie tearing open a fresh wound. Downstairs I'd been totally unaware of what was happening. The first I knew of it was when Debra walked into the front room in tears. She said she'd just spoken to Michelle who had told her things which meant our relationship could not continue. She said I was a bastard and a pig and she wanted me to leave. I tried to talk to her, but through her tears she just kept telling me to leave. I was too numb even to pack a bag. I just walked out the door, got in my car and drove to my flat in south London. I was distraught.

Over the next few days I felt like paying Michelle a visit – and hurling her head-first through the window of her first floor flat. But I reasoned that I might only make things worse by confronting her – she might continue to call Debra to fill her mind with stories. I knew Michelle was more than capable of saying cruel and inaccurate things about our time together, and I didn't want her dredging up more sludge than she already had. I thought it better to allow her that one revenge call without retaliation rather than risk provoking more.

In fact, over the next few days, and without any provocation from me, she kept up her calls to Debra. During one call she claimed I'd allowed one of my young children to have a lengthy telephone conversation with her when Debra was out one day. I was ringing Debra regularly myself to try to find out what was being said. Each time I called, Debra would relate, often tearfully, the latest poison from Michelle. I told Debra not to listen to her, that she was simply trying to cause trouble between us. But Debra wouldn't listen. She said Michelle knew enough about our relationship to prove I'd betrayed confidences. She said that Michelle was really friendly to her, that she wanted to be her friend, that she wanted to meet up with her and the children, that she wanted to let her know the sort of man I really was. Around three days after moving out I rang Debra who told me that, at Michelle's suggestion, they were going to meet up for a drink. Debra said: 'I want to find out the truth.'

I slammed the phone down and drove to Debra's house. When I got there I telephoned Michelle and screamed down the line: 'Keep out of my fucking life! Stay away from Debra and our children! I want fuck all to do with you! Stay away!'

Michelle put the phone down on me. A short time later Ray called. He wanted to know why I was upsetting Michelle. I could hardly believe his cheek. He hadn't contacted me since I'd left him that note, and I'd been too busy to follow up my attempt to get back the money he owed. Now the cheeky bastard was ringing me with a grievance. I shot a load of abuse down the phone and told him I was still hoping to meet him soon. He rang off.

Almost immediately the phone rang again. It was Lisa. She wanted to know why I was threatening them.

'I'm not threatening anybody,' I said. 'I'm stating facts. Tell your fat fuck of a boyfriend I'm looking for him.'

'What makes you think he isn't looking for you?' she said.

She'd pressed the red button. I flipped. I screamed that they were all 'wrong-uns' and I was going to 'do them all'.

'I'll put you all fucking six feet under,' I said. 'I will kill Michelle and Ray first, and then you.' What was more, I said, I was going to do it now: I was going to drive to their flat as soon as I put the phone down. Within seconds I'd walked out the door and was driving towards London and their flat. Debra told me later that Michelle had telephoned again shortly after I'd left. She'd wanted to know what I was doing. Debra said: 'He's on his way to your flat.'

Michelle couldn't resist a final stab: 'He's been seeing other women as well as me. A woman called Donna and a girl in Battersea.' Debra put the phone down.

As I drove at raging speed down the motorway I kept asking myself why Michelle couldn't leave me alone. It was as if, not content with making a total mug of me, she now wanted to rub it in. What was wrong with her? Was she trying to drive me to kill her in the way she'd killed Alison? The way she was going, she was going to get her wish. That thought of Alison suddenly made me see parallels between Michelle's relationship to Alison and John and her relationship to Debra and me. In both cases she'd been sleeping with another woman's man; in both cases she'd tried to befriend the woman; in both cases she'd wanted to punish the man by getting at his woman. At least in this case she'd only stabbed Debra with words. I realised, too, with a chill, something else about Michelle: how she really liked to get up close when causing pain. It hadn't been enough for her to stab Alison to death – she'd needed to be there too when John discovered the body. She must have wanted to see his pain at the moment of its greatest impact. She must have wanted to be right up there close to witness his collapse. With Debra too, it wouldn't have been enough just to write her a letter – she must have wanted to hear Debra cry, and she must have wanted to hear her crying over and over again.

I got to the flat in half the time it normally took. As I parked the car I looked up at the flat's window. Lisa, Michelle, Ann and Ray were standing there, peeping out from behind the unwashed lace curtains. I got out of the car and gestured to Ray to come outside. He looked away. I walked towards the flat; they all stepped back from the window. I banged on the door, but, not surprisingly, I couldn't hear the sound of feet on the stairs. I wished I still had a key. I considered kicking in the door, but I knew they'd call the police before I could get at them. Instead, I scribbled a note for Ray and put it through the letterbox. It read: 'I am told you are "looking" for me, fat boy. Silly move, because now I shall save you the trouble. See you soon, dough boy.' I walked back to my car. Before I got in I turned to look up again at the window. They had all re-appeared. I formed my right hand into the shape of a pistol and, pointing it at them, pretended to shoot them, one by one. I got back in my car and drove to my flat.

That same day Debra started receiving nuisance phone calls. As soon as she picked up the phone the caller would ring off. After about a week of receiving these sort of calls at all hours she telephoned Ann Taylor. She told me later that she'd said to Ann: 'Tell Michelle that if she calls my home, at least say something. Don't just put the phone down.' Ann said she knew nothing about such calls.

Back in my flat I tried to get used to living on my own again. I spoke to Debra several times a day, but she seemed in no hurry to let me move back. When I'd hurriedly cleared out my stuff from Michelle's flat I'd just dumped it in a pile on the floor. One day, with time on my hands, I decided to sort it into some sort of order. Amongst the pile I found a cassette tape I didn't recognise. I put it in my coat pocket. I would have played it then, but I couldn't, because my stereo was at Debra's. I forgot I had it on me until, that night, on the way home from work, I came across it in my pocket. Out of curiosity I stuck it in the car's cassette machine. I could hardly believe what I started to hear. There was one voice on the tape, a female voice.

The person started by greeting Michelle warmly. Within seconds, from a few incidental details, I'd established that this person was a prison officer. She was making a tape-letter for Michelle to listen to in her cell, and she was making it while walking around her own home before her next prison shift. She was telling Michelle how much she was missing her and how much she was looking forward to seeing her soon. She began talking with sexual explicitness about what she wanted to do to Michelle; what, indeed, she would be doing to her next time she saw her. She didn't leave anything to Michelle's imagination. I thought I'd plugged in to one of those 0898 filth lines. After a few minutes the love-letter reached its romantic end. As I wound it back I wondered if this was the prison warder I'd met that day at Michelle's family house. No wonder she'd looked like she'd wanted to bash me – I was taking away her woman. I wondered if Michelle had been carrying on with her during our relationship. I thought of all those times I'd had to listen to Michelle's bleating about the need for loyalty, trust and openness as the basis of a solid relationship. And, worse, all that crap she'd bombarded me with about not being able to trust anyone again, not being able to have a relationship with anyone again. Yet again I felt deceived.

Despite the lateness of the hour I pulled up at the first call box I came to. I rang Michelle at her mother's. As soon as she came on the line I said: 'You're a fucking liar, Michelle.' She asked me what was the matter. I said: 'You, getting all high and mighty, going on about openness and honesty, going on about never going with anyone other than John. You're a fucking liar.'

She said she didn't know what I was talking about. She said: 'I've only ever been with you and John.'

'Wait there! Just fucking wait there!' I shouted. I went to the car, opened the door and turned the tape on at full volume. The prison officer's voice boomed out. I went back to the phone and held up the handset. I let the prison officer get into her explicit stride, then I put the handset to my mouth and said sarcastically: 'Had you forgot this one, 'Chelle?'

Michelle was silent. Then she said: 'I'm sorry. Please turn it off.'

I said nothing. I put the phone down and walked away.

Debra stopped getting nuisance calls. Within a week she'd let me move back in. There was only one condition she attached to my return: I must never, ever, mention the word 'Taylors' in our house again.

THIRTEEN

Silent Nights

Over the next eight months I didn't hear anything more from the Taylors. Then I got a phone call. A man claiming to be a senior detective from Scotland Yard rang me one morning in July 1994 to say he was at Basildon Police Station and wanted to speak to me urgently. I thought it was a wind-up – I got them all the time – and, after telling the caller to fuck off, put the phone down. He rang back. He said his name was Commander Griffiths and he needed to talk to me. I said I was John the Baptist and didn't need to talk to him. Again I put the phone down. Again he rang back. This time he told me to ring Basildon Police Station and ask for him. I realised he might be genuine. I agreed to ring him back, but first I rang my 'business associate' from Raquels, Tony Tucker, to discover if anything had happened that might warrant Scotland Yard's attention. Tucker had many interests, most of them illegal, and the police tried to keep an eye on him. Since I'd invited Tucker and his firm to become involved in running security at the club, life had become more dangerous. Tucker and his lieutenants had ambitions to become major players in the drugs world. Unfortunately, their plans usually involved double-crossing other drug-dealers, so I didn't think a bright shining future lay ahead of them. Life at Raquels had always been violent, but intrigue and paranoia had now become part of the mix. I'd started feeling extremely uneasy. I couldn't see a happy ending for any of us. Tucker said he wasn't aware of anything that would merit a visit from Scotland Yard. He told me to find out what they wanted and get back to him.

I arranged to meet Commander Griffiths at Basildon Police Station. When I got there he introduced me to his colleague, a detective superintendent. They took me into a small room. The superintendent said: 'We've had problems locating you, Bernard. I think some people were rather hoping we wouldn't.'

I still didn't have a clue what they wanted. I sat down, and they explained that they wanted to talk to me about Michelle and Lisa Taylor. Apparently, the sisters had made an official complaint about the conduct of police officers. Commander Griffiths had been appointed to investigate their allegations. These were, first, that police officers had tried to pervert the course of justice by suppressing evidence from one of the witnesses and by coercing or intimidating two other witnesses; second, that officers did not pursue lines of inquiry which would have assisted the sisters' case; and third, that certain officers had behaved discreditably in commenting about the sisters, had used undue force during the arrest of Michelle and had established improper relationships with journalists. I had to stop myself laughing out loud; apart from the undue force whilst making an arrest, the Taylors' complaints represented a pretty accurate list of everything we'd done in the run up to the appeal. Commander Griffiths said they had to re-interview everyone connected with the murder inquiry – witnesses and police officers. In short, he was carrying out an investigation of the murder inquiry. He said that several witnesses had already mentioned that I'd asked them to alter their evidence. I sat there in silence. I knew that perverting the course of justice carried a likely prison sentence.

'Sorry. Not me,' I said.

Griffiths said his job was not to prosecute anyone: he wanted merely to establish whether there was any substance to the complaints. I could have said nothing and walked away, but I realised that by doing so I'd be effectively helping Michelle. I hadn't thought about her in a long while. In some ways I'd been trying to blank the whole embarrassing experience from my mind. A sudden surge of anger and contempt surprised me: anger at the way I'd been conned, and contempt for the person who'd conned me. Not content with getting away with murder, she was now trying to punish the people who'd rightly pursued her. What was she after? Then I realised her goal – money. Making an official complaint was probably her first step towards getting compensation for her supposed miscarriage-of-justice ordeal. When I lived with her, she'd talked about compensation as if it were a dead cert. She thought applying for it would just be a formality. With a nice tax-free sum from the Metropolitan Police she planned to fund two things: a holiday for her family and the start-up of a catering business. What compensation would Alison's family be getting for their grievous loss? With hindsight, I then made an extremely rash, even foolish, decision: I decided to talk to the police. Although I could well have been talking my way into prison, the easiness of my decision surprised me. If I could summarise the dominant thought behind my impulsiveness it was: 'Fuck her. I'm going to put a stop to her little game.'

Over the next few hours I told them everything I'd got up to on behalf of the 'Justice for Lisa and Michelle Taylor' campaign. They eagerly scribbled down my words, hardly pausing to ask any questions. I found the experience strangely enjoyable. Embarrassment and guilt had ensured I hadn't told anyone – not even Debra – of half the things we'd done, and I had a sense of unburdening myself. I'd never spoken so honestly and openly to policemen. The only thing I didn't mention was that Michelle had confessed her guilt to me: there wasn't any point. It was pretty much my word against hers, and she'd deny she said it. Besides, she couldn't have been charged again with murder, nor would I have wanted to participate in any prosecution of her. I wasn't an informant – and my business associates would take a dim view of my adopting such a role. I just wanted a little bit of revenge – for myself, for Alison's family and even for the police officers. My account would help the police dismiss the Taylors' complaints – and screw up their chances of getting any money out of the system. I imagined Michelle's rage when she found out what I'd done – it gave me great satisfaction. I knew that, despite Commander Griffiths's assurances, I was running the risk of being prosecuted for attempting to pervert the course of justice, but I didn't really care. In a way I felt I was helping to bring everything to a final conclusion. Once the police had dismissed the Taylors' complaints the whole business would be at an end.

I rang Tucker and told him the reason for Scotland Yard's visit. He said: 'Why are they bringing that up again?'

'Fuck knows,' I said. 'The Taylors have made a complaint against the police. You'd think they'd leave it.'

Tucker said he'd have a word with Lisa's husband, Ray, who was employed at one of his West End clubs. Tucker didn't want Scotland Yard sniffing around for whatever reason. But I told him it wasn't worth it: 'It's done with, Tony. It's over.'

However, it had only just begun. Soon after I made my statement to Commander Griffiths someone started making menacing silent phone calls to my house. They were always made in the early hours of the morning when I was at work, so the caller knew they'd be bothering my family, not me. Even the scum I dealt with in the club wouldn't have done that. Yet I knew instinctively that the Taylors or their mates were behind the calls. I remembered how much pleasure Michelle and Lisa had got from hearing about the similar silent calls with which JJ Tapp had been bombarded. I contacted British Telecom to see if they could trace the calls. They said the owner of the phone, Debra, would first have to lodge a formal complaint with the police. I thought that such a course might involve me in a court case that could drag me into further unwanted dealings with the Taylors. So I decided to ignore the calls in the hope that the callers would grow tired of their games and go away. They didn't. The calls intensified. Debra became seriously concerned for the safety of herself and our two young children. I decided that if we wanted to prove who was making the calls, and to stop them, Debra would have to make an official complaint to the police. I wasn't happy about having to do this, but the calls were really beginning to spook her and the kids. Even I began to feel alarmed; I knew my family was safe when I was around, but I wasn't always there. Was this the first stage of a campaign that might escalate into something more sinister and dangerous? I didn't think anyone would hurt my children, but I didn't need to ask John Shaughnessy about the danger to my wife. As far as I was concerned, Michelle and Lisa were capable of anything.

BT put a trace on the line: it could be activated by pressing the number five on the phone's keypad. The calls kept coming, perhaps four times a week. There was always silence, apart from heavy breathing and the sound of traffic in the background. BT said the calls were coming from public phone boxes in central London. I marked down each location using an A–Z street map. Within a week my 'pest map' told its own damning story. The club where Lisa's Ray worked was in Charing Cross Road in the heart of the West End. The first call had been made from a box only 50 yards from its door. The other calls had been made from boxes on the route Ray would have taken to get home. All the evidence pointed to Ray, but I couldn't understand why he'd do it. Why terrorise a woman and two young children? I thought perhaps Michelle and Lisa had been at the club with Ray and they'd all decided to do it for a laugh on the way home. I was determined to discover the truth: they'd started it, but I'd finish it.

In December 1994 I was at home one night when the phone rang 20 minutes before midnight. Silence. I activated the trace and said nothing for about five minutes. For some reason I felt sure it was one of the Taylors.

Finally I said: 'Who's that? A fucking murderer? Did you enjoy stabbing her 54 times, you bitch?'

Still silence.

I laughed and made taunts, but the caller kept silent. After 15 minutes the caller put the phone down. The next day BT told me the call had been made from a residential address in south London, but because it was residential they couldn't give me any further details at that stage. I felt sure the resident at that address would turn out to be either Michelle or Lisa. Unusually for me, I decided to do everything by the book. I asked BT if they'd set up secret video cameras in some of the most frequently used phone boxes. They refused. I decided to do it myself. I was going to film the pest, or pests, making their nuisance calls. To be safe, I informed the police of my intentions.

Debra came along with me to hold the video camera while I drove. Her mother agreed to babysit; she would also activate the trace if the pest rang. We hoped that the time of the nuisance call would correspond to the time on the video.

Ray left the club after the last revellers had spilled out. I was almost overwhelmed by the urge to get out and bash him, but I resisted. He got in his car and drove off towards south London. I followed him, but at some point he spotted us. As we approached Brockley he suddenly turned off his lights and sped away, disappearing around a corner. I'd only been planning to film him secretly, but suddenly I felt gripped by anger. I decided I would bash him, after all. I sped round the same corner, but there was no sign of him. It was a long, straight road. I drove up and down, but couldn't find his car. He must have parked at the rear of a house or in a garage. At least I now knew the street where he lived. I felt angry and elated – angry because I couldn't physically grab him, but elated because he knew I was onto him. I parked the car and got out. Although it was the early hours of the morning I started shouting: 'You fucking gutless bastard. I'm coming for you.'

Lights in nearby houses were being switched on. A man opened a window and shouted: 'D'you know what bloody time it is?'

'Tell that murdering bitch and her fat fuck of a boyfriend that I'm coming back for them' I shouted back. The poor man must have wondered what I was on about. I got back in my car, slammed the door and drove off, still shaking with fury. Debra looked out the window, raised her eyes and shook her head.

I had enough information to ring Ray. I rang him at work and said: 'Why do you keep ringing my house, fat boy?'

He denied having anything to do with nuisance calls. He said he'd try to find out who was behind them. I told him it was him. He kept denying it. I couldn't control my anger. Eventually the conversation descended into an exchange of threats – and my vowing to make him pay for persecuting my children. 'I'm on my way to get you, fat boy,' I screamed, before slamming down the phone.

I found out later that as soon as Ray replaced the receiver he told the manager he had to go home immediately, because I'd threatened his wife who was on her own. Before I could get in my car and drive to Ray's club,

I got a call from Tucker. He said the manager at Ray's club had rung him to tell him about the dispute. He asked me not to bother Ray while he was working. I didn't want to fall out with Tucker as well, so I agreed to leave Ray alone while he was at the club.

On New Year's Eve I got a call at ten in the morning from Ann Taylor. She asked me why I'd been following Ray. I told her he'd been making nuisance calls to my house. She said she didn't know about any nuisance calls; she certainly didn't think Ray or her girls were responsible. I said that the BT trace told a different story. I gave her details of the calls – when they'd been made, where they'd been made from, and their duration. She said she'd see what she could find out and would get back to me. When she hadn't got back after a few days, I rang her. I asked her what she'd been able to find out. She said she hadn't had a chance to talk to Ray and Lisa. I told her I wanted an apology from them. She said she'd ask them to ring me. Again, I didn't hear anything. So this time I wrote a letter to the Taylors saying that if I didn't hear from them within a few days I'd assume they were denying making the calls – and I'd take 'appropriate action'.

A few days later Lisa rang me. I could tell by her tone of voice that I wasn't about to get an apology for the months of aggravation. At the same time, though, I hardly expected the cock-and-bull story she told me. She admitted that she'd made one late-night call to my house – the 15-minute silent call which I'd answered and which BT had traced to a residential house in south London. She explained herself by saying that Ray had been receiving nuisance calls at work. He'd pressed 1471 to get the number of the caller – and my number had come up. Neither of them had recognised it. He'd then asked her to call that number to see if she recognised the voice on the other end. That was how she'd come to make the call.

Her story was beyond pathetic; it was also demonstrably untrue. First, my number, being ex-directory, was withheld automatically, so therefore couldn't be retrieved by pressing 1471, even if I'd been making nuisance calls to his club, which I hadn't. Second, Ray had been my best friend for about 18 months and during that period had rung my number nearly every day. He knew it by heart. Even if he'd forgotten it, he'd hardly ring his wife, who was home alone, to ask her to phone an unknown number at twenty to midnight to see if she recognised a voice. Anyway, Ray would at least have recognised the area code as Basildon's. Who did Lisa know in Basildon, apart from me? Third, why did she then stay on the line in silence for almost 15 minutes? I'd have thought that even she'd have been able to see the ridiculousness of her explanation. But the more I thought about it, the more I realised she was behaving entirely in character. She'd foolishly made a nuisance call from her own phone – and her response to being caught out was to produce a lame excuse. It wasn't the first time she'd done this after being caught out; she'd done the same when the police found her fingerprints at the murder scene she'd denied ever visiting. She hadn't fooled the jury then – and she wasn't fooling me now. I finished the call by saying I wanted an apology from Ray for the other calls to my wife and children. I warned her that if I didn't get that apology I'd do something about it. She asked if I was threatening them. I said I was just making a statement.

The calls had stopped, but I wanted revenge. For the time being I decided to pursue the matter through the law. The police took a statement. They said they'd have to pass it on to the Metropolitan Police as the calls had been made in London. At the end of January 1995 Tucker asked me what was happening with Ray. I told him the police were investigating the nuisance calls. He wasn't happy: 'You can't involve the Old Bill, Bernie. It ain't right.'

I told him I didn't give a fuck who I involved when it concerned my children. He suggested a way of sorting it out. He said he'd arrange for Ray and me to have a fight (a 'straightener'). I told him that nothing would give me greater pleasure, but I said Ray wouldn't have the bottle to face me. A few hours later he rang me back.

'You were right. The geezer's a wanker,' he said. 'He was shitting himself. He said he couldn't come out, so I've sacked him.' He told me to deal with him in whatever way I wanted.

About a month later I was called in to Basildon Police Station. They told me they were investigating a complaint from a Mr Ray Buck that I had been making nuisance calls. They took a statement from me, but I didn't hear any more from them about Ray's complaint. I didn't hear any more from them about mine either.

During this time Gary Jones, of the *News of the World*, had been in contact with me. We often spoke and I regarded him as a friend. He knew I'd fallen out with the Taylors more than 18 months earlier, but I'd never told him the reason. He'd always said that the sisters were guilty of murder and that I was a mug to become involved with them. The quashing of their convictions hadn't altered his opinion. In my embarrassment following Michelle's confession, I hadn't wanted to tell him how right he'd been. I'd certainly not sought to sell any stories about the sisters, even though Gary would have been extremely interested in what I had to say. I felt a fool for having run their campaign; I had no desire to publicise the full extent of my foolishness. I'd mentioned the nuisance calls to Gary, and that the police were supposedly investigating. But by May 1995 I knew the police had almost certainly dropped the matter. Gary mentioned a television documentary that was about to be broadcast about nuisance calls. He asked me if I'd like to do an article with him about my experience with Ray and Lisa. I said it was up to Debra – she was the one who'd been tormented. Debra, who was as keen as I was to exact revenge, knew the Taylors would hate to see their new image as innocent victims tarnished. So she agreed to tell Gary the story.

On 28 May 1995 the paper published an article with the headline: TWISTED SISTERS MADE MY LIFE HELL: CHEATED WIFE TELLS OF TAUNT AFTER MURDER-CASE GIRL STOLE HER HUSBAND. It took up most of the page. The article focused largely on the calls, but the last few paragraphs quoted from a letter Michelle had written me. I'd warned the Taylors that if they didn't apologise for making the calls, then 'appropriate action' would be taken against them. This was that appropriate action – a quick burst of public humiliation. I knew it would hurt them more than almost anything else I could do. But at the same time, as far as I was concerned, that was the end of the matter. I had no plans to tell any more stories about the 'twisted sisters'.

Debra and I were jubilant. Our jubilation didn't last long.

FOURTEEN

Gagging the Truth

No one was to know that the 'twisted sisters' article would set in train a legal battle that would last two and a half years. I got a call from the *News of the World* two days after it appeared to say they'd received a threatening letter from the Taylors' solicitor. In it he'd demanded the paper give an undertaking not to publish a second article the following week based on my information. He would issue proceedings if such an undertaking was not forthcoming. Everyone was puzzled by the request, because no further articles had been either flagged or planned. There wasn't another story to tell, apart from the one about my attempts to pervert the course of justice for people who'd duped me, and I had no intention of publicising my idiocy. But who would have run the story anyway? I was a self-confessed criminal admitting to criminal behaviour; the sisters were the supposedly innocent victims of a miscarriage of justice. The paper told the Taylors that no other story was in the offing and so refused to give any undertakings. Again, I thought that was the end of the matter.

However, the 'twisted sisters' article must have put the Taylors in a panic. A fortnight later I got a call at home from the manager of Raquels. He said two well-dressed people had been at the club asking questions about me. As we were talking there was a knock on my front door. The knocking rapidly became more insistent. I wasn't going to answer: I thought it was the police. Before I could look out the window to identify the caller I heard the clatter of the letterbox and the sound of footsteps retreating down the footpath. I went downstairs to find a bundle of A4-

size papers lying on the floor. I picked them up and started reading. I could hardly believe my eyes. The Taylors had issued me with a writ. They were seeking an injunction to stop me publishing the contents of either their letters or the book we'd written; they also wanted to stop me divulging confidential information about their private lives or private conduct. So that was what they were worried about. They were terrified I was going to tell newspapers everything I knew about them. But I'd had no intention of going beyond what had been said in the 'twisted sisters' article, which referred largely to the nuisance calls.

I wasn't sure what to do. I wouldn't be able to afford a lawyer to defend me in what could be an expensive High Court battle. The ringing of the telephone interrupted my thoughts. A female voice on the other end said she was from the *South London Press* (the Taylors' local paper). She said she'd been informed that the sisters were seeking an injunction to prevent me from stalking them.

'*Stalking* them?' I said incredulously.

She outlined a distorted account of my pursuit of Ray over the nuisance calls and asked me if I had anything to say.

'Plenty,' I said. I explained what had happened and that my version of events could be backed up by British Telecom and the police. All the same, I had a gut feeling that this was the beginning of a period of major grief for me. I decided to contact the *News of the World*'s legal department which had dealt with the first legal letter. I was invited to the headquarters of News International in London's Docklands. I was interviewed by a lawyer who asked me if I wanted to contest the writ. I said I did. I wasn't going to let the Taylors dictate to me; I wasn't going to spend my life with a gag over my mouth. I didn't properly consider the possible repercussions for myself and my family, although if I'd known the battle that awaited I might have stepped back. The lawyer said that, as the writ had arisen from a *News of the World* article, the paper would at that stage be willing to pick up the bill to defend me. However, he couldn't give any guarantees that they could continue to fund my defence. I said I didn't mind: I thought it was more than decent of them to fund me initially. I didn't expect an open-ended commitment from them.

A few days later I reported to the Covent Garden offices of Olswang, the solicitors' firm that represented the *News of the World*. The firm was based in a huge modern office block with shiny windows and shinier security men. I was more used to visiting solicitors in dilapidated rooms above High Street chip shops. I felt apprehensive as I climbed the steps to the security desk, where I was given a sticker with my name on and told to take the lift to one of the upper floors. When the doors opened I found three smartly-dressed and well-scrubbed people standing before me. I think it was at that moment I realised that my little spat with the Taylors might turn into something bigger than I'd imagined possible. A friendly woman extended her hand and said her name was Caroline Kean – she would be representing me as my solicitor. She introduced the other two people as her assistants. We went into a large boardroom where they began questioning me in great detail. Michelle had sworn an affidavit giving a ludicrously inaccurate version of everything that had occurred between us. My legal team wanted my version.

It was early afternoon when we started, but I didn't leave the building until ten that night. I told them in great detail the story of my involvement with the Taylors. At first I held back from mentioning Michelle's confession. I did so for much the same reason I hadn't wanted to tell the police: it seemed pointless – Michelle would only deny it and she couldn't be charged again for the same offence. She told me I had to disclose everything.

Caroline pressed me about whether I'd set out to sell stories about the sisters. I denied strongly that I'd ever had any intention of doing so. I told her that if I'd wanted to sell stories about them I'd have done so when they were in the media spotlight. I then made a throwaway remark which Caroline seized upon. I said I knew for a fact that Michelle had murdered Alison, because she'd confessed to me. However, I added, this knowledge wasn't of any use because she couldn't be tried again. Caroline almost fell out of her seat. She asked me if Michelle had given evidence at the trial. I said she had. Caroline said that in that case she could be tried for perjury.

There was a pause. Caroline asked if I realised the seriousness of the allegation. I said I did. She got me to tell her what had happened. As I spoke, I felt uneasy. What trouble was this going to cause me? What could I lose? And what could I gain? I couldn't find answers to those questions, just as I couldn't find an answer to the question of what the Taylors hoped to gain by bringing the action in the first place. Surely they could see they'd be forcing me to disclose things that none of us wanted in the public arena? By the end of the day I felt drained. It was Thursday. Caroline said the case was due to be heard the following Monday, so we had little time to prepare a defence. She wanted me to come back the next day to continue the preparation.

I had a sleepless night. Early next morning as I got myself ready to return to London for another grilling, I got a call from my brother Michael. He told me that one of our uncles, Tommy, had been found dead. He didn't know how to break the devastating news to our mother, who'd been very close to her brother. I told him I'd travel to Wolverhampton immediately to tell her personally. I telephoned Caroline Kean to explain the situation. She said she'd ask the Taylors for a 24-hour adjournment. I thought, given the circumstances, it would be a formality. I travelled into London to get the train to Wolverhampton. At the station I picked up a copy of the *South London Press* (9 June 1995). There was an article headlined, TAYLORS' ORDEAL:

> Two sisters cleared of killing a 21-year-old bank clerk are involved in a legal battle with the man who led their bid to freedom. Michelle and Lisa Taylor are furious with Essex club bouncer Bernard O'Mahoney who was once a trusted friend and ally.
>
> Police in both Catford and Basildon in Essex are investigating counter claims by the Taylors and Mr O'Mahoney that they were stalked. And now the sisters believe that they have been hoaxed by a man who befriends prisoners then capitalises on their notoriety by selling stories.

The article mentioned my dealings with the Yorkshire Ripper Peter Sutcliffe and the child-killer Richard Blenkey. This was a tactic the

Taylors would consistently use to try to discredit me in and outside court. The problem with it – something they always managed to keep from journalists – was that I had letters from Michelle showing that she not only knew about my dealings with Sutcliffe and Blenkey, but approved of them. The article ended with news of their other legal actions:

> The sisters are set to face another courtroom hurdle next month when they take on four national newspapers. They made legal history by successfully challenging a decision by the Attorney General not to take action against the papers which it is recognised prejudiced their murder trial and led to their successful appeal.

The sisters had certainly grown fond of the law. Getting away with murder must have convinced them they were invincible. If they'd taken on the Attorney General, they must have thought I'd be a doddle. I rang Caroline later in the day from my mother's house. She sounded a bit embarrassed. She said the Taylors' solicitor wanted to verify I was telling the truth about the family bereavement. He'd sent a fax asking me to identify the name of the relative, the time he'd died and his relationship to me. I was astonished and infuriated. I bit my lip, though, and passed on the details of the police station that was dealing with Tommy's death. In the meantime I was dealing with my mother's grief and my uncle's funeral arrangements. Caroline rang me later to say the Taylors' solicitor wanted further undertakings before agreeing to the adjournment. I wasn't going to be humiliated further, so I told Caroline to forget about it: we'd go ahead with the Monday hearing. But it meant I had to travel back home on Saturday. I'd wanted to stay longer with my mother, especially as relatives were arriving from as far afield as Ireland for the funeral. I was raging.

On Sunday I got a call from another journalist. He said he was from the *Daily Star*. He was under the impression the sisters were taking me to court to stop me 'stalking' them. I said they were taking me to court to stop me talking, not stalking – the attempted injunction was for alleged breach of confidence. I gave him my side of the story, and put the phone down. The *South London Press* story had been bad enough, but was I now going to appear in the national press as a 'stalker'? On Monday I travelled into London for the court hearing. As I made my way to the Royal Courts of Justice in The Strand I bought a copy of the *Daily Star*. Inside was the banner headline: WE'RE BEING STALKED, SAY MURDER CASE SISTERS. If the sisters had deliberately set out to boost my determination to fight them, they couldn't have done a better job.

Outside the court were lots of photographers and reporters. I walked up the steps into a lightning storm of exploding flash bulbs. Reporters shouted questions, but I ignored them. I headed for the courtroom. As I approached it I saw Michelle and Lisa outside with members of their legal team. I couldn't see their mother or Ray, although the latter's absence didn't surprise me. Both sisters looked ill: Lisa had lost weight and Michelle looked stressed-out. We made eye contact. I smirked at them sarcastically. Lisa smirked back, but she lost her bravado when my solicitor arrived. I think they were surprised to see I had a solicitor: they'd probably thought I'd just cave in. But Caroline Kean's presence signalled I was going to put up a fight. The sisters looked uncomfortable. The last time I'd stood there with the Taylors had been two years earlier on the day they'd walked to freedom. Then we'd been firm friends, bonded by our secrets. Now we were bitter enemies, using those very same secrets to try to destroy one another. None of us was enjoying the experience. Michelle kept looking over at me, a little-girl-lost look in her eyes, as if inwardly pleading with me to let the matter drop. Her eyes searched mine for the 'good old Bernie' of old. But that 'good old Bernie' was dead – through her actions she'd buried him, and spat on his grave.

We were called into court. I glanced over at them as we made our way to the door. Michelle looked away, but Lisa looked straight back at me, her face filled with contempt. Inside, the sisters sat in the row in front of me, slightly to my right. Neither spoke. They just sat there, stony-faced, staring straight ahead. The Taylors' lawyer asked the judge to order that I return a cassette tape which he said had been given to Michelle by a prison officer. The tape was described as containing a woman addressing

Michelle in 'passionate and sexually explicit terms'. It was the tape I'd played to Michelle from the call box after we'd split up. I agreed to hand it back; I wasn't interested in her private life. The case was then adjourned for two days for the swearing of affidavits and the production of other documents. No more than ten minutes after sitting down, we were all leaving. Outside the court I watched Michelle and Lisa go into a whispering huddle with their legal team. Moments later the group walked off. Soon they'd disappeared from sight. I wasn't to know that that would be the last time I'd see the Taylors in the flesh. From then on I'd see only the members of their legal team. When I returned to court on Wednesday the two sides agreed to a temporary injunction preventing Michelle, Lisa and myself from discussing the case. This injunction would only last until the issues could be properly dealt with at a full civil trial. It was also agreed that all future hearings would be held behind closed doors to prevent journalists from reporting the details of the case.

Later that week Caroline Kean and I sat down for more long sessions to hammer out my defence. I had never met a solicitor like her. She believed in me and was as determined as I was to fight the case. She was genuinely disturbed by the thought that the Taylors had got away with murder. By this stage Michelle had sworn two affidavits. The fact that her story differed significantly from one to the other did not seem to embarrass her. I wasn't surprised that she told lies. I was, however, surprised that her lies were such transparent and provable lies. In her first affidavit she tried to suggest she hadn't known about my criminal background for a long time and had only 'subsequently discovered' my criminal convictions for violence. However, in her second affidavit she produced a text which she said I'd sent her in prison and which she described as a summary of my life to date, listing a series of violent crimes and other incidents. In her first affidavit she suggested she hadn't known at the time about my writing to the Yorkshire Ripper and the child-killer Blenkey. In her second she revealed in passing that she had. She indicated she'd been conned by the aliases I'd used, although she'd written letters to me using some of those aliases. I felt from reading her affidavits that she had to be assuming either that I'd got rid of our correspondence or that

I'd be too embarrassed to produce the letters as evidence, perhaps as mine contained matters concerning my partner Debra. Why else would she include falsehoods which she knew her letters could disprove? She was making it up as she went along, just as she'd done during the murder investigation. She wasn't thinking things through. I couldn't wait to face her in a trial. Yet even at that early stage I felt sure she'd never again risk going into the witness box. She and her sister would do everything they could to avoid another trial. Subsequent events proved me right.

The most interesting, and potentially important, parts of her affidavits concerned her version of why our relationship ended. In her first affidavit she said that during the autumn of 1993 (that is, following her release and while we were living together) she began to hear reports that I might not be all that I appeared to be. She said that 'David Smith, a journalist' told her I'd previously contacted other people in the public eye and sold stories about them. According to her, our relationship then became strained and she broke it off, asking me to leave the flat. In her second affidavit she elaborated on this story slightly by saying that when she discovered I had a 'record of deception' she became upset, confronted me over it and asked me to leave the flat. Her account was laughable. Not only could I prove from her letters that she'd known about my 'record of deception', but now she'd given another hostage to fortune by naming the journalist who'd supposedly told her about me – David Smith. I had a vague recollection of meeting Smith during the campaign. I hoped that by tracking him down I could get him to destroy Michelle's lie. However, at that stage I was unable to approach him because of the nature of the injunction. I wasn't allowed to talk to anyone other than lawyers about the case. I mentioned him to Caroline and she said she'd contact him in due course.

Caroline took me through the pros and cons of continuing with the action. By this stage she'd read the correspondence between Michelle and me. She said the letters would be vital evidence, but there would have to be full disclosure: all the incidental personal matters would be brought into the open too. She said it was therefore important that Debra – who might also be a witness – should read the letters in their entirety. That way there'd be no surprises at the trial. I felt sick. I wasn't sure I'd still have a partner once Debra read the letters. I'd said many things I didn't want her to read. Caroline told me to bring Debra to the office the next day. That night I asked Debra if she'd come to London to swear an affidavit. I didn't have the courage to tell her what really awaited her. Once again the Taylors had guaranteed me another sleepless night.

The next day I drove with Debra into London. I parked the car in a meter bay near Lambeth North Station and we got the tube into town. We didn't talk much. I got the feeling that Debra suspected I hadn't told her exactly what was in store. I introduced Debra to Caroline; there were strained smiles all round. Caroline led us into the boardroom which was fast becoming my second home. Debra and I sat next to each other at the gleaming boardroom table; Caroline sat opposite. She started out by asking Debra about the nuisance calls, then explained she might have to give evidence and that certain aspects of my relationship with Michelle might also be raised.

'You need to be prepared for some pretty unsavoury questions, Debra,' she said. 'You'd better look through these.' She pushed the pile of Michelle's letters towards Debra. The bundle zipped across the highly-polished surface like an Exocet missile on its way to target. Debra began to read. I excused myself from the room. Outside in the corridor I despised myself for what I'd done to the mother of my children. I paced up and down for perhaps half an hour, then took a deep breath and went back into the room. I felt like I'd walked into a storm cloud – the sort you see on documentaries called things like 'The World's Greatest Natural Disasters'. Debra didn't even look at me. She just stared straight ahead, expressionless. Caroline said we'd done enough for one day.

In the lift downstairs, and on the tube journey back to the car, Debra couldn't bring herself to talk to me. As we walked from the tube station towards my parking space she suddenly stopped walking and started crying. I tried to console her, but she didn't want me near her. I hated myself, but I hated the Taylors more. At that moment my will to win became magnified tenfold. I had to right all the wrongs I'd done, starting with the misery I'd caused my family.

The parking bay was empty. My car had been either stolen or towed away. It was the final straw for Debra. She broke down completely. As I used my mobile to discover if my car had been towed away, Debra began hitting me. Two police officers on the beat tried to intervene. I told them to get lost, and they threatened to arrest me, but eventually walked away. Amid Debra's blows I'd managed to establish that the car had indeed been towed away. I had to travel across London to the car pound to pay an extortionate fee to get it released.

My thoughts about the Taylors became even darker.

FIFTEEN

The Policeman's Story

My battle with the Taylor sisters soon turned into the legal equivalent of trench warfare – long periods of inaction broken by bursts of heavy bombardment. I'd hoped the case would be quickly brought to trial, but I was soon disappointed. The Taylors showed no signs of wanting to come out from behind their line of fortifications. I realised they'd dug in for the long haul and hoped to grind me down with distracting skirmishes. But both I and my solicitor Caroline Kean kept busy behind the lines, preparing for the big breakthough – and what we hoped would be the final push to victory.

Part of Caroline's work on the case involved her meeting the man who'd led the investigation into Alison's murder, Chris Burke. She rang me after spending several hours with the former detective superintendent at his home in Surrey. He'd retired from the police three years after the sisters' release. His experience at the appeal left him so disillusioned that he lost enthusiasm for the job; and the stress was undermining his health. Caroline said his summary of the case against the Taylors devastated their claims of innocence. Her few slight doubts about the sisters' guilt had been dissolved in the acid of Burke's minutely detailed account of the investigation. He'd given her the full background to all the most contentious aspects, throwing light on much that had been obscured both at the Court of Appeal and in the media reports at the time. Caroline sounded very upbeat, but there was too much to tell me over the phone. She said she'd write up her notes and send them to me.

A few days later her notes arrived. I read through them eagerly with the stinging sensation of being made aware of my foolishness in having been taken in by the Taylors. I felt like a traveller being led across familiar ground by a guide who not only knew the terrain better than I did, but also had the power to make me see what I'd previously ignored. Over the following days as I read and re-read the notes I rang Caroline frequently to get her to elaborate on certain things that had been said. The following account of Burke's investigation is based largely on Caroline's notes, my conversations with her about them, documents from the original police investigation, and transcripts from the trial and the appeal.

Chris Burke had been a policeman for 22 years when he took charge of the investigation. For the first eight weeks Detective Superintendent Tom Glendinning had been the top man. Burke took over when Glendinning went on annual leave prior to promotion. Burke had a passing familiarity with the case from his Monday morning meetings with Glendinning and the area's other detective superintendent, when the three would sit down with the chief superintendent to discuss progress in their various murder inquiries. So when he went in for his first meeting with the team at the incident room in Earlsfield Police Station he knew the inquiry had fallen into the doldrums. Burke had already gleaned that the victim's husband had been having an affair and that he and the mistress had found the body; he knew there'd been some stranger attacks on women in the area over the previous months; and he also knew that Barclays Bank had offered a substantial reward which hadn't resulted in any significant new information.

Burke was surprised by the subdued atmosphere in the office at that first meeting. Officers seemed reluctant to say anything. So he took them to the pub where he hoped the more relaxed atmosphere might get them talking. Burke said around 98 per cent of murder victims knew their murderers, so you always started with a metaphorical pin in the body and worked outwards. Several members of the team felt Michelle Taylor and John Shaughnessy hadn't been investigated sufficiently. They told Burke that their former chief had effectively cleared Michelle and John, because both had seemingly watertight alibis. Glendinning had become convinced that an opportunistic stranger had murdered Alison. On the day of her murder a nanny had been pestered by a stranger on a common not far from the murder scene. Then, a few weeks later, in nearby Clapham South a woman had been accosted on her doorstep by a stranger: he tried pushing her into the house, but she screamed and he ran off. The descriptions of these two men tallied. Several members of the team felt, perhaps wrongly, that Glendinning was so absorbed in the stranger-attack theory that he'd become less interested in their suspicions about Michelle and John, although the gossip at the clinic was that they were lovers. Burke was open-minded. He knew Glendinning was a dedicated and conscientious policeman, and he could understand why the focus might have shifted, but he reassured the team that he came with no baggage. He would look freshly at all their theories.

As Burke familiarised himself with the details of the investigation he discovered that when the team did their first house-to-house enquiries they'd asked people the question: 'Did you see anything suspicious in the road on that day?' All the neighbours said they hadn't. Burke felt the team had made a fundamental error. What might neighbours have regarded as 'suspicious'? A man coming out of a flat with a knife in his hand, or 'M for Murder' on his chest, or horns on his head? He decided to send the team back to re-interview the neighbours – and this time merely to ask people what they remembered seeing in the road on that day. Although two months had now passed since the murder, Burke felt confident that people might still remember things. His confidence was based on what he called the President Kennedy Syndrome: everyone knew what they were doing at the time they heard of President John F. Kennedy's assassination. And so, on a smaller scale, if someone gets murdered in your street you tend to remember that day with a special clarity. That Sunday he intended sending the team back to knock on every door in Vardens Road.

In the meantime Burke had gone through the small mound of paperwork that had so far been generated. He clarified in his mind what they knew: on Monday evenings John Shaughnessy earned extra money at the clinic by doing the flower-arranging. John would buy up to forty pounds worth of flowers at the stall near Waterloo Station owned by Buster Edwards. John's movements at the time of his wife's murder had been verified by both Buster and staff at the clinic. Michelle would usually help John with the flower-arranging because, she said, her long-term ambition was to start her own catering business, and the ability to arrange flowers would be an asset in that field. On the evening of the murder Michelle helped John with the flowers between 6.20 p.m. and 8 p.m. Then, as usual, she drove John home. She said she had a stomach upset and, before leaving the clinic, went to the toilet. The journey to Vardens Road took 15 minutes at the most. She entered the flat with John. She said, because of her stomach upset, she'd wanted to use the toilet again before returning home. She claimed she'd also intended having a quick chat with Alison. On top of that, John wanted her to take back to the clinic two flower pots too large for him to carry on the train. When John put his key in the communal door he found the mortise lock was not on. This was so unusual he remarked on it – Alison always kept it locked. He entered the flat, accompanied by Michelle, and found his wife's dead body.

Michelle was first seen by the police at Vardens Road: on the night of the killing. She appeared very distressed. She answered questions, but she did not, at that stage, mention her relationship with John. Indeed, she did not mention it until she was interviewed at length almost two months later on 24 July. In a statement of the same date, Lisa said that she and Michelle had gone to Bromley to shop for a party dress around 3 p.m. They returned to the clinic around 5 p.m. to the room of a work colleague and friend, JJ Tapp. While Michelle went to do the flowers with John, Lisa played Monopoly with JJ in her room until around 7.30 p.m. Lisa said she'd never been to the flat at Vardens Road: she didn't even know where it was – she thought it was somewhere in Clapham. JJ confirmed the sisters' story. She'd been in her room when the Taylors arrived at 5.10 to 5.15 p.m. She could be sure of the time because she was waiting for *Neighbours* to start on

BBC1 around 5.30 p.m., and the programme hadn't started by the time the Taylors arrived. If JJ was telling the truth – and at that stage the police had no reason to believe she was lying – then the Taylor sisters couldn't have committed the crime.

However, within less than a fortnight of Burke's arrival the Taylor sisters had been charged with murder. The train of events that led to this outcome happened rapidly. When he first took charge Burke had an open mind, but as soon as he went through the small details of the case he found himself becoming extremely suspicious of Michelle and John. In particular, regardless of their reticence about the affair, he found Michelle's behaviour on discovering the body quite peculiar. By her own account, she'd walked into the flat behind John and had run up the stairs after him when she heard him shout, 'Alison! Alison!' His wife was at the top of the second flight of stairs, lying on her stomach with her head on one side, resting against the kitchen door. John felt Alison's hand for a pulse and put his hand on her forehead, which he said was still lukewarm. Michelle also felt for a pulse in Alison's neck, but in addition put her hand underneath Alison's head and tried to lift up the body. She found it stiff. She noticed Alison's bloodshot eyes and the cuts on her legs. She also saw blood around Alison's mouth and ears. John, who didn't touch the body again, was in shock and said repeatedly: 'I don't know what's happened.'

Michelle kept touching the body before saying, 'She's all stiff', and starting to scream. John said he was going downstairs to use the neighbour's phone to call the police. He knocked on the neighbour's door. However, instead of staying with John and waiting for a reply, Michelle ran into the street – supposedly to find a police officer she had seen just before entering the flat. Michelle said she couldn't see the policeman, so she ran several hundred yards up the road to a pub (past a call box) and, crying hysterically, told a barmaid and customers to call the police because someone was dead. People rushed to comfort the distraught woman. She then took a group of three or four people back to the flat. When she got there John and the neighbour had already phoned the police. A few of the men went upstairs, followed by

Michelle. They stood looking at Alison without touching her, then went back downstairs. Michelle, however, stayed alone with the body. She knelt down next to Alison, stroked her hair away from her face and pulled down her skirt, which had ridden up to expose her underclothes. Michelle now had blood on her hands which she washed off in the bathroom (although despite her 'stomach upset' she didn't go to the toilet). She also went into the front room with John to see if anything had been touched: everything seemed normal and undisturbed. On her way back downstairs she opened the window on the landing because, she said, she felt sick and wanted some fresh air. She made a point of saying that the clasp on the window seemed loose. That window overlooked a flat roof at the back of the house.

Burke said he found Michelle's actions bizarre. He said everyone was instinctively wary of touching a dead body. John had briefly touched Alison's hand and forehead when he thought she might still be alive, but as soon as he knew she was dead he didn't touch the body again. Yet Michelle not only repeatedly touched her lover's wife's body, but even tried to lift it up. Then later, while everyone else was keeping clear, she returned to it, stroked the hair, rearranged the clothes and got blood on her hands. She had contaminated the crime scene: no forensics could now be linked to her. She had also opened a window near the body and made a point of mentioning its supposedly loose clasp. Her implication was that perhaps someone had got in the window after climbing onto the flat roof. However, John remembered checking recently that the window was firmly locked. Also, the only way of accessing the flat roof would have been by a hazardous scaling of the drainpipe. Burke said no one could have clambered up it without leaving some signs of interference. Yet forensics found no such signs on either the drainpipe or the window. Nothing had been disturbed.

Burke also felt alarmed by the pathologist's report. Bruising showed that Alison had received a karate-style chop between her upper lip and nostrils which would have momentarily stunned her. Then 54 stab wounds had been delivered in rapid succession: nine to her chest, ten to her throat and more than 30 to her back. One had pierced her right hand as she tried to ward off the blows: the nail of her little finger had been almost torn off. A lot of the blows had been delivered with great force, others were mere pin-pricks. The pathologist thought the murderer could have done them in two to three minutes. The two significant wounds were the one to the throat which slashed her windpipe, and another to the left side of her back which pierced her lung. She died through a combination of loss of blood and asphyxiation as it flowed into her lungs. Burke noticed there had also been a few stabs wounds in the vaginal area – as if the murderer had wanted to make a point about that part of her body. Generally, the savage nature of the attack suggested to him a personal motive. This suspicion was bolstered by the clear evidence that Alison had known her killer or killers. The mortise lock on the front door was unlocked, contrary to Alison's security-conscious habit of closing it. This pointed to her having let in somebody she knew and whom she expected to leave shortly afterwards. Moreover, Alison had picked up the mail from the communal hallway and carried it upstairs, along with her keys, handbag, umbrella and coat. All very relaxed and normal. She would hardly have done this if a stranger had pounced as she'd opened her door: there'd have been a struggle in the hallway which would probably have continued up the stairs. All the signs were, however, that she entered the flat normally and that someone whom she knew (and who she knew was coming up behind her) had attacked her suddenly as she was about to enter the kitchen.

Neighbours didn't hear screams or sounds of distress; police found no evidence of sexual interference; and there were no signs of robbery – neither the flat nor her handbag had been ransacked. John Shaughnessy thought that two low-value gold chains were missing, one of which he believed Alison wore on her wrist (the other he thought might have gone missing some time before). However, the suggestion that the murderer had stolen a chain could be countered by the fact that a bigger, more visible gold chain around her neck was untouched. The nature of the attack was obviously different to the recent stranger attack nearby. In that case the victim had been pushed violently from behind as she opened her front door on arriving home; the assailant had then tried to drag her into the hallway, but she screamed and he ran off.

Burke said that at first Lisa Taylor had not really been in the picture. Only when suspicions began to intensify about Michelle did Lisa move inevitably into the frame. After all, she was providing part of her sister's alibi. During this period officers spoke to several of Michelle and John's work colleagues at the clinic. There were two statements in particular which raised further questions about the Taylors. The statements put serious doubt in Burke's mind about the sisters' claims to have been shopping in Bromley between 3 and 5 p.m. Nurse Carol Healey said she finished work at the clinic at 4 p.m. on the day of the murder. As she left, between 4 and 4.30 p.m., she saw Michelle Taylor (whom she knew) driving out of the clinic in an estate car. Sitting beside Michelle was a young, slight woman with her hair in a pony-tail. Lisa had had her hair in a pony-tail that day. This sighting contradicted the sisters' story that they'd been in Bromley at that time. Then, Mrs Valerie McDonald, who was also employed at the clinic, left work at 6 p.m. exactly. She saw a stationary car at the end of the driveway near the exit: sitting in it were Michelle and Lisa Taylor, whom she knew. They exchanged waves. If Alison had been attacked as soon as she arrived home around 5.37 p.m., and the attack had only taken a few minutes, then the two sisters could easily have driven back to the clinic to be seen by Mrs McDonald around 6 p.m.

Burke said that in the week before he took charge the team had searched the Taylors' family home and Michelle's room at the clinic. They took away various items, but a few days passed before they realised the potential significance of one of those items – Michelle's diary for 1990. The officer reading through it came upon the entries in which Michelle said she hated Alison, described her as an 'unwashed bitch' and expressed her desire for Alison to 'disappear as if she never existed' so Michelle could give everything to the man she loved. Burke now had a clear, and clearly expressed, motive for murder. He looked back over Michelle and Lisa's previous statements and could see how both had clearly lied about the true nature of Michelle's feelings for Alison. Michelle had deliberately tried to mislead the investigating officers. She described how she first came into contact with John and how they then became 'friends'. She explained how she learnt John was engaged to a girl called Alison and how she then became 'friends' with her. She told detectives that her friendship with the engaged couple had grown to such an extent that she'd been invited to their wedding in Ireland. She told how she'd often watched television with Alison and John in their room when they lived at the clinic; how Alison would visit her room; how the three of them would go out together; how she would sometimes go out just with Alison for a drink and a pizza when John was working. And, to ensure there was no doubt in the detectives' minds about her friendly feelings towards John and Alison, she repeated: 'My relationship with both of them was good friends.'

Michelle later claimed she didn't mention her affair with John because she didn't want her mother finding out she'd had an affair with a married man. Lisa said in her statement that Michelle had been upset by John's engagement to Alison but had told her that so long as John was happy she was happy. She added that Michelle thought Alison was a nice girl and had said she'd have been more upset if Alison hadn't been such a nice girl. She finished her statement by saying she came from a close family in which people readily discussed problems; they didn't keep secrets from one another.

But the most startling development came on Friday, 2 August. The results of fingerprint tests at the flat came through. A fingerprint expert had found three fingerprints belonging to Michelle on the banister. This was only to be expected. However, he also found a few fingerprints belonging to Lisa on the inside of Alison's front door – the sort of fingerprints that would be left by someone closing the door behind her. Burke said: 'Bingo!' Lisa had denied ever being in the flat and had even suggested she didn't know where it was. Both Michelle and the sisters' mother had backed her up, stating categorically that Lisa had never been there.

The expert estimated that the prints, taken on the day after the killing, were relatively fresh, probably no more than 48 to 72 hours old. There's no definitive scientific way of proving the age of fingerprints. The expert, who had 27 years in the job, said it was more of an art than a science. He made his judgement on the basis of three factors: the fact that they were clear; the ease with which they took to the aluminium powder and the absence of any damage to, or interference with, them (which you might have expected if they'd been in that position for more than a few days).

Another interesting development was about to come from the door-to-door team's second round of interviews on Sunday, 4 August. On the Monday morning Burke read through the papers logging the details. A team member drew his attention to what a doctor said he'd seen. Doctor Michael Unsworth-White said he left the hospital where he worked at 5.30 p.m. to cycle to his home in Vardens Road. He reached there around 15 minutes later. As he rode down the road he noticed two girls coming down a short flight of steps to his right. They were in their late teens or early twenties. At first – and this later became crucial – he said he thought one of the girls 'may have been black'. However, without any prompting from the interviewing officer, he immediately retracted the suggestion. He said he was mistaken. Both of them were definitely white.

Burke didn't need anyone to point out that the two young women could have been the Taylor sisters; they could have been in the flat and out again in a few minutes. If it had been them, they'd have arrived back at the clinic at the time Valerie McDonald saw them sitting in the stationary car in the driveway. He assigned an officer, as a matter of urgency, to take a full written statement from the doctor that day. In his statement the doctor provided fuller details of what he had seen. He confirmed once again that the two young women had been white. He described their hair as blonde and said they had been wearing what looked like joggers' tracksuits. He said one of them had her hair tied back in a pony-tail. His attention had been drawn by the girl with the pony-tail: he said she was prettier than the other one. His description of their appearance tallied with the sisters' own descriptions of how they looked that day. The doctor said they'd come running or jogging down the steps into the street. One of them was carrying a bulky bag. His impression was that they were taking clothes to the laundry, but then he thought that strange, because the launderette was at the opposite end of the street. The second girl reached the bottom just as the doctor went past. The doctor walked back down the street with the police officer. It turned out that the steps he'd seen the girls coming down were Alison's.

Burke now felt he had enough evidence to arrest the Taylors. Furthermore, if JJ Tapp was providing them with a false alibi, then she had to be part of the conspiracy; he'd arrest her too. An important question was whether John Shaughnessy was also involved. He had a watertight alibi for his movements at the time of the murder, but he'd been less than frank about his relationship with Michelle. They might have been in it together. However, Burke knew there wasn't enough evidence to arrest John: he could only be invited to attend the station as a witness.

Around 5.40 a.m. on Wednesday, 7 August, the police arrested the Taylor sisters and JJ Tapp. The Taylors were arrested at their family home. As they were read their rights they both denied having had anything to do with the murder. They were each taken to separate police stations – Lisa to Battersea, Michelle to Wandsworth. JJ was arrested at the Churchill Clinic on suspicion of conspiracy to murder. She was taken to Tooting Police Station. Within a very short period of time JJ said she wanted to tell the truth. She said she'd lied about her movements on the day of the murder. She'd not been in her room from 5 p.m. In fact she'd not arrived there until 7.15 to 7.20 p.m. She said she'd lied because her good friends Michelle and Lisa had assured her they'd been waiting for her in her room, and she had no reason not to believe them. She said in mid-afternoon she'd gone shopping at a supermarket some distance from the clinic. After shopping she went to her mother's house nearby where she stayed with her mother and two sisters until around 7 p.m. Then she walked back to the clinic, arriving around 15 minutes later. As she walked up the clinic's driveway towards her house she saw Lisa Taylor standing on the balcony outside JJ's room. Lisa waved at her. She wasn't surprised to see Lisa there; Michelle had a key to her room and it wasn't unusual for Michelle or Lisa to enter when she wasn't there. As JJ reached the door Lisa came down the stairs and opened it for her. They walked upstairs. Lisa said she and Michelle had been in JJ's room since around 5 p.m. and that Michelle had left at 6 p.m. to do the flowers with John.

Lisa said she'd recorded some tapes for JJ's birthday party, which was due to be held in the near future. JJ said that Lisa didn't seem to be her usual self – she was fidgety and kept pacing around the room, whereas normally she just sat down and chatted. At around 8 p.m. Michelle came to her room. She said she couldn't stay long because she had to drive John home. However, she had a cigarette and some water, and mentioned in passing that she and Lisa had been in JJ's room since just after 5 p.m. She didn't mention anything about a stomach upset. Michelle then left to drive John home.

Some time later a porter shouted up to say there was a phone call for Lisa on the pay-phone downstairs. The two of them went down. Lisa picked up the receiver, went white and said something like, 'Alison's been killed' or 'Alison's dead'. They went back upstairs and the internal phone rang. It was Michelle. She asked for Lisa. During the conversation Lisa started crying. She put the phone down and said Alison had been stabbed and that Michelle and John had found the body. JJ said Lisa had cried almost hysterically. She'd really been in a bad way, even though she'd hardly known Alison. JJ phoned Lisa a cab, gave her ten pounds and sent her off home. JJ noticed Lisa had left behind a plastic bin-liner which was a quarter full. During the night JJ said she looked inside the bin-liner and saw a nightdress and a make-up bag on top, but didn't go through the rest of the contents. Burke said they thought the bin-liner might have been the bag the doctor had seen the two girls carrying – it might have contained the murder weapon and bloodstained clothing. To my mind, Lisa's act of leaving behind the bag was a move the police would never have anticipated if she or Michelle had been considered as suspects from the moment

Alison was found dead. By leaving the bag in JJ's room, Lisa had ensured that any search of the Taylors' car or home, or Michelle's room at the clinic, would prove futile.

The next morning JJ went into work and told her boss about Alison's murder and how Michelle and John had found the body. Later on that morning she got a call from Michelle, who sounded a little annoyed. She said to JJ: 'Who've you told?' Michelle had been speaking to one of the hospital's bosses and had been surprised to discover he already knew about the murder. Around midday that same boss rang JJ to say Michelle was at the clinic and wanted to pick up something from JJ's room. JJ went down to meet her in the foyer. Lisa was there too. They said they wanted to pick up the bin-liner they'd left behind. This wasn't making easy reading for me: I was reminded of another of Michelle's lies. When explaining to me in a letter why Carol Healey had told police she'd seen Michelle and a pony-tailed girl driving out of the clinic around 4 p.m. (when the sisters were supposedly shopping in Bromley), Michelle said Healey must have seen them the *next* day when they'd gone to pick up the overnight bag from JJ's room. Yet they'd clearly picked up the bag around midday, not late afternoon. Michelle hadn't disputed the later sighting of them sitting in a stationary car in the clinic driveway around six: she explained that she and Lisa had gone to the car to use the stereo to sort out the tapes Lisa had recorded for JJ's party. I realised once again what a fool I'd been to lap up her lies.

I read on: the three of them walked up to JJ's room. Michelle looked upset and tired. They had a brief conversation in which Michelle said emphatically: 'We was here just after five.' They picked up the bin-liner and left. Michelle rang JJ a few days later to say the police would soon be calling to see her and that she should ring her as soon as they'd been. The Sunday after Alison's murder the police called on JJ at the clinic. JJ was told that a statement would be required from her, but in the meantime she should write down everything she'd done on the day of the murder. She was also asked to recall how long Michelle and Lisa had been with her and at what times. When the police left, JJ felt very frightened; she was unsure of what she should say. If Michelle and Lisa said they were in her room from 5 p.m., why should she doubt them? Moments after the police left she phoned Michelle to tell her about the visit.

Sensing JJ's dilemma, Michelle said: 'We were really at your flat just after five. We are not lying. Tell the police you were with us at that time.'

JJ, frightened and confused, decided to believe her friends. Before putting the phone down she agreed she'd say what Michelle wanted her to say. JJ said she really believed the sisters had been there when they said they were; Michelle had been a good friend to her and, to the best of her knowledge, had never told her lies. Later, after JJ had made a written statement she phoned Michelle to tell her what she'd said. Michelle just said: 'Okay.'

A couple of days later she spoke again to Michelle, who asked her if anyone else at the clinic had been interviewed. During this conversation Michelle said once again that she and Lisa had definitely been in JJ's room since just after 5 p.m. JJ felt Michelle was trying to reassure her. However, after a few weeks the police went back to JJ for a second statement. JJ said by this stage she was really worried about two things: first, that she was lying to the police and, second, that things just didn't seem to be right. She became very stressed – and felt she was more stressed about everything than Michelle. Despite those feelings, she believed her friends and felt she had to stick to her story. After JJ's second interview Michelle phoned her to ask if she'd stuck to her statement. JJ said she had. About a week later JJ went to Michelle's house and spoke to the sisters' mother. JJ told Ann Taylor she hadn't actually arrived back at her room at the clinic on the day of the murder until after 7 p.m. Mrs Taylor didn't say much, but seemed surprised. They didn't discuss the matter further, because Michelle arrived home a few minutes later. Some weeks later JJ went again to the Taylors' house on her way to a car-boot sale. Mrs Taylor made a point of bringing up the matter of JJ's movements on the day of the murder. She asked JJ if she remembered shouting 'hello' to her on the phone when

Lisa had telephoned her that day. JJ said she definitely hadn't: she hadn't gone to the phone with Lisa at that time, because she hadn't got back to her room until after 7 p.m. JJ said Mrs Taylor kept saying: 'I'm sure you were there. I'm sure it was that day.'

Burke didn't conduct any of the interviews himself, but received regular progress reports. When he was told what JJ was now saying he knew her evidence was dynamite. It showed that the Taylor sisters had been trying to create an alibi for themselves at least an hour before the body's discovery. Why create an alibi before the body's been found? Who but the murderers would know the exact time of death and therefore the period for which they'd need an alibi?

Burke said that the interviewing officer had asked JJ why she'd lied. She replied that, in addition to her belief that the sisters had been telling the truth, she'd stuck to her story because the Taylor family frightened her. She said Michelle had told her about a protective uncle who was capable of violence. Michelle's martial arts background also made her fearful. JJ had genuinely believed the Taylors would hurt her if she changed her statement, although they had never made such threats. I felt a twinge of sympathy and guilt as I read about JJ's fears. I had experienced her fear, even contributed to it, that night when I phoned her to try to get her to change her statement. But she'd stuck by the story she told in court. She'd cried as she pleaded with me to believe her. I'd just sneered at her, convinced she was lying from fear of what the police might do to her. I could hear her voice in my head; I had the urge to contact her to apologise, but I didn't think she'd be pleased to hear from me – and I had already caused her enough stress and upset.

Burke expanded on JJ's reference to Michelle's martial arts training. He said that both sisters had been taking lessons in martial arts for around five years. Both had been learning ju-jitsu – Lisa had earned a blue belt, Michelle a superior purple belt. In one of her earlier statements before her arrest, Lisa had mentioned how they had been thrown out of one club following an incident in which Lisa had allegedly thrown scissors violently on a table. She said she and Michelle used to get quite a few bruises and scratches during those classes, especially when they were doing 'weapon defence'. According to Lisa, they trained with wooden weapons, although she added that all movements were made into the air and not towards any person. Under further questioning, however, she admitted they did sometimes train with a small metal dagger-type knife with a pronged handle. Apparently, you're supposed to use it to defend yourself against attackers wielding Samurai swords. Fortunately, there aren't too many of those in south London.

While JJ was telling the police her story, Michelle and Lisa were also being interviewed. However, Lisa answered almost every question with the reply: 'No comment.' In her morning session, before the lunch-break, Michelle had been willing to answer questions. But after the long lunch-break, she too answered almost every question with the words: 'No comment.' Both sisters were represented by solicitors from the same firm. Burke thought this shouldn't have been allowed. I could imagine Michelle and Lisa sitting there sullenly refusing to answer questions. What had happened to Michelle's heartfelt wish that the killers of her 'friend' be caught? I cringed as I remembered those newspaper reports of Michelle's tears over Alison's coffin. If they had done no wrong, why on earth would they refuse to answer questions about the murder of Michelle's dear friend?

As Burke looked back over Michelle's early statements another discrepancy suddenly jumped out at him. In her first statement she described how on the night she drove John home to discover the body she'd parked a little way past the flat in Vardens Road. But in her second statement she said how there weren't any parking spaces in Vardens Road, so she had turned left to park in a side road. Burke realised she'd made a slip-up. She'd been in Vardens Road twice that day – the first time to murder Alison (when she'd parked in the road itself) and the second time when she drove John home (and had parked around the corner).

Meanwhile, in their interview rooms Michelle and Lisa maintained their silence, and gave no sign they were likely to crack. Lisa, in particular, astonished officers with her icy composure throughout her two days of interviews. They thought she behaved as if she'd been on a terrorist anti-interrogation course: she avoided eye contact with the detectives, usually by staring at the floor or at a spot on the wall, and answered monotonously: 'No comment.' No fear, no tears, no emotion of any kind. Burke knew a decision had to be made, so he made it – he was going to charge the Taylor sisters with murder. He gave the order for Michelle to be brought over to Battersea Police Station from Wandsworth. Burke stood at the desk as Lisa was brought out first from her cell. She showed no emotion. Then Michelle arrived looking nervous and flustered. She was brought down the steps to where Lisa stood waiting. Burke said he thought she was about to burst into tears. However, Lisa turned and gave her a hard look, as if to say, 'Pull yourself together.' Michelle composed herself. They were both charged with murder. Neither said a word, and they were taken back to separate cells.

Burke and the team were elated: no one doubted they'd caught the murderers. For Burke, and the other officers, the sisters' silence since their arrest merely underlined their guilt.

SIXTEEN

Pain Magnet

The Taylor sisters were charged on the Wednesday; John Shaughnessy went in voluntarily to the same police station on the Friday. Burke said he still wasn't sure about John's possible involvement. He told the team to give him a thorough going-over. They had to establish once and for all his innocence – or guilt. The officers looked forward to their task; none of the team thought much of him. Everyone, especially the women, regarded him as shallow and insincere, a bland nonentity with a double life. They all felt his selfish sexual pursuits had, at the very least, started the sequence that ended with the butchering of his young wife. They also didn't like the fact that until then he'd only hinted at his affair with Michelle. They resented the way that, even with his wife lying in the morgue, they'd had to drag every piece of information out of him. But now they were ready to drag it out in a way it hadn't been dragged out before. They knew that under a death-benefit scheme for employees' spouses Barclays Bank was going to pay John a lump sum of nineteen thousand pounds with an annual pension of two thousand pounds for the rest of his life. So, as he was only 29, if he lived until he was 70 he'd have earned around one hundred thousand pounds from his wife's premature death (although the police soon established he'd had no prior knowledge of those provisions). But what had really astonished everyone was John's asking them to return his wife's annual rail card. He wanted to get a refund on the remaining few months' travel Alison would no longer need.

Since the murder John had moved out of his flat to live with Alison's parents. He'd not even had the decency to tell them himself about his affair. They'd only found out from the police shortly before John's grilling. During the first day of his major interrogation, detectives told John that Alison's family now knew what he'd been up to. They left it to him to make his peace with them. Alison's mother was ill – sick with grief – when John went home that night. He went into her bedroom, stood at the end of her bed and said: 'I was winding it down.' That was all: he didn't explain himself further, nor did he apologise, let alone beg forgiveness.

John was interviewed all day Friday – then the following Monday, Tuesday and Wednesday. By the end of that gruelling process, in which he often broke down sobbing, the police had wrung from him a 73-page statement. It contained every detail of his life – from the circumstances of his birth to the sex he'd had with former girlfriends. By the end, he'd convinced the police he'd had nothing to do with his wife's murder.

Burke had talked to my solicitor about the content of John's statement. When I discussed with her what had been said I found myself coming to know John and Alison much better. Until then, both had been one-dimensional characters: John, the womanising Irish charmer with slick good looks; Alison, the naïve and unsuspecting young wife – stock types, not rounded people. But as I read the details of their backgrounds and their life together I could feel for them both, and sympathise with them, in a way I hadn't before.

John's childhood home was in Ballintober, County Roscommon. He was the eighth of eleven children – four brothers and six sisters. His father worked for the local county council. John left technical school at 18 with no formal qualifications. For the next few years he stayed in Roscommon, working as a shop assistant and also in unskilled jobs for the county council and a steel company. He was a religious young man; he'd been an altar boy and later joined a Catholic charitable group called the Knights of Malta. The group had awarded him medals for taking invalids on pilgrimages to the shrine of Lourdes and to the

Vatican in Rome, where he'd once seen the Pope. At one stage he'd even considered becoming a priest. At 23 he moved to England and worked in a Leeds warehouse as a general labourer. A cousin who owned a London florist's invited him to come and work for him. However, after six months John became homesick and returned to Ireland, where he began setting up all-inclusive coach trips to pop concerts. He had a few relationships after leaving school, including one with a local girl which lasted around 18 months. In September 1986 a friend who worked at the Churchill Clinic informed him of a vacancy for a porter. He successfully applied for the post and started working there in October 1986.

Burke said Alison was the sort of girl you'd want your son to bring home. She came from a lovely family – kind, warm, decent people who lived modestly. She was born near Crouch End, north London, to Irish parents in 1969. Her father was a bus driver, her mother a nurse. She had an older sister and two younger brothers. She left her all-girl Catholic school at 16 and, after a few stop-gap jobs, started working as a clerk at Barclays Bank. Although London-born, she loved Ireland and spent her summer holidays there picking fruit, usually staying with relatives in her parents' village of Piltown, County Kilkenny.

Everyone who knew Alison described her as shy, kind and caring. She often went out dancing, but she rarely drank alcohol and never smoked. She liked embroidery, crafts, Irish dancing, television soap operas and reading – John said she read at least a book a week. She was also deeply religious and a regular church-goer. In October 1986 Alison went with a friend to an Irish pub called the Archway Tavern in north London. Her friend struck up a conversation with a handsome Irishman. Alison said hello, introduced herself and then stood quietly sipping her Coke as the other two chatted. At closing time the man said goodbye and left. A few weeks later Alison was back in the Archway Tavern with the same friend. On the way to the ladies she bumped into the young Irishman who'd been chatting to her friend previously. She was surprised he remembered her name. He said his name was John Shaughnessy. That night the three of them went on to a late-drinking pub in nearby Holloway Road. They stayed until around 1.30 a.m. During the evening John and Alison exchanged phone numbers. In the cab home Alison was extremely happy; she told her friend she'd just met the man of her dreams. The romance blossomed, and they began seeing each other every Wednesday and every weekend. He was her first proper boyfriend. John had been surprised to discover she was only 16 (he was 24) but Alison had said: 'Age isn't everything.' John thought she was mature for her age and, although shy, easy to talk to. He said that once you got to know her she was a happy person. At times she had a quick temper, but was always quick to apologise and never held a grudge. John said Alison was very selective with friends. She didn't like people who were bitchy or who talked behind others' backs, although she'd never ignore anyone and got on well with everyone. She was very good with children and enjoyed being with them. After two years of going out they talked about getting engaged. However, John was worried that she hadn't had any real boyfriends before him. He suggested they break up for a time so she could be sure of her feelings for him before making a lifelong commitment. Alison disagreed vehemently. They compromised by agreeing not to see each other so often. They began meeting only once or twice a week instead of the usual three times. But that arrangement only lasted a month before, at Alison's instigation, they returned to the way they'd been. They got engaged in May 1989.

Burke said that around the time John first met Alison he also became aware of Michelle Taylor. She worked in the Churchill Clinic's accounts department. John would pass the time of day with her when he saw her, exchanging pleasantries and idle chat, but he didn't consider her as anything more than a work colleague. In his statement he said he found her to be a pleasant, outgoing person, but not pretty – unlike Alison, who he thought was beautiful. John became responsible for purchasing stock and this job brought him into more regular contact with Michelle. They spoke at least twice a day. When Michelle was admitted to the clinic as a patient to have an operation on her knee, John visited her a few times to ask how she was. Around this time John also attended Michelle's 18th birthday party at her family home where he met her parents and her sister Lisa. He didn't bring Alison with him to the party, although by this time they'd been going out for just over two years and were discussing marriage. Over the next few months John drifted into what he thought was a casual sexual relationship with Michelle. Burke said John couldn't even remember who'd made the first move. They just ended up having sex one day in his room at the clinic. From the dates in John's statement it would seem he started sleeping with Michelle about two months before his engagement to Alison. John said he couldn't remember Michelle's reaction to his announcement that he was getting engaged. He said there certainly hadn't been a row or a scene. This was not Michelle's recollection: she told me – as if the memory had been seared on her brain – that John had taken her out for a cheap meal to break the news to her, and that she'd fled the restaurant in tears. She claimed she hadn't realised John was even going out with Alison, so this news from the man she'd just started sleeping with – and who she also thought was the man of her dreams – had devastated her. She said she then didn't speak to him for several months. John, however, said the clinic's matron threw an engagement party for him in her office; Alison attended. And so did Michelle.

Alison bought John a gold engagement ring with a black stone on which was inscribed a gold 'Playboy' motif. Alison said she wanted to get married in Ireland in the church in Piltown where her parents had got married and where she herself had taken her first Holy Communion. The wedding was booked for June of the following year, 1990. However, some months after the engagement John and Michelle started having sex again. This would usually happen about twice a month in his room in the staff accommodation after the Monday flower-arranging.

Around May 1990, only a month before the wedding, Michelle moved out of her family home and into a room at the clinic. John said Michelle told him she left home because of rows with her father. She claimed he had a drink problem and used to come home and argue with his wife. On at least one occasion, according to Michelle, he'd picked up a kitchen knife and threatened his wife, but Michelle had got between them. She claimed that in the past he'd assaulted both her and his wife. Burke said he found that suggestion hard to believe: his impression was that Mrs Taylor dominated the family. His officers often joked: 'Watch out for Mum!' Even physically, she was significantly larger than her husband. Burke couldn't imagine Derek Taylor threatening her – unless he was very drunk and careless of his own safety. I also couldn't imagine Del threatening Ann – I couldn't see him raising his voice to her, let alone a knife.

In early 1990 Lisa Taylor had also got a job in the Churchill Clinic accounts department. It was her second job after leaving school at 16 with one qualification – grade one in her English oral exam. Her first job had been as a sales assistant in the Muscle and Fitness Pro Shop in Forest Hill. John said he didn't have much contact with Lisa Taylor. He knew that she and Michelle were close, because Michelle often talked about her. Michelle wore around her neck a heart-shaped locket containing mini-photos of them both. She said they'd both had problems at school with teachers and their mother had often had to take time off work to talk to teachers. Lisa lasted less than two months at the Churchill Clinic. Her work was regarded as sub-standard and she had a personality clash with her boss. At first, John liked her, but he grew to dislike her. He didn't like the sort of people she seemed to hang around with and he found her to be cheeky and a know-all.

With Michelle also living in the clinic, John and she now had two rooms in which to have sex. John admitted that, although Michelle did most of the running in the relationship, he initiated sex as often as she did. He said that at no time did he and Michelle ever go out as boyfriend and girlfriend. On the morning of her arrest – while she was still answering police questions – Michelle said that in the first few months of their relationship she'd regarded John and herself as girlfriend and boyfriend. The detectives asked her why, as girlfriend, she hadn't wondered why her boyfriend never saw her at weekends. She didn't have a proper answer. To me, that fact revealed how Michelle had deluded herself about the nature of the relationship – just as she'd deluded herself about ours. John thought they were nothing more than occasional casual lovers. He said the sex was just something that happened. It wasn't planned and he always felt guilty afterwards, telling Michelle they should stop seeing each other, that they should just be good friends and that she should find someone else. However, he said things somehow kept going back to the way they were. Again, I felt reminded of my own relationship with Michelle: it had followed a similar pattern. In our attitudes John and I had treated her in almost exactly the same way – as someone to sleep with every now and again, but as casual friends, not committed partners. Both of us had been ignorant of the deep emotions we were stirring within her; neither of us had any real sense of her fantasies.

John and Michelle also started attending weight-training and aerobics evening classes; Michelle even did tap-dancing classes for a while, but gave them up. John had invited Alison along to the classes, but she hadn't wanted to go. Burke said some people at the classes remembered John introducing Michelle as his wife, but John vehemently denied doing so. For his birthday that year Michelle bought John a gold-plated chain, but he didn't buy anything for hers. In fact, he said he didn't even know when it was. By this time Alison and Michelle had started to get to know each other; John thought they were quite friendly. However, he said that after a while Alison noticed Michelle was always hanging around and had begun to wonder why. In fact, she even started making comments like, 'We know what she's up to.' But in the months preceding the wedding Michelle and Alison seemed to become friendly again – and both John and Alison invited her to the wedding. Michelle organised and paid for John's stag night in a pub near the clinic; she also did the catering for it and invited Lisa along. Most bizarrely, Michelle even joined John and Alison in their hire car for the drive over to Ireland for the wedding. I felt astonished by Michelle's masochism. To watch the man of your dreams getting married to someone else must have been painful enough. So why intensify the pain by spending perhaps twelve hours stuck in a car with the happy couple? Twelve hours of watching their happiness up close as they drive towards their joyful union. Michelle was a pain magnet.

John described his wedding day as the happiest in his life. Almost exactly one year later the same church would be the venue for Alison's funeral. In his statement John said that on the night before his wedding Michelle had joined him in his hotel room. There were two single beds: she lay on one, he on the other. They chatted for a while and she fell asleep, but woke up and went to her own room. He was adamant they hadn't had sex. Michelle, however, said at her trial: 'I stayed there the night. We slept together.'

The newlyweds returned to London to live in John's room at the clinic while they looked for a place of their own. They found that Michelle had cleaned and tidied the room – and even decorated it with balloons and good-luck messages. Michelle also invited them to dinner with her family. John remembered sitting down at the table with Mr and Mrs Taylor, Michelle and her youngest sister. Burke said that previously Alison had been out of sight, popping into the clinic occasionally, but living most of the time with her parents on the opposite side of London. Her absence must have eased the burden on Michelle's mind. But now the mistress had to watch the wife taking up residency in John's room. Michelle started dropping in on them occasionally to watch television. However, if Michelle thought she'd lost John, her hopes of holding on to him in some way received a boost when less than two months after his wedding he started having sex with her again. According to John, they continued having sex about once a fortnight, usually on Monday nights, until three weeks before the murder. Burke said John claimed to have tried several times to tell Michelle the sex had to stop, but that they could still be friends. John said they occasionally argued about this, because Michelle didn't seem to grasp what he was trying to say. However, at other times she'd agree with him. Then, after a short while, things would somehow return to the way they'd been. He remembered telling her one night that he loved her, but he said he'd been drinking and didn't mean it. He said he loved Alison but only 'cared' for Michelle, who knew he would never leave his wife. Once again I felt John could have been describing my own former relationship with Michelle.

John and Alison settled down into a happy married life. They would watch American football at Wembley Stadium and go to pop concerts and the cinema. They spent a bank holiday weekend in Jersey and also visited Leeds Castle in Kent. But Michelle was never far away; she tried continually to weave herself into their lives. Occasionally she went for a drink with the Shaughnessys, and one time they all went for a curry at the Imperial Tandoori opposite Kennington Police Station. John remembered Alison and Michelle going for a drink together perhaps twice, but by October 1990 they only saw each other rarely, and John felt their friendship was cooling. In the seven months leading up to the murder John noticed an atmosphere between Alison and Michelle on the occasions the three came together. He said he knew they didn't like each other, although nothing to that effect was said. John's interpretation was that they didn't really have anything in common (apart from him, he failed to add). Sometimes John would tell Alison certain things Michelle had done or said. Alison wouldn't say anything, but even John could tell she wasn't happy about Michelle's prominent presence in his life. One time Alison found some cards Michelle had sent John: she tore them up and put them in the bin. But, for all that, John told detectives he was sure his wife hadn't suspected the full extent of his relationship with Michelle. He claimed he'd even considered getting it 'off his chest' by telling Alison about his affair.

Burke said Michelle had clearly expressed her torment in her diary. He said that after the appeal some newspapers had suggested Michelle's words of hatred for Alison had been ripped out of the context of an otherwise innocent teenage diary. This was not the case. In her diary she recorded the disturbing depths of her anguish. Most interestingly, the entries covered the six-month period when Michelle had to endure the sight of her rival living in John's room. Burke said you could clearly trace the development of Michelle's feelings as they moved from despair to anger and hatred. She'd poured her heart out to her diary because common sense would have told her there was no one else to confide in. The only advice those closest to her would have offered was to forget John and to find a man of her own. But for Michelle that would have been advice she didn't want to hear. For her, there was no man other than John.

On 1 October 1990, eight months before the murder, John led Michelle into the gardener's shed in the grounds of the clinic. There, among the potting plants and the lawnmower, he had sex with her. Afterwards she wrote how she felt used and degraded, sick with herself. She didn't have the strength to refuse John's advances, although in her mind she desperately wanted to. She knew he was using her, but she wanted to believe he loved her. They made love again four days later. On 7 October her desperation and pain filled that day's entry. She wrote how she loved him being with her for a long time, how all she really wanted was for him to sleep the night so she could have him to hold. Instead, she had to sleep alone knowing the man of her dreams was fulfilling another woman's dreams only yards from her bed. She often asked him to go away with her for the weekend, but he always refused. On 15 October John had sex with Michelle again. A few days later the couple had sex in Michelle's room. On 18 October Michelle said she was writing her entry in tears. She described the incident that had made her reach for the hankies: John had a bad head at work, so she got him a bacon sandwich. Later, when she knocked on his door to make sure he was okay, she entered to find him in bed with Alison. She said she felt used. On another occasion she glared at John after watching him kiss and cuddle Alison; she recorded how only minutes earlier he'd been trying to kiss her in the shed. The diary showed what an emotional wreck she was: one day feeling sorry for herself, the next consumed with hatred. She wanted respect from John; she wanted to be wanted by him. In her desperation she tried to make him chase her. She thought if she flirted with other men she might make him jealous. She hoped he might realise he could lose her and come rushing back. Unfortunately for her, John couldn't have cared less what she did, so long as she was still there for the occasional rushed encounter. And worse – he actually encouraged her to forget about him and to find a man of her own. In fact, she subsequently went out with another staff member for four months (January to April 1991), but wouldn't have sex with him. Michelle tried to convince herself John didn't mean it, but entries in her diary showed she knew in her heart she was losing her already-weak grip on the man she loved.

On 31 October John had sex with Michelle in his own room on the bed he shared with his wife. Michelle wrote that she loved him, but she asked herself what she had to show for it. She then answered her own question: memories was all she had. It was as if she was finally accepting the situation, painful as it was. But such moments of lucidity were rare in Michelle's tortured mind. Before long she was thinking of how she could change the situation, and have for herself the man whose love she craved.

On 2 November she wrote about her dream solution for Alison, 'the unwashed bitch'. On 6 November John tried to seduce Michelle but she refused his advances. She said she refused because it would have been Alison's birthday after midnight. She couldn't understand how John could tell Alison he loved her, yet have sex with someone else. Michelle had often heard John telling Alison he loved her, because – unknown to them – she was privy to some of their most intimate moments. She'd sneakily found a way of eavesdropping on them. Her friend JJ's room was next to John's, and Michelle had a key. Occasionally, Michelle would press her ear against the thin wall to listen intently to the cooing of the lovebirds. Then she'd record bitterly in her diary what she'd heard. More anguish, more agony, more pain. I felt cold as I imagined the bitterness and resentment stewing up inside her. On 7 November she wrote down all the birthday presents John had bought for Alison. She also wrote how she had listened to John's singing 'Happy Birthday' to Alison. She heard him tell her he loved her and ask her if she loved him. Michelle's ears had been filled with the sounds of Alison's laughter and delight. In her diary Michelle wrote the word 'sick' several times. I could imagine how those sounds of happiness must have torn through her, especially as her own birthday was only five days away. She must have known that John wouldn't be buying her a present, or singing her 'Happy Birthday' as she lay in his arms. The most she could expect from him was a card, but even that was unlikely. In her diary entry for her own birthday she wrote that John hadn't bought her anything. She added that that showed her something.

Burke said Michelle made sure Alison didn't have another birthday.

SEVENTEEN

The Perfect Wife

John may not have celebrated Michelle's birthday, but a month later she was eagerly on hand to celebrate his. On 7 December she went out with him and Alison to mark his 29th. Afterwards, while Alison waited for her husband in their room, John tried to have sex with Michelle. He started to undress her, but she said no. When she refused, John became annoyed. She knew now she had a way of getting at him. More importantly, these attempts by John to have sex with her gave her fresh hope. They told her he still wanted her – needed her, even. As always, she was deluding herself.

She tried to dig herself deeper into his life. At the wedding six months earlier she'd met John's niece, 18-year-old Edel Slattery. Edel was very close to Alison. John decided to spend Christmas 1990 in Ireland with his wife. They were surprised when Michelle suddenly announced that she too would be spending a few days in Ireland at the same time. She told them she was going to stay with Edel, the daughter of John's sister, in Loughrea, County Galway. She knew John would be dropping in to offer the season's greetings. John assumed the two had been writing to each other and that Edel had invited Michelle over. The Shaughnessys were together for most of their time in Ireland, but towards the end they decided to visit some of their respective relatives separately. So while Alison stayed in Kilkenny, John went to Loughrea to visit Edel and other relatives. Michelle was waiting for him. John told police they saw each other briefly before Michelle returned to London on Christmas Eve. Not only had she made a point of befriending John's sister's daughter, who she knew was also close to Alison, but she'd then managed to manoeuvre things so she could spend time on holiday with John without Alison being there. He'd always refused her requests for weekends away, so this was as close as she could get to what she wanted. It wasn't much, but for lovesick Michelle it must have meant a lot.

Shortly after returning from their Christmas break John and Alison moved into the flat in Vardens Road. Michelle used her car to help them move, and over the next few weeks brought over their belongings in dribs and drabs. One night, when Alison had gone to stay with her parents, Michelle dropped off some more stuff. Then she asked if she could stay the night. John claimed he made her sleep on the couch, even though she asked to sleep in his bed. He said he didn't inform Alison of his hospitality. Shortly afterwards Alison herself invited Michelle to the flat for a meal to thank her for her help with the move. Michelle said to me, and to the jury, that she'd hated John since the end of 1990, yet there she was jetting off at Christmas to where she knew he'd be, then working as an unpaid removals person in January, before finally trying to sleep with him in his new flat. A strange way to express hatred.

According to John, the illicit sex with Michelle continued to happen once a fortnight, usually on Mondays after the flower-arranging. John told police he never paid Michelle anything for her two hours' work, whereas Michelle made a point of saying in her statement that John sometimes gave her five pounds. In Burke's eyes Michelle had clearly been trying to draw attention away from the fact she was so besotted she'd do two hours' unpaid work just to be with him. But whether she received payment or not she'd still, through her own choice, spend two hours with the man she claimed she hated and then drive him home. After flowers on 13 May – three weeks before Alison's murder – John said he and Michelle had sex for the last time. Michelle claimed they'd stopped having sex at the end of 1990, more than six months earlier. Then he delivered a blow: he said he was giving up the flower-arranging to spend more time with Alison. He told police that part of his motivation was his desire to stop the affair, because by then their brief encounters only occurred on Monday evenings.

In that same month before the murder John and Alison discovered that Michelle had invited Edel Slattery to London. John said Alison wasn't at all happy. She told him that if Edel came over she should stay either with them or with her parents. John rang Edel and asked her to stay with them. Edel then wrote to Alison and said that of course she'd be staying with them and that Michelle must have been joking if she thought she'd stay with her. Another snub for Michelle. However, that little disappointment was nothing compared to the blow she was about to suffer. She'd heard worrying rumours around the clinic. She asked John about them. And he confirmed they were true. He was planning to return to Ireland with Alison to start a family.

In Burke's mind this news sealed Alison's fate. Not only was John walking away from those Monday sessions – Michelle's sole remaining quality time alone with him – he was walking completely out of her life. And who would be holding his hand as he strode off into his bright future? Alison. Alison would be taking him away to play happy families. Burke said John had signed his wife's death warrant, because at that point Michelle's fantasy world must have collapsed. Until then, she'd been able to deny the reality that she was simply a bit on the side. Until then, she'd been able to maintain her conviction that John loved her and in his heart wanted to be with her. To her mind, the fact that he kept wanting sex with her must have proved it. After all, if he was genuinely happy with Alison, why would he be seeking sex elsewhere? Yet now he'd provided Michelle with incontrovertible proof that he loved Alison and wanted to be with her. But perhaps Michelle's delusions didn't collapse that easily. Perhaps she thought that John did still truly love her and did still truly want to be with her. She'd said to JJ before the wedding that John had told her he didn't want to marry Alison; she'd also told another work colleague that the marriage wouldn't last because Alison wasn't the right girl for John. So perhaps now, with the planned move to Ireland, Alison was thwarting John's true desires. It was Alison, 'the unwashed bitch', who was making sure John would never be with her. Michelle's 'dream solution' had been for Alison to disappear so she could give everything to the man she loved. But Alison was not going to disappear – John was.

Now her dream solution would never happen – unless she herself acted to turn her dream into reality.

The way I saw it, killing Alison would have struck Michelle as a dream solution in several ways: first, it would punish Alison for coming between her and the man of her dreams; second, it would thereby leave John free to have her as his ideal partner; and third, it would at the same time punish John for the way he'd treated her. She wanted John to feel the pain she felt. She wanted him to know what it was like to have someone you loved snatched away from you. By killing Alison, Michelle would break John's heart – even though she must have felt sure she'd be the one to mend it.

Alison spent most of her last weekend alive at her parents' home. She and John arrived there on Saturday and stayed the night. They headed back to Battersea early Sunday evening, stopping for something to eat in McDonald's at Victoria on the way home. John said they made love and had a bath, then around 9 p.m. they went to a local pub, where they stayed until closing time. Returning to the flat, they watched television for a bit before going to bed around midnight. The next morning they followed their usual routine: Alison got up first around 7.30 a.m., John got up 20 minutes later after she'd finished in the bathroom. While he was shaving she went downstairs to get the milk from the front door. They got dressed together. Alison put on a floral patterned skirt, a black sweatshirt, a blue denim jacket and black shoes. They had a quick breakfast of a bowl of cereal and a cup of tea, then left the house together around 8.20 a.m. to walk to nearby Clapham Junction Station. John was carrying his black briefcase, Alison her black box-handbag. The post hadn't yet arrived. They didn't have long to wait for a train. They managed to get seats next to each other, but on the 15-minute journey to Waterloo they didn't speak. Outside Waterloo Alison grabbed one of the free magazines being handed out, then spotted her bus. She gave John a quick kiss before running to the stop where the bus had already started taking on passengers. John walked in the same direction and passed her as she waited in the queue. He said: 'I'll see you later.'

She said: 'I'll ring you.'

It was the last time he saw her alive.

John had a busy day. Michelle phoned him around 3 p.m. to say she wasn't sure if she'd be able to do the flowers with him that night. She said she had to pick something up from her mum's house; she didn't mention anything about shopping in Bromley with Lisa. She said if she got back in time she'd do them. John was busy when Alison phoned from work around 4.30 p.m., so he didn't speak to her for long. He said she sounded her normal self. She mentioned some minor task she had to do on the way home, but he couldn't remember what it was. He said: 'I'll see you later.'

Alison said: 'Take care. Mind yourself.' It was the last time they ever spoke.

Around 6 p.m., John picked up the flowers as usual from Buster Edwards's stall and took them back to the clinic. As he was sorting them out Michelle arrived at about 6.20 p.m. He joked that he'd have to sack her for poor time-keeping. They chatted about things in general as they did the flowers. Michelle seemed her normal self. About an hour later Michelle said she had to see Lisa about something. She returned around 7.45 p.m. They started to tidy up. John said Michelle only started driving him home after the flower-arranging about three months before the murder. Before then, he used to get the train home. He said that 75 per cent of the time Michelle just dropped him off and left. He could only remember her coming into the flat perhaps twice. Burke said this clearly contradicted Michelle's claim in one of her statements that it was 'quite normal' for her to go into the flat after dropping him off. Burke said Michelle hadn't wanted the police to be suspicious about her being there when the body was found.

When they'd finished tidying-up Michelle said she'd see John at her car at 8.15 p.m. to drive him home. Michelle didn't mention to John that she had a stomach upset or that she needed to use the toilet. Before she left, John gave her a small bunch of flowers to put in her car. They weren't for her – John told her they were for Alison. I felt a chill as I imagined Michelle placing the flowers on the car's back seat. She knew the only flowers Alison would now be getting were the ones for her grave.

As they drove to the flat John thought Michelle was quieter than normal. She hardly said a word. In a letter to me, though, Michelle claimed they'd argued. According to her, John asked her why she always had Lisa or Tracey staying with her on Mondays. She also claimed he said she'd changed towards him and that he thought she had someone else. They'd then argued, but she couldn't remember what had been said. Obviously, she'd been trying to convey to me a sense of the distance between herself and John, who, by this stage, she supposedly hated. She'd also claimed (and this was important for her defence) that she'd stopped having sex with John at the end of 1990. She'd written to me of how she'd try to have Tracey or Lisa in her room if she thought John was going to be around – her strategy for deterring his unwanted sexual advances. I may be warped, but if someone I 'hated' (and with whom I didn't like to be alone) asked me to work two hours for free (alone with them) and to give them a lift home at my own expense (again, alone with them) and to take two large flowerpots back to the workplace to save them the trouble, I think I'd probably decline their requests.

After entering the flat, John found Alison's body at the top of the stairs. Burke said John and Michelle's descriptions of what happened next tallied in all significant respects.

In Alison's bloodstained handbag the police found an unfinished handwritten letter to Edel Slattery:

> I'm glad you are coming over and staying with us. I could give you pages on Michelle, but I would rather wait until I see you. Don't let on to anyone, especially Michelle, of this. At Laura's confirmation, when everyone was saying what a nice girl she is, I felt like shouting out: 'No she isn't, you don't know her at all.' Don't tell anyone this, I will fill you in on the whole story when I see you. John told me Michelle is over [to Ireland] for a weekend in a couple of weeks' time. I'm saying nothing until she does. God I'm such a bitch. I'm starting again. I must stop. I'm starting to rave now, aren't I?

As the murder hunt began the police drove John and Michelle to

Battersea Police Station for questioning. Both made brief written statements. Around 3.30 a.m. the police took them back to Michelle's car. Mrs Taylor had joined them at the police station. The Taylors offered to drive John to Alison's parents in north London, but he declined, saying it was too late. Instead, he asked if he could spend the night with the Taylors at Forest Hill. Michelle readily agreed. John sat up all night talking to Mrs Taylor in the front room. Michelle fell asleep in a nearby chair.

A memorial service was held for Alison at St George's Cathedral in Southwark. Michelle, Lisa and their mother attended. Another service took place at St Peter-in-Chains Church in Stroud Green, north London. It had been Alison's parish church when she was growing up. Again, Michelle, Lisa and Mrs Taylor attended. Michelle cried as she joined mourners filing past the coffin. Lisa walked behind her, stony-faced. Both dipped their fingers in a bowl of holy water and flicked small drops onto the coffin. Michelle cried throughout the service and hugged Alison's relatives afterwards. Alison's brother remembered her saying: 'It's such a terrible shame.' The following day Alison's remains were taken to Ireland for burial.

A week after the funeral John, who was staying with Alison's aunt in Kilkenny, received a message. Michelle had telephoned to say she was in Ireland and was staying with Edel Slattery. One of John's brothers was getting married the following week. John learned that his brother had verbally invited Michelle to the wedding. However, he didn't have to wait until then to see Michelle, because when he drove up to his brother's house in Roscommon she was already there waiting for him. Despite the invitation, Michelle told John she'd been planning to return to London a week before the wedding, but there'd been a problem with her ticket, so she had to delay her stay in Ireland until it was sorted out. Fortunately, she said, this meant she would be able to attend the wedding with John. Over the next few days they stayed with various relatives, sleeping in separate bedrooms.

On Saturday, 6 July, Michelle travelled with John to the wedding. At the hotel reception John had a bit to drink, but wasn't drunk. Before

Alison's murder a room for the wedding night had been booked at the hotel for John and his wife. It had a double bed. During the reception Michelle approached John and told him there were no vacant rooms in the hotel. Could she put her suitcases in his room while she sorted something out? Her cases were securely locked in his car, but he gave her the keys to the car – and his room. After putting her cases in his room she went back downstairs. As she gave John the key back she asked him if she could stay in his room that night as all the other rooms had been taken. John told police he wasn't keen on the idea, but he didn't want to start an argument. He said she could stay, but only as somewhere to spend the night.

Michelle went up to the room around two to three hours before him. John didn't get there until about 4 a.m. He thought Michelle would be fast asleep, but when he opened the door he saw the bedside light was on. Michelle was in bed, awake and wearing nothing on top. John undressed down to his underpants and got into bed. He said he turned his back to Michelle and prepared to drop off to sleep. Michelle had other plans. She told him she wanted sex; John said he just wanted to sleep. Around 7 a.m. he was awoken by Michelle's fondling his genitals. He became aroused and she removed his underpants. Then, naked, she got on top of him. She inserted his penis inside herself and they started to have intercourse. But John told her it wasn't right and pulled himself out of her. He said she dismounted, got back on her side of the bed and huffed. As he drifted back to sleep he heard her getting up, dressing and leaving his room. At her trial Michelle claimed John had tried to seduce her and she had rebuffed his advances, telling him he was confused and needed to sort himself out.

When John got up around 11 a.m. he saw Michelle in the hotel foyer with a few of his nieces. Later on that day Michelle caught the coach to Dublin airport and flew back to London, the problem with her return ticket apparently sorted out. Michelle had often said she had hated John up to six months before the murder, that she tried to make sure he wouldn't be able to get her by herself, and so on. But, yet again, as I read John's account I could see how her behaviour throughout 1991 – from the flower-arranging to the evening classes – told a different story. Her behaviour in Ireland capped everything. Burke added a final twist: his officers had taken a statement from the friend, Patricia Keane, who'd flown over to Ireland with Michelle. Their holiday had been booked several weeks before the murder. At the time of booking, the plan had been for Michelle to stay with Patricia's relatives. But when they'd got to Ireland Michelle had headed off to John's niece, Edel Slattery, leaving Patricia to go her own way. Patricia had still expected to fly back to London with Michelle using their pre-booked tickets. However, Michelle hadn't turned up at the airport and Patricia had flown back alone.

John returned to London to live with Alison's parents. When he saw Michelle at work he just said hello; they were never again alone together. Michelle phoned him twice before her arrest. The first time she phoned him was after her police interview on 24 July. She told him she wasn't happy about some of the things she'd been asked; she felt she was being accused. She phoned him again about a week later and said she didn't want him to give her the cold shoulder; she wanted them to be friends. By this stage John had got wind of the police's suspicions about Michelle. He remembered saying to her: 'God help the person or persons responsible for this.' He also said: 'You wouldn't hurt Alison, would you?'

Michelle said: 'You don't think I had anything to do with this?'

John didn't answer, leaving her to do the talking. The last thing Michelle said was: 'I hope they catch those responsible. That was a poor innocent person.'

Burke said John was genuinely astonished when they presented him with Michelle's diary. He'd been unaware of how obsessed with him she'd been. He was shocked to read her description of Alison as an 'unwashed bitch'. He tried to explain it to police by saying Michelle was very quick-tempered and, when she lost her temper, she could do or say anything without thinking. He said he found Michelle's comments about her wanting Alison to disappear frightening and disturbing. He had no idea of the depth of her feelings towards him or Alison.

Reading through Burke's detailed account of the evidence I realised that every part of it fitted in with the confession Michelle had made to me. Her and Lisa's lies glared at me from every page. I felt as guilty as they were.

Burke said that after John had undergone his four days of grilling, the team's earlier hostility to him had softened somewhat. Most officers felt sorry for him, although several still regarded him as a loathsome shit. In his statement John said he'd loved Alison dearly and that she was his best friend. They had rows but they never lasted long, and they always made up quickly. He said that, without doubt, his days with her had been the happiest of his life. He regarded their relationship as perfect in every way, both in the way they got on together and on the physical side.

To him, he said, she'd been the perfect wife. Sadly for Alison, he'd been a less than perfect husband.

EIGHTEEN

Beyond Reasonable Doubt

By the time of the sisters' trial the police felt confident they'd constructed a powerful case against them. Burke said that although the evidence was largely circumstantial, it was compelling none the less. He'd felt sure the prosecution could prove to a jury beyond reasonable doubt that the Taylor sisters had murdered Alison.

Once the sisters had been charged, the police continued building up evidence against them. Some interesting material came from investigating their martial arts background. Lisa had admitted they'd trained with weapons, including a small metal dagger-type knife, at their ju-jitsu clubs. At their first club in Brockley, Michelle had developed crushes on two married men, one of whom was her instructor. The wife of the other man remembered an incident between herself and the sisters in 1988. The woman had been trying to enter the building with her daughter. Michelle and Lisa were in her way. She asked them if they were going in. Michelle's response was to snarl: 'I'll kill you, you fucking cunt.' The sisters then followed the woman into the club in a way which frightened her. She saw the sisters six months later in a newsagent's in Forest Hill. They didn't say anything to her, but behaved in an extremely threatening way. The instructor said both sisters were competent at ju-jitsu. He described Michelle in combat as being aggressive, but in control. Eventually, after a number of incidents on and off the mats the instructor asked the sisters to leave. Burke thought the sisters' martial arts training was relevant because of the bruise found under Alison's nose and above her lip. It was the sort of bruise that had been caused by some sort of assault move, perhaps a sideways chop of the hand, on one of the body's weak points. Burke thought it showed evidence of an attacker with some sort of combat training. The blow would have forced back Alison's head to expose her neck, which was then stabbed several times, one of the blows piercing the windpipe.

An employee at the clinic said that in 1989 Michelle had described to her in detail how she'd broken someone's arm. John Shaughnessy also mentioned a story from 1989: Michelle had phoned him at work to tell him she'd been involved in a fight in a pub car park. According to her, three black girls (one with a knife) had approached her. Michelle said she'd used a ju-jitsu kick to knock one of the girls flying off her feet. The girl had then lain on the ground screaming that her leg was broken. Burke said that, at the very least, those stories would have shown Michelle's capacity for violence and her history of aggressive behaviour. This evidence would have countered the impression of Christian innocence she tried to convey as she sat in the dock clutching her Bible and crucifix. However, the judge ruled as inadmissible all references to the sisters' martial arts training. He thought such evidence might prejudice the jury against them.

There were other things that didn't come out at the trial. The police took statements from two of Alison's closest friends (one of them her cousin). Both remembered Alison saying she disliked Michelle. Alison had lived with John for six months at the clinic. During that time some of her clothes in the washroom had been damaged or stolen. She confided to her friends that she suspected Michelle was responsible.

The police worked hard to disprove the sisters' Bromley shopping alibi. The Taylors said they'd visited seven or eight clothing shops, yet couldn't name them or even describe one shop assistant to whom they might have spoken and who might have corroborated their story. The only shop they could both name was The Body Shop. Burke said the sisters hadn't dared name the shops, because they feared the police could have got film from their closed-circuit cameras. The Body Shop didn't have cameras. Burke said there weren't many women who, after shopping for clothes, wouldn't later be able to name a good few of the seven or eight shops they'd visited. Michelle called two witnesses to back up the Bromley shopping story. Both were friends of Lisa. The first was Tessa Jordan, who said Lisa had asked her to go shopping with them. She'd planned to do so, but on that afternoon her mother said she wanted her to deliver some advertising cards door-to-door for her father's mini-cab office. Tessa further stated that Lisa had phoned her – apparently from Michelle's room at the clinic – at 5.30 p.m. that day to say they hadn't bought anything in Bromley. Tessa's mother, a close friend of the Taylor family, confirmed her daughter had sought permission to go to Bromley that afternoon. She also said Tessa had received a phone call from Lisa around 5.30 p.m.

The second witness was a man called Philip Beeson, another friend of Lisa. The police had wanted to speak to Philip as soon as the sisters mentioned him in statements. The Taylors claimed they'd met him outside McDonald's in Bromley. However, they couldn't supply any details about him (surname, address, phone number) and the first time the police encountered him was when he popped up a year later as a defence witness. In her statement Lisa said she only knew Philip vaguely to say hello to. She described him as a dreadlocked Rastafarian with a small beard and a woolly hat. She said he was driving past in his car when they saw him. He shouted to ask them what they were doing in Bromley. She added that she knew this was about 4.20 p.m., because she'd looked at her watch. Michelle, however, said Philip had stood on the pavement when he spoke to them. She had a different recollection of what he'd said, but, like Lisa, she remembered the time as being about 4.20 p.m. The police questioned Lisa about this after her arrest. The interviewing officer put to her:

> You can't remember what he said; you can't remember an awful lot
> about Philip, but strangely enough you can remember the time. You
> saw Philip and thought, 'I'd better look at my watch just to confirm
> I've seen Philip at twenty past four.' It's not the sort of thing a normal

person does, is it? You see people in the street, you say hello and salute them, you don't go round looking at your watch every two minutes to say, 'Well, I saw so-and-so at twenty past four. I'll make a note of that or I'll remember that.'

Now bearing in mind that your statement was taken on 24 July and we are talking about an incident that occurred on 3 June, which in fact is six to seven weeks after the incident – say six weeks – and yet six weeks later, Lisa, you can remember what time you saw a man called Philip in Bromley. You can't remember what was said, you can't remember the shops you visited for the dress, but you can remember what time you spoke to Philip. Don't you find that rather strange?

Lisa's response to that question (as to almost all other questions) was: 'No comment.' She maintained her silence throughout the trial, refusing to go into the witness box. Burke said that if the sisters had been innocent they would surely have gone out of their way to help the police track Philip down. Even if they hadn't wanted to answer any other questions, they should have seen Philip as their saviour – if he could have verified their alibi he would have set them free. In their statements they'd indicated he was the vaguest of Lisa's vague acquaintances. But JJ Tapp remembered him visiting Lisa at least twice when she worked at the clinic. Then the police found a guest list for JJ's forthcoming party. Among the names were two that were linked together: 'Lisa and Philip'. In the witness box Philip was of very little use to the sisters. He confirmed having a brief accidental meeting with them outside McDonald's in Bromley in 1991, but he couldn't even remember the month, let alone the day.

Burke said that, apart from their supposed shopping trip to Bromley, the other part of their defence depended crucially on whether the jury believed the Taylors or their former friend JJ. Burke felt JJ was impressive in the witness box: under intense cross-examination she stuck by her story. The defence tried to suggest the police had bullied her into changing her story. However, her interview had been taped and on the tape JJ could be heard talking freely and naturally without being browbeaten by the interviewer. In court she remained adamant that she hadn't got back to her room in the clinic until about 7.15 p.m. Her mother and two sisters also swore statements that she was with them between 5 and 7 p.m. The jury obviously realised the cardinal importance of her story. During their deliberations they sent out two notes asking for further clarification about her evidence.

Burke said mistakes had been made in the initial investigation which had undermined their chances of getting forensic evidence. He was disappointed that on the night of the murder the police hadn't stood back from the horror and treated the finders of the body with more detachment. He said, at the very least, the police should have taken Michelle's car away for forensic examination. If they'd been more rigorous in checking out her alibi they might even have ended up in JJ's room, and so found the plastic bin-liner. Unfortunately, it was almost two months before they searched Michelle and Lisa's property, so there was plenty of time to clean up. When the search did take place, the police found what Burke was sure was the murder weapon hidden in a mop among Del Taylor's work gear. It was a metal ruler that had been sharpened to a point. The police carried out forensic tests on it, but could only find traces of industrial cleaning fluid. Del Taylor said he kept the knife as anti-mugger protection. He was charged with possessing an offensive weapon. A few months before his daughters' trial he appeared in court on that charge, pleaded guilty and was fined one hundred pounds.

The police's failings on the night of the murder meant their forensic expert had to go into the witness box to say there was no scientific evidence to connect the sisters with the murder. The expert said he'd taken samples of hair from the scalps of both Michelle and Lisa, but had been unable to match them with any trace evidence at the scene of the crime. He'd also examined a number of items of footwear from the girls' wardrobe, but had found no traces of blood on the soles. However, he also pointed out that, despite the frenzied stabbing, there'd been very little blood at the scene. He assumed that most of the bleeding had been internal: the external bleeding had been largely absorbed by the several layers of clothing worn by Alison.

But on the forensics front the sisters still had to explain why Lisa's fingerprints had been found on the door of a flat she'd claimed never to have visited. Burke said the prosecution had no advance warning of Michelle's defence – otherwise they could have exposed it as a lie. Michelle said in court that, at John's suggestion, she and Lisa had gone round to the flat on a Saturday about three weeks before the murder to clean the windows. John wasn't there, but Alison was. Michelle claimed Alison had been a bit puzzled to see them because John hadn't told her they were coming. Alison said she could do the windows herself. Then, according to Michelle, she invited them in and showed them her photo-album. When asked why she had lied about Lisa's ever being there, she claimed she'd wanted to shield her younger sister; she felt bad about being the cause of all the oppressive police attention and just wanted to leave Lisa out of it.

But, as Burke said, if she'd wanted to leave her sister out of it, surely telling the truth would have been the best way? Furthermore, how could Michelle possibly leave Lisa out of it if she was putting her forward as part of her shopping alibi? John Shaughnessy said Michelle's story was fantasy. He categorically denied he'd ever asked Michelle to clean his windows and described as ridiculous the idea that Alison would have invited them in and shown them her photo-album. I felt that 'ridiculous' was certainly the best word to describe that whole cock-and-bull story. By Michelle's own account, she hated John by this stage. Yet, on a Saturday, when she would have been working with her father until noon, and working at the clinic from three, she supposedly headed off – in the break between her two jobs – to clean the windows of a man she hated. Burke felt the story was so implausible that the jury would see it as a pathetic and transparent lie. After the trial, Alison's family proved with photos that she and John had in fact been in Ireland for a christening on the weekend Michelle claimed she'd gone to clean the windows.

Burke said the defence made good use of evidence which could have put doubt in jurors' minds. The house at Vardens Road had two other occupants: 61-year-old Michael Casey and 72-year-old Christina

Wright. Both were too ill to give evidence, but their statements were read to the court. Mrs Wright said Alison had come home between 6 and 6.30 p.m. She claimed she was certain of the time because she was watching the *Six O'Clock News* on BBC1, which had not yet finished. She accurately described the clothes Alison was wearing. She was definite that Alison had arrived alone. She put the arrival home of Mr Casey that evening at about 5.30 p.m. If her evidence was right as to when Alison came home, then Michelle and Lisa couldn't have killed her. Mr Casey said he arrived home between 5.40 and 5.45 p.m. As far as he recalled, the mortise lock on the front door was on. The defence used these statements together with John Shaughnessy's memory that when Alison had phoned him that afternoon she'd mentioned she had something minor to do on the way home. The defence said that, taken together, this evidence suggested Alison couldn't have arrived home within the necessary timescale for her to have been murdered by the Taylors. However, Burke thought Mrs Wright was mistaken in her belief that she'd been watching the BBC news. He was sure she'd been watching ITV's news at 5.40 p.m. (which ended at 6 p.m.). There was a potential witness who could have backed up his belief, but in the hectic atmosphere of the inquiry Burke failed to spot her. He said he blamed himself for missing the piece of paper that could have undermined Mrs Wright's evidence. Mrs Wright said a friend had visited her that day and that this friend left at 6 p.m. The police visited the friend and a note was made of what she said. However, its importance was overlooked. The friend was adamant that she'd left Mrs Wright at 5.30, not 6 p.m., and that Mrs Wright had the television switched to ITV, not BBC, at that time. At the very least, if Mrs Wright was wrong about the time her friend had left the house, then she could equally have been wrong about the time Alison had allegedly arrived home. Moreover, John Shaughnessy said that, more often than not, his wife arrived home between 5.30 and 5.45 p.m.

Despite everything, when the jury went out to deliberate, Burke was confident they'd convict the sisters. The jury's unanimous verdict delighted him and the team. A few officers had become close to Alison's family; they felt pride in having been part of the team that had got justice for them.

Burke assumed the sisters would launch an appeal, but he had no fears. After all, what could possibly go wrong?

NINETEEN

A Game of Chance

Until two days before the appeal hearing Burke had no inkling of the bombshell that was about to explode. The appeal was due to start on Thursday, 10 June 1993. On the Monday of that week Burke and three members of his team had a meeting with the prosecution barrister from the original trial, John Nutting QC. He was confident they'd win the appeal and anticipated no serious problems. But next day everything changed.

In the early evening of Tuesday, Burke was at Earlsfield Police Station when he got a message to ring Nutting at home. He did so immediately and found a terse voice on the other end of the line. Nutting got straight to the point: he wanted Burke to go to his chambers the next day to explain why he'd deliberately withheld a document. Burke was astonished. He didn't know what he was talking about. Nutting explained that the Taylors' defence team had found a document which had not been disclosed to them at the original trial. Nutting refused to discuss the matter over the phone. Instead, a conference was arranged for the next day.

Burke discovered that the document related to Doctor Michael Unsworth-White, a near neighbour of the Shaughnessys in Vardens Road. At the trial he'd given evidence that he'd seen two white girls, one with a pony-tail, running down the steps of Alison's flat at the relevant time. The initial brief 'message' written by the female officer who'd spoken to him noted that at first he said one of the two girls 'may have been black'. She also noted that he'd immediately retracted the suggestion and said both girls were definitely white. The next day another officer took a full statement from him in which he again stated categorically that both girls were white. Burke said that the initial 'message' hadn't been disclosed to the defence at the original trial, because it hadn't been regarded as relevant.

Burke had disclosed everything required of him by the guidelines operating at the time – the Attorney General's Guidelines for the Disclosure of 'Unused Material' for the Defence (1982). However, shortly before the Taylors' trial, a woman called Judith Ward, who'd been convicted for an IRA bombing, had had her conviction overturned on appeal. One of the key issues had been the police's non-disclosure of certain documents to the defence. Burke had known that as a result of that case the guidelines on disclosure were about to change, so before the Taylors' trial he'd contacted the Crown Prosecution Service (CPS) to ascertain the current position. He was told to follow the 1982 guidelines. He did so. Altogether there were around 1,500 other pieces of paper that weren't disclosed to the defence.

Burke hadn't even regarded the doctor as an especially significant witness – he'd failed to pick out either of the sisters at an identity parade (although he'd pointed to Lisa as one of two possibles in the line-up), and at the trial the defence had picked up on the fact that his partner had applied on his behalf to Barclays Bank for the reward. Burke said there was nothing improper about a witness applying for a reward. However, the defence had tried to insinuate that the seeking of a reward was somehow disreputable. In fact, before the trial Barclays Bank had written to Burke to ask if Unsworth-White was entitled to the reward. Burke said no. He wrote to Barclays to say that the doctor's information hadn't contributed significantly to the arrest of the Taylors. At the trial itself Burke didn't feel the doctor's evidence had been of much use. Indeed, in his summing up the judge had appeared to attach little significance to what the doctor had said: he'd pretty much told the jury to disregard it. Mr Justice Blofeld said: 'There is no eyewitness account that either of these two defendants killed Alison. There is no eyewitness account that puts them at the flat at the relevant time. There is no evidence that puts them in the street at the relevant time.' Yet now it seemed the unfortunate doctor was about to find himself centre-stage at the appeal: the defence was planning to use his first immediately-retracted observation to suggest that not only was his evidence unreliable, but also that the police had tried to hide its unreliability.

Burke was gobsmacked – and another, harder, smack in the gob soon landed. He discovered that, without consulting him, Nutting had asked someone from the CPS to visit Unsworth-White to clarify the reason for the apparent discrepancy between the initial police report and the doctor's signed statement. In a nutshell, Nutting wanted to know if there'd been any skulduggery: had the police leaned on him to drop his suggestion that one of the girls may have been black? The CPS man was advised by his seniors not to approach Unsworth-White in case the CPS man himself became a witness in the case. An approach was subsequently made to Burke's area commander, who was asked if he could instruct a senior police officer unconnected with the case to carry out the task. Burke never found out if anyone went to see the doctor.

Burke was furious. He and two colleagues went to see Nutting the next day. Burke immediately launched into him. He said he was extremely unhappy with the way he'd dealt with the matter. As the officer in charge of the murder inquiry, he should have been the first person Nutting contacted if there were any queries about the investigation's conduct. He felt that Nutting, by going instead to third parties, had attacked his integrity and damaged his reputation by effectively insinuating that he might have behaved in a dishonest manner. Nutting slammed down his papers and said the case was over. He said they were going to lose the appeal on the grounds of 'material irregularity'. He wanted Burke to write a statement to be read out in court the next morning.

Burke was lost for words: at their meeting only two days earlier Nutting had been confident of victory. And (although Burke, to his regret, did not become aware of this until after the appeal) the day before that last confrontational meeting Nutting had himself written and signed a document to show that what the police had done was *not* a material irregularity. In that document Nutting wrote that, first, Unsworth-White had retracted his assertion that one of the girls may have been black; second, that he'd retracted it within a very short period of time and within the same conversation; and third, that he'd thereafter asserted that both girls were white – an assertion he'd repeated in his written statement. Nutting also wrote that Unsworth-White's evidence was of little effect in the case; therefore the failure to disclose the piece of paper, though regrettable, did not constitute a material irregularity. At that angry meeting Burke felt that Nutting was refusing to take on board his insistence that he'd acted entirely in accordance with the prevailing guidelines.

Burke had a sense of impending doom. Just before he went into court on the first day of the appeal Nutting's barrister assistant asked him if he regretted what had happened. Burke said yes, meaning that he was regretful of the predicament they were in. As the proceedings got underway, Nutting stood up and said to the three judges that Detective Superintendent Burke wished to offer his sincere apologies for his part in withholding the Unsworth-White document. Burke was astounded. He couldn't believe what was happening. He hadn't apologised for anything because, as far as he was concerned, there was nothing to apologise for. But it was too late. From that point everything went downhill.

Burke's nightmare was only beginning. He felt that on several significant points Nutting either conceded or failed to argue the police's case vigorously. For instance, Michelle's barrister, Richard Ferguson QC, stood up and said that only through the tenacity of his two junior counsel had they found the Unsworth-White document buried in the police archives. He insinuated that the police had acted at least unprofessionally, if not criminally. Burke knew that this was crap – the piece of paper had been discovered by the defence at some point during two visits in the previous fortnight to Earlsfield Police Station. During those visits the defence team had the assistance of two police officers who helped them view all of the unused material. But Burke waited in vain for Nutting to stand up and say (in appropriate legal phraseology) that

Ferguson was talking crap. He wanted him to explain that the police had had nothing to hide and had willingly opened up their files to the defence team. Burke wanted Nutting to say, at the very least, that the police's honesty had led to the discovery of the piece of paper. But what Burke most wanted Nutting to explain was the insignificance of what the defence suggested was highly significant. The defence was arguing that Unsworth-White was the key witness upon which the prosecution's case relied. Discredit the doctor, and the case would collapse. Nutting, despite having signed a document only two days earlier denying a material irregularity had occurred, conceded that there had been a material irregularity. The judge's later ruling underlined the extent of Nutting's capitulation. Lord Justice McCowan said:

> Mr Nutting, for the Crown, conceded that he cannot possibly argue that a failure to disclose a previous inconsistent description is not of real significance. He further conceded, therefore, that there was a material irregularity. It must be made plain, incidentally, that neither the prosecution counsel at trial, nor the Crown Prosecution Service, had any idea of the existence of this document.
>
> The Detective Superintendent in charge of the case did, however, know of the existence of the document and its significance, but decided there was no need for him to disclose it to the prosecution legal team. He was, of course, as Mr Nutting agrees, completely wrong in so thinking. We can only conclude that he did not disclose it to the prosecution team, because he knew that if he did, in accordance with the Bar's highest traditions, they would in turn disclose it to the defence.

To Burke, Nutting seemed to behave as if the appeal had already been lost. At one stage, as the sisters' convictions looked well on their way to being quashed, Burke had pleaded desperately with Nutting to do something, anything, to stop the sisters' slide to freedom. Bizarrely, Nutting had put his hand on Burke's shoulder and said he represented neither Burke nor the Metropolitan Police. So, Burke asked, who was he representing? The highest traditions of the Bar, presumably. After the first day, Burke went home and wrote a statement that he wanted Nutting to read out in court the next day. In it he said that neither he nor his team had set out to mislead; that the prevailing guidelines had been adhered to; that absolutely no impropriety had taken place; and that he didn't regret a single action carried out by himself or his team. Next day he showed it to Nutting and requested that he serve it on the court. Nutting refused. He said the statement was 'dynamite', and that if Burke persisted with it, then the judges would crucify him.

There had been around 13 points of evidence which, taken together, had led the jury to convict the sisters. Yet in Burke's eyes the appeal judges glided over everything else of significance to focus on the insignificant. Burke said that if they'd looked at all the other points in the same detail and with the same focus, and had then decided that, on balance, the Unsworth-White document still tainted everything, then he'd have been, if not happy, at least accepting of the ways of the law. Instead, he'd had to watch as the Taylor sisters swaggered to freedom wearing T-shirts emblazoned with the picture of the convicted murderer Winston Silcott. For Burke, the final irony had been Michelle's little speech on the steps of the Royal Courts of Justice. She'd said: 'We will not say that by being released justice has been done . . . ' Burke said that, knowing her twisted mind, that sentence was probably a sick little in-joke for her and Lisa – they both knew well that justice hadn't been done.

The other main ground for the appeal had been the 'unremitting, extensive, sensational, inaccurate and misleading' press coverage of the original trial. Burke felt a cogent case could still have been made against the contention that the coverage had affected the jury's verdict. But, as Lord Justice McCowan later said, 'Mr Nutting has not sought to persuade us otherwise.' Burke's last desperate hope as the convictions were quashed was for a retrial. But that was not to be. Lord Justice McCowan said:

> We were troubled, at one stage, by the fact that defence counsel did not, at trial, ask the judge to discharge the jury because of the press coverage. Mr Nutting has, however, with typical fairness, provided the answer.

This is what he said: 'Asking for a retrial puts defence counsel in a hopeless situation, where young girls had spent considerable time in custody, and where to dispel the publicity, it would be necessary to postpone the trial for a further long period.' We accept that.

The judges' ruling devastated not only Burke, but the whole police team. In parliament, David Mellor, the soon-to-be-disgraced Conservative minister, said that Burke should be forced to resign. In a show of cross-party unity the future Labour sports minister, Tony Banks, agreed with him. On television the former Labour MP turned presenter, Robert Kilroy-Silk, also called for his sacking. Burke later heard that even a Metropolitan Police assistant commissioner had been pushing for his suspension. In fact, as a result of remarks made during the appeal judgment, and following allegations about police conduct made by the Taylor family, the police launched two investigations. One, for the Police Complaints Authority, looked at the specific allegations made by the Taylors. The other was a review of the murder investigation itself. After 18 stressful months both investigations cleared Burke and his team of any wrongdoing. The conclusion of one of the investigating officers, Detective Chief Superintendent William Hatfull, was that the original investigation had been highly professional and painstakingly thorough. Hatfull said that all the most compelling evidence discovered during the course of the investigation pointed towards the murder having been carried out by the Taylor sisters. He found no other credible suspect or line of inquiry worthy of further exploration. He concluded there was no justification in reopening the investigation. The Police Complaints Authority also rejected the Taylors' complaints. There were a few minor procedural points that resulted in Burke's being offered words of advice. But when the investigating officer arrived in Burke's office with a piece of paper containing the words of advice, Burke told him to cut off the corners, get some Vaseline and stick it up his arse.

A few years later Burke left the police, totally disillusioned. It was around the same time that John Nutting QC got his knighthood. Burke said that, unlike Sir John, in the wake of the Taylors' appeal the only 'honour' he'd been likely to get was the DCM – Don't Come Monday.

The only bit of solace for Burke was that the Taylors didn't get a penny compensation for their alleged wrongful imprisonment. Burke said that that fact in itself made them unique among those set free after alleged miscarriages of justice. Even the Taylors' friend, Winston Silcott, whose conviction for murdering a policeman was quashed, could sit out his other life sentence for murder knowing that on his release there was fifty thousand pounds from the Metropolitan Police waiting for him.

Burke said the case had poisoned his view of the British justice system. He now saw 'justice' as a farce — there was a National Lottery on Wednesdays and Saturdays, but there was an even bigger lottery every time you walked into court. He said the judicial process wasn't a search for the truth, as it should be, but a technical game of chance played by clever barristers. He thought the system was environmentally unfriendly, because all it did was to recycle nasty villains so that privileged barristers in their well-paid closed-shop could make more and more money at the expense of the victims of crime.

What Burke didn't know was that the Police Complaints Authority's investigation had started a time-bomb ticking under the Taylors. It had led the police to the witnesses I'd tried to nobble, and they, in turn, led the police to me.

TWENTY

Malicious Falsehood

My legal battle with the Taylors can be summarised as two and a half years of delays, setbacks, frustration and misery. It soon became apparent that the sisters were in no hurry to have the case brought to trial. Months passed in a blur of often indecipherable legal jargon – interlocutory injunctions, Sealed Orders, Unless Orders – and I seriously wondered whether the end would ever come. The Taylors erected every possible hurdle in my path. I got the impression (although perhaps it was just my imagination running away with me) that they'd do anything to prevent the evidence being tested in court.

The *News of the World* stopped funding me after the first hearing. I successfully applied for Legal Aid, only to have the Taylors (themselves on Legal Aid) successfully oppose it. I appealed, and got it reinstated, only to have my enemies oppose it yet again. Sometimes I had to represent myself in court. Common sense often told me to quit, but I disregarded common sense. Driven by anger and the will to right the wrongs I'd done in the Taylors' name, I spent my free time studying civil law, reading the evidence, travelling to court hearings, swearing affidavits, attending Legal Aid appeals and sitting in conferences with my solicitor Caroline Kean, who continued to work with me despite the fact she wasn't being paid.

When I wasn't either immersed in paperwork or in the company of members of the legal profession, I was out hunting down new evidence. Sometimes this involved approaching people I'd formerly approached on the Taylors' behalf – people I'd once asked to tell lies. Now I was asking them to tell the truth. I often felt embarrassed, even ashamed, but nothing was going to stop me achieving my aim of defeating the Taylors. In her first affidavit Michelle said she'd ended our relationship after a journalist called David Smith told her I'd previously contacted other people in the public eye and sold stories about them. I knew this had to be nonsense, so I set about tracking Smith down. When I finally found him he totally dismissed Michelle's story. He went further. He wrote me a letter to say he hadn't had contact with them in any form. He said his only dealings with the case had been through me. He hoped his letter would be 'of some help'. As far as I was concerned, his words were explosive. His letter proved Michelle was lying about the break-up of our relationship – it proved she was hiding the truth.

In November 1995 the nightclub at which I worked, and where I'd introduced Lisa Taylor to her future husband, was catapulted into the headlines when a teenager died after taking Ecstasy. The tablet that killed 18-year-old Leah Betts had been bought at Raquels. In the following month media scrutiny became more intense with the fatal shooting in a Range Rover of my 'business associate' Tony Tucker (whose 'firm' I'd invited into the club to help run security) and his two lieutenants, Pat Tate and Craig Rolfe. For a while I became chief suspect. I wouldn't be surprised if Basildon police had to install new phone lines to handle the number of anonymous callers denouncing me. But I'd had nothing to do with the murders, and the police soon knew I was innocent. However, for me those events brought to an end my criminal way of life. I'd never been a drug-dealer, but my role in charge of security at Raquels meant I was effectively a cog in the machine that delivered drugs to those who chose to take them. I turned my back decisively on that past when I reluctantly became a prosecution witness at the trial of the man accused of supplying Leah Betts with the Ecstasy tablet that killed her. For my troubles I received death threats that forced me to uproot my family and live with panic alarms connected to a police station. I've written about that story in my book *Essex Boys*. It has relevance to my battle with the Taylors in that my forced movement away from criminality made me determined to tell the truth about all my past misdeeds – and my attempt to pervert the course of justice on the Taylors' behalf was high among them.

The saga of my on-off Legal Aid caused me to lose my barrister Gavin Millar QC. He had to take on another case during one of my periods without funding. I was sorry to lose him, but when my funding was reinstated my solicitor managed to secure the services of Ian Mill QC. His most recent high-profile success had come when he'd represented the singer George Michael in a dispute with his record company. Mr Mill brought a fresh eye to the case, and his new ideas lifted my demoralised spirits. After my first conference with him I felt we were sure to win – and soon.

The supposed purpose of the Taylors' action against me was to stop a breach of confidence. However, my legal team had earlier seen a clever way to defeat this. In court they argued the following: if Michelle said she never confessed to the murder, how could she then say I'd be in breach of confidence if I told a third party? There can be no confidence in something you claim you've never said. If I went on to say something that Michelle claimed was a lie, then she could sue me for libel – a course of action for which there was no access to the Legal Aid which had funded the Taylors' action from the beginning (and would do to the end). The Taylors' legal team realised they were in a predicament. They amended their case to prevent any attempt to make public the confession. To do this, they decided to allege 'malicious falsehood', which is allied to libel, but, unlike libel, it can be pursued on Legal Aid. However, this amended action was to be their downfall. In a case of malicious falsehood the claimant has to prove that the words are both untrue and spoken with malice. This meant that my legal team could now defend the claim on the ground that what I'd said was true – that Michelle had confessed to murder – and they could seek to introduce evidence to prove this. This made the case totally different from the initial action, which had a much narrower focus, concerning itself largely with the question of whether there'd been a breach of confidence. Something else in the new plea added to our delight: the Taylors' legal team said I was claiming not only that Michelle confessed to murder, but also that she'd actually committed the murder. People unfamiliar with the workings of the law might wonder what the difference is. However, in legal terms, by pleading that I'd alleged that she'd done it (and not merely claimed to have done it) the Taylors gave my legal team the scope to use the evidence from the criminal trial – something that wouldn't have been possible otherwise.

In October 1997 – two years and four months after the Taylors started the action – Ian Mill QC went into court and argued cogently that the Taylors had now themselves put in issue the question of whether they'd committed the murder. Therefore, he said, all the documents relating to the murder trial should be disclosed. This was necessary, he said, because the jury in these proceedings would need to consider the evidence from the murder trial in order to determine whether, on the balance of probability, the Taylors were guilty of murder – and whether, therefore, it was more likely than not that Michelle had confessed to me.

The Taylors' barrister said that evidence from the criminal trial was irrelevant. But, to my delight, the judge agreed with my barrister, and made an order granting access to the original evidence held by the Crown Prosecution Service. My team would now be able to seek corroboration for Michelle's confession. His ruling also meant I'd be able to call all the witnesses from the original trial. My barrister said the trial would probably last 15 days. It was provisionally scheduled for March 1998. Effectively, it would have amounted to a rerun of the original murder trial.

At the heart of the new case was Michelle's confession to murder, which had been prompted by my discovery in her papers of the legally privileged letter written by one of her legal representatives. Michelle, naturally, denied both the existence of the letter and her subsequent confession. During that same October 1997 court hearing the judge remarked that I was obviously an intelligent man, so if I'd invented the confession he didn't think I'd have included the detail of the legal letter, because its existence or non-existence could surely be easily proven by the Taylors' former legal representatives. He ordered the Taylor sisters, and three named people from the solicitors' firm that originally represented them, to swear affidavits detailing any solicitor, legal executive or clerk who had ever given advice to the sisters throughout the course of the police investigation, their criminal trial and the Court of Appeal hearing. This was a key step towards establishing definitively whether the incriminating letter existed.

At an earlier stage in the case one of the Taylors' solicitors from their original firm, Michael Holmes, did swear an affidavit denying he had written the letter. But he wasn't the only person from that firm to have represented them – and the other remained silent.

Around three weeks later I got a call from my solicitor Caroline Kean. 'The Taylors have caved in,' she said. 'They want to do a deal.'

I suspected it was another time-wasting manoeuvre – and, as the days passed, they didn't make any significant efforts to reach a deal. Both the Taylors and the three named people from their original legal team failed to comply with the judge's order to swear affidavits. My barrister applied for the case against me to be struck out. A date was set for the hearing.

On Monday, 24 November 1997 I sat up late into the night preparing myself for the next day's hearing. Could it really be over? The Taylors had enjoyed tremendous good fortune throughout the case. I'd been branded a dodgy crook; they'd been portrayed as the innocent victims of a miscarriage of justice. I wasn't stupid: I knew how my relationship with them must have looked to the outside world. Yet the seemingly righteous didn't want the facts tested in court. For me, that fact said it all: they were far more dodgy and crooked than I could ever be. I got up, dressed and left my home while it was still dark; I wanted to avoid the rush hour in London. I arrived at Aldwych tube station around 8.30 a.m. and went to sit in the same café I'd sat in before the last day of the sisters' successful appeal hearing. I drank my tea and watched the commuters streaming off to their workplaces.

I arrived at the High Court feeling apprehensive. What obstacle would the Taylors lay before me this time? I couldn't believe the case might be about to end. I knew the sisters themselves wouldn't show; they never did. They'd only ever bothered to attend once. I met Ian Mill and

Caroline Kean: they both assured me that today would be the final day. We were allocated a courtroom and a period of time for the case to be heard. We would have 90 minutes starting at 2 p.m. – an hour and a half to finalise the years of misery and frustration that had gone before.

I walked out of the High Court and wandered around aimlessly. I had three hours to kill before the hearing. I soon found myself in The Strand at the Barclays Bank where Alison had worked. Still there was the television displaying financial information and the exact time and date. It had featured in all the videos I'd made trying to challenge the police's timings for Alison's journey home. At that moment I truly hated myself. I was filled with remorse. What on earth had I done? Thinking about the way the Taylors had duped me turned my self-pity to anger. As I started walking back up The Strand, though, my negativity lifted. Whatever happened that afternoon in court, I'd continue fighting the Taylors until I won.

Caroline wished me luck as we entered the courtroom. The Taylors' barrister stood up first. He said his clients should be allowed to discontinue their action against me. However, if they could fund the matter in the future, they should be allowed to start up the whole process again. I could hardly believe the request. They were asking the judge to allow them to pull out of the case just as it had reached a crucial and difficult stage for them. Yet they also wanted a licence to start it off again when they saw fit. Their barrister said: 'We all live our lives with the weight of the law hanging over our heads. Why should Mr O'Mahoney be any different?' Mr Mill stood up and efficiently demolished that argument. He said it would be unethical for them to abandon, and then restart, the case after I'd gained such an advantage.

At 3.42 p.m. the judge began to read his judgment. I should have been transfixed with suspense, but instead I was daydreaming. I couldn't hear the judge's words, although his voice registered like a drone in the background. However, I snapped out of my reverie when I heard him say: '[The Taylor sisters' barrister] has said all that could be said on behalf of his clients but in my judgment his approach is profoundly unsatisfactory.'

That line rang in my ears. I knew I'd won. It was finally over. The judge continued:

> The writ in these proceedings was issued in 1995 and proceedings have up until now taken two and a half years, during most of which [O'Mahoney] was under restraint in respect of confidentiality and infringement of copyright. Since May, he has also been restrained in respect of the claim of malicious falsehood. Litigation of this sort is a matter of anxiety for both sides and must be so for [O'Mahoney]. Once this advanced stage in proceedings has been reached, for the [Taylors] to say that they cannot go on with it now due to lack of funds but would like to in the future, is close to an abuse of the process of the court. It is entirely unsatisfactory that the [Taylors] should be given that liberty.

Ever since the start of the case I'd thought about the conclusion. I'd always known the Taylors wouldn't face me in a trial; there were far too many questions they couldn't answer without incriminating themselves. I'd imagined myself emerging from the High Court, fist clenched, standing on the very steps where the Taylors had stood on their release. But this time I'd be telling the media pack: 'Yes, they were guilty.'

However, the street outside was empty. There were no journalists – and I was pleased. Now that I'd won I suddenly felt mentally exhausted. I didn't think I could face another conversation regarding the Taylors. I didn't even feel relief. I was subconsciously preparing myself for their backlash. I knew they hadn't yet played their final card.

I arrived home late that evening. Debra and the children were asleep. I sat in the kitchen wondering what I should do next. It might sound odd, but I wasn't sure I wanted to go anywhere with the story. After an hour or so Debra came downstairs. I explained what had gone on that day in court. I told her I was now free to tell the world of their guilt. As we talked, it soon became clear that she thought it was time to let the matter rest. She said further publicity would just cause ourselves and Alison's loved ones more anguish. I wasn't sure; part of me wanted revenge. Yet my previous instinctive decisions relating to the Taylors had been terribly wrong. Debra and I agreed to think things over. Technically the injunction wouldn't end for several more days. Only then would I be able to discuss the case with third parties, anyway. So a cooling-off period was welcome.

On 4 December, the day after the injunction was finally lifted, I got a call from a journalist friend. 'Hello, scoopmonger,' he said. I asked him what he was talking about. He told me to go and buy a copy of *The Guardian*. I asked him why.

'Because they've just done a huge two-page spread slagging you off as something called a "scoopmonger",' he said. Unfortunately, I wasn't living in a *Guardian*-friendly area, so I had to drive several miles before I found a shop that stocked it. I sat in my car and skimmed quickly through the paper. Sure enough, I turned the pages to be slapped in the face by a two-page feature with the stark headline JUDAS OF FLEET STREET. Half of one page was filled with a recent photo of Michelle and Lisa; there was a smaller picture of me, unshaven and in doorman gear, in the top left-hand corner. The feature was introduced with the ominous words:

> Bernard O'Mahoney is a scoopmonger – a double-dealer who befriends vulnerable people in the news, then sells their secrets to the tabloids. His latest victims are the Taylor sisters, acquitted of murder four years ago but powerless to stop his whispering campaign today.

The writer of the article was Nick Davies. I had to laugh. Davies had been the 'nice' journalist who'd written the four-page feature in the same paper promoting the sisters' innocence a week before their appeal. At that time the Taylors and I had been extremely grateful to him, particularly as he'd given great prominence to what we secretly knew was a nonsense story about the homeless man. I'd tried to contact him during the civil case to see if he'd be willing to verify that I'd threatened him over his plans to track down the homeless man. However, he hadn't replied to my letter or phone calls. Now I understood why.

As I read the article I realised swiftly that the Taylors had not fully briefed him on the facts. He said they'd 'abandoned' the legal struggle against me, whereas they and their legal team knew that the judge had struck out the action and awarded costs against them. But that was only one of many inaccuracies and distortions. In fact, the article's essence had already been printed in the *South London Press* when the Taylors first issued their writ. It was the familiar charge that because I'd written letters to the Yorkshire Ripper and a child-killer I was not to be trusted. Davies also explained to his readers why the Taylors were innocent: according to him, the prosecution's case had been 'demolished' at the Appeal Court and by members of the 'quality press', such as himself. Like his earlier article, his summary of the case for the Taylors managed to leave out a lot of the significant evidence against them. And you can make any criminal seem innocent if you omit or distort the significant facts that point to their guilt. However, the most striking omission was his failure to tell his readers how he himself had worked with the scoopmonger. Why didn't he give them his own experience of the scoopmonger's wickedness? Why didn't he tell them how he had shared with the scoopmonger a prison visit to the Taylors during which I'd threatened him? Of course, that would have been difficult for Davies, because then he would have had to tell his readers about his own earlier 'scoop' regarding the homeless man as suspected murderer – the suspect supposedly ignored by the incompetent police. But by that stage even Davies must have known 'the homeless man' story was bullshit, albeit bullshit that had been convincing at the time – so convincing, in fact, that Davies had placed it centre-stage in his 'Rough Justice' article a week before the appeal. And his scoop had been eagerly followed up by other members of the quality press.

As I read on, I realised Michelle couldn't have shown him either her sworn affidavits or several of her letters, otherwise he surely wouldn't have printed one sloppy and provable lie about the ending of our relationship. Davies said Michelle threw me out after discovering I was still involved with my former girlfriend. During the civil case she'd never given this as a reason for our parting. In her first affidavit she said she threw me out after David Smith, a journalist, told her I was a criminal who had befriended other prisoners. Michelle had also written me letters when I left her in which she blamed herself for my leaving.

The one thing that didn't seem to occur to Davies in his constant references to 'the scoopmonger' was the number of obvious 'scoops' I'd missed. If, as he alleged, I'd become involved with the sisters purely in order to get stories about them to sell to newspapers, why hadn't I sold those stories at the times when they would have been most valuable? In the run up to the appeal, for instance, or when I'd fallen out with them in October 1993? However, the central irony of Davies' feature was that he published the essence of the story that the Taylors had just spent two years and five months trying to suppress.

I felt sorry for Davies. I knew he was a nice, quality journalist who wouldn't deliberately lie to his readers, but – like me before him – he'd been duped by the Taylors into becoming a mouthpiece for their lies. All the same, I knew the article was extremely damaging to me. Not because it came anywhere close to the truth, but because most people, including would-be publishers and documentary makers, were more likely to take the word of a respectable *Guardian* journalist than that of a former violent criminal. For me the only positive consequence of the article was how it breathed new life into my determination to tell the truth about the Taylors. At the end of the civil case I'd seriously considered walking away from the whole business. But now I knew I'd have to write the book, because only in a book could I tell the full story in a way which would expose the Taylors, and their lies, once and for all.

And for that, at least, I had to thank the nice man from *The Guardian*.

Afterword

After *The Guardian* published Nick Davies' 'scoopmonger' article my collaborator on this book, Mick McGovern, wrote to the satirical magazine *Private Eye*. He enclosed a brief article outlining why Davies might have been so keen to rubbish me. He was contacted by the *Eye* contributor and miscarriage-of-justice campaigner Paul Foot. McGovern had reservations about talking to Foot: he knew Foot was a long-time supporter of the Socialist Workers' Party, whose newspaper had campaigned for the Taylor sisters and whose members had given them a rapturous reception at a rally after their release. Foot had even shared a platform with the sisters on that day. However, Foot put McGovern at ease by saying that, although he'd written about almost every other significant miscarriage of justice of recent years, he'd avoided writing stories about the Taylors, despite many calls from their mother. He'd always felt there was something odd about the whole business. None the less, he said, he'd be reluctant to print the story about Davies, although the editor was interested. He said that by printing it *Private Eye* would effectively be saying the sisters were guilty of murder. He thought such a story might let 'the genie out of the flask': it could start an avalanche of negative reporting about alleged miscarriages of justice. Tabloid newspapers might start saying, 'All those other people you said didn't do it, did do it', whereas Foot knew for sure that he'd only ever helped the wrongfully convicted. He asked whether – regardless of the story's possible truth – it was really worth writing about. McGovern said the victim's family would think so.

Foot said: 'If a couple of girls who did a revenge murder are not in prison I don't feel terribly upset about that. I'm more upset about people who are in prison who shouldn't be there. That may make me sound rather unsympathetic to the girl they murdered – if they did.'

Private Eye didn't print the story.

I wrote a 17-page letter to *The Guardian* pointing out what I considered to be Davies' many errors and distortions. My solicitor Caroline Kean also wrote a letter to them in which she said some of Davies' statements were not just inaccurate, but libellous. Having been involved with me in the civil case, she knew first-hand that Davies' account of how and why the action had ended was incorrect. She received a letter from *The Guardian* editor's office agreeing to her request that a copy of her letter be filed with the article in the newspaper's library 'so that everyone is made aware of your comments'.

In March 1998, three months after his 'scoopmonger' feature, Nick Davies was honoured at the British Press Awards as 'Feature Writer of the Year'. The following year the judges of the What the Papers Say Awards acclaimed him as their 'Journalist of the Year'. Last year Davies generously agreed to give a masterclass in reporting skills to those possibly less talented than himself. In a *Guardian* article he wrote that he'd been inspired by his fear that reporting skills in this country were 'choking to death' in a 'sediment of incompetence'. Would-be investigative reporters were invited to a 48-hour crash course at the University of Sussex in which Davies and fellow investigative superstars would 'expose the techniques we use'. Among the teachers was Paul Foot who was going to 'look back at notorious miscarriages of justice'. Foot started his miscarriage-of-justice career in 1966 when he became convinced that James Hanratty had not been guilty of rape and murder. Unfortunately for Foot, a few months after his masterclass, modern DNA techniques linked Hanratty with the crime for which he was hanged. HANRATTY WAS GUILTY, said the *Daily Mail* headline, although in his *Guardian* column Foot dismissed the new evidence and stuck to his conviction that Hanratty was innocent. Another campaigner for

Hanratty is Bob Woffinden. He'd also helped promote the idea of the Taylors' innocence. He wrote a major article in *The Independent* a few months before the appeal. In March the police dug up Hanratty's body to get a better DNA sample. According to newspaper reports, it seemed to prove his guilt even more conclusively. Paul Foot wrote an article in *The Guardian* titled 'Hanratty may still be innocent, OK?' In it he gave an insight into his approach to new evidence. He said: 'Bob Woffinden and I, who have written books claiming Hanratty's innocence, were asked about these tests and could only say that the case for Hanratty's innocence is stronger than it ever was, and that if the DNA suggests otherwise there must be something wrong with the DNA.'

As the director of the Victims of Crime Trust, Norman Brennan, said: 'Had the DNA results said Hanratty was not guilty, I am sure the family and their solicitors would be rubbing all our noses in it.' Interestingly, the Taylor sisters are now with the firm of solicitors who've represented the Hanratty family for the last 33 years, Geoffrey Bindman and Partners. I hope the latter aren't hoping for a 33-year commitment from the Taylors, because the sisters have got through three other sets of solicitors in the last eight years alone.

McGovern also met the former BBC *Newsnight* reporter Miriam O'Callaghan. She said she'd worked on the first *Newsnight* film to raise doubts about the Taylor sisters' guilt. She told McGovern that when she first looked at the case she felt the sisters were probably guilty. However, she'd gone out to dinner with Michelle Taylor's barrister, Richard Ferguson QC, and some time between the starter and the dessert he'd persuaded her of their innocence. She said Ferguson convinced her by focusing on the timings. He made her feel sure that Michelle and Lisa could not have carried out the murder and driven back to the hospital in the time alleged by the prosecution. O'Callaghan is now the main presenter on the Irish equivalent of *Newsnight*. Richard Ferguson QC went on from his victory at the Taylors' appeal to represent Rose West, wife of mass-murderer Fred. Sadly for him, and for Mrs West, he failed to convince the jury of his client's innocence. If only he'd had the chance to take them out to dinner.

Another member of the Taylors' legal team also became involved in another controversial case. The solicitor Michael Holmes found himself representing some of the men accused of the racist murder of the black teenager Stephen Lawrence. Interestingly, the Macpherson Report on the police's investigation into Stephen Lawrence's murder questioned the long-standing principle of British law that no one can be tried twice for the same crime (the so-called 'double jeopardy' rule). Following this, the Law Commission (the official law reform body for England and Wales) has recommended abandoning the rule in cases of murder, thus allowing people who have been acquitted to stand trial again if new evidence emerges. So Mr Holmes might yet find a few former clients back knocking on his door.

McGovern also met a freelance television director, Leo Telling, who in 1993 had been a researcher on the Channel Four programme *Hard News*. This programme was devoted to investigating the misbehaviour of newspaper journalists (especially tabloid ones). After the Taylors' release a *Hard News Special* had looked critically at the tabloids' coverage of the original trial. Telling had been the researcher on that film. He told McGovern he'd had a big row with the producer about which details should be included. Telling thought it was important for viewers to understand why the tabloids might have been so convinced of the sisters' guilt. For instance, he wanted to include a mention of how Lisa's fingerprints had been found at Alison's flat, although she'd initially denied ever having been there. The producer thought putting in that sort of detail would be tantamount to playing the tabloids' game.

In June last year, on the tenth anniversary of Alison Shaughnessy's wedding, the *Daily Mail*'s Jo-Ann Goodwin re-examined the Taylors' case. She wrote a three-page feature under the headline: WHY I BELIEVE THEY ARE MURDERERS. She'd looked at the trial evidence, spoken to the policeman who led the investigation, spoken to me, to Alison's family and tried to speak to Michelle and Lisa. The sisters refused to talk to her. Despite the article's damning conclusion, the Taylors failed to sue for libel to restore their shredded reputations, although they constantly threatened to do so. Instead, their parents complained to the Press

Complaints Commission (PCC). In February of this year the PCC said it was unable to adjudicate in such a complex case. Only in court could the claims and counter-claims be properly tested. Therefore, it thought the proper course would be for the Taylors to institute libel proceedings. However, instead of suing for libel, the Taylors sought to obtain a judicial review of the PCC's decision. Their bid prompted another article in *The Guardian* in March. The writer this time was the former tabloid editor and writer on journalistic ethics, Roy Greenslade. One of his sources was 'Journalist of the Year' Nick Davies, who was revealed as having supported the Taylors' complaint to the PCC. Davies attacked the original *Mail* piece as 'a highly partisan reworking of the prosecution case' (as opposed, presumably, to his own earlier highly partisan reworkings of the defence's case). He also said that he and the Taylors were outraged that the *Mail* had given the Taylors very little time to respond to 'O'Mahoney's allegations' (although the article had contained a lot more than my 'allegations'). Apparently, Mrs Taylor had only been phoned the day before publication. He claimed that this had resulted in a one-sided article. Laugh? I nearly cried. At least Mrs Taylor had been given a chance to respond; Davies hadn't given me any chance whatsoever to respond to his 'scoopmonger' allegations before publication – a clear contravention of basic journalistic standards. Perhaps I should ask media moralist Roy Greenslade to investigate him.

The Taylors and their many friends in the media, aware that this book was in the pipeline, launched another attempt to frighten publishers off me. In November last year *Private Eye*, sometime home of miscarriage-of-justice campaigner Paul Foot, attacked the *Daily Mail*'s feature by trying to rubbish me. It said the paper had accused 'two innocent women of murder on the word of a con man' who specialised in writing letters to high-profile prisoners and then selling the correspondence to newspapers. It said the paper hadn't mentioned this – 'Nor did the *Mail* story mention that O'Mahoney hates Michelle Taylor, who kicked him out of her bed, and nor that he has been waging a war on the Taylor family ever since.' He said Jo-Ann Goodwin should have known all this because it had been exposed at length by Nick Davies in *The Guardian* in December 1997. However, the writer saved the best bit for the end. He said the Taylor sisters had gone to a solicitor to sue the *Mail* (although *Private Eye* failed to point out that four months later a writ had still not been issued).

> Their parents, meanwhile, filed a complaint with the PCC, citing the 1997 *Guardian* story. The *Mail* smugly replied that *The Guardian's* own cuttings library had attached a solicitor's letter to the file warning that Davies' story was unreliable. Alarmed, the Taylors spoke to *The Guardian*, which said there was no such letter in the cuttings file. The *Mail* then seemingly trumped them by producing a letter to O'Mahoney's solicitors from *Guardian* editor Alan Rusbridger. It acknowledged a complaint from Bernard O'Mahoney and agreed that his solicitor's letter should be attached to the offending cutting as a warning. Match point to the *Mail* – except the 'Rusbridger letter' was a forgery.

The article didn't say who had forged the letter, but presumably it could only have been me or my solicitor. You might have thought that before making such an allegation the magazine would have contacted one of us for a response. But such a simple procedure was too much to expect. My solicitor Caroline Kean was naturally a little upset at the implication that she'd been party to a forgery. She wrote immediately to *The Guardian*:

> I enclose a copy of the letter that was sent by post from this firm on 8 December 1997. I enclose a copy of the letter dated 9 December 1997 on the Editor's notepaper which you can see from the date stamp was received by my firm, again by post, on 10 December 1997. I have the original on file. Obviously I do not know whether Alan Rusbridger signed the letter personally or if it was signed on his behalf (although presumably with his authority) and I cannot account for the fact that you have no record of either of these letters, but the fact of the matter is that they were exchanged, and Bernie O'Mahoney relied on the promise in the letter dated 9 December 1997 that my firm's letter would indeed

be filed with the article. You are welcome to inspect the original letter from *The Guardian* if you wish, but I hope you will agree it is inconceivable that the letter is, as claimed, a 'forgery'.

I rang *Private Eye* to speak to the writer of the article. He gave his name as Tim Minogue. I expected to have a rational discussion with him about the case. I'd have put to him certain facts of which he was clearly unaware. I wasn't intending to blame him for his ignorance; I assumed his knowledge had come from the Taylors' camp. Unfortunately, Mr Minogue – in common with some other quality journalists I'd encountered in the past – didn't seem to want to discuss any facts that pointed away from a conclusion he'd already reached. Instead, he sounded tired, then became extremely emotional. He slammed down the phone after shouting: 'Grow up, and leave those poor girls alone.' I did try calling him back in the hope that he'd calmed down, but he refused to take my call.

As for 'the poor girls' themselves, they've both now got children of their own, although Lisa's husband has left her. The final irony of this story is that, despite all the efforts of the Taylors and their supporters to prevent me telling the world of their guilt, it was an attempt by Michelle Taylor to scare off a publisher that resulted in my securing a book deal. Michelle wrote to Mainstream Publishing to say she'd heard I was writing a book about her and her sister. She said if the book made libellous allegations that they were guilty of the murder, then they'd take advice from their lawyers with a view to instructing libel proceedings against Mainstream and obtaining an injunction to prevent publication. She understood the book was to be called *Dream Solution*. She said this title was taken from a phrase she used in her diary and which we couldn't use without her permission. I'd mentioned this book to Mainstream's managing director, Bill Campbell, a few years ago. He'd published my book, *Essex Boys*. At that time he said it wasn't for him. When Michelle's letter landed on his desk he couldn't even remember the story. He rang me to ask if I knew what she was on about. I reminded him of the story and he asked me to send him a few sample chapters. I was delighted, because I hadn't been planning to send them to him. He had, after all, already rejected the book several years earlier, as had several publishers after reading Davies's *Guardian* feature. When he read the sample chapters, he agreed to publish. I considered sending Michelle a thank-you letter, but I thought she might not appreciate it. I hadn't decided finally on the book's title, but Michelle's letter settled the matter for me. It would be called *The Dream Solution*, which, as she said, was taken from a phrase she used in her diary. It was also the title I'd chosen for the book I'd been writing for her back in 1993.

Meanwhile, the only poor girl in this story, Alison Shaughnessy, lies in her grave next to the church in Piltown, County Kilkenny, where she was married. Her gravestone is inscribed with a poem she wrote herself. Titled 'Seven Days', it reads:

> Long long ago, when all was darkness, no rain or snow,
> God first made Heaven then the earth,
> The sun and moon he gave them birth,
> This then made light, for the day, for the night,
> May there be land, may there be seas,
> May there be beasts and birds in the trees,
> He then made man, women too,
> He made them just like me and you.

Alison's mother told journalists after the Taylors' trial: 'The poem was just typical of Alison. She was such a gentle, warm and lovely person who would not have hurt or upset anybody.'

The last word should go to the miscarriage-of-justice campaigner Bob Woffinden. He concluded his *Independent* article in the run-up to the Taylors' appeal with the prescient words: 'At the end of the trial, the parents of Alison Shaughnessy expressed a feeling of relief that it was all finally over. Sadly, one suspects that they haven't yet endured the half of it.'